THE INTERNET GENERATION

Civil Society: Historical and Contemporary Perspectives

Series Editors:

Virginia Hodgkinson   Kent E. Portney   John C. Schneider
Public Policy Institute   Department of Political Science   Department of History
Georgetown University   Tufts University   Tufts University

Henry Milner, *The Internet Generation: Engaged Citizens or Political Dropouts*

Bruce R. Sievers, *Civil Society, Philanthropy, and the Fate of the Commons*

James Longhurst, *Citizen Environmentalists: Women's Activism and Air Pollution in Pittsburgh*

Janelle A. Kerlin, ed., *Social Enterprise: A Global Comparison*

Carl Milofsky, *Smallville: Institutionalizing Community in Twenty-First-Century America*

Dan Pallotta, *Uncharitable: How Restraints on Nonprofits Undermine Their Potential*

Susan A. Ostrander and Kent E. Portney, eds., *Acting Civically: From Urban Neighborhoods to Higher Education*

Peter Levine, *The Future of Democracy: Developing the Next Generation of American Citizens*

Jason A. Scorza, *Strong Liberalism: Habits of Mind for Democratic Citizenship*

Elayne Clift, ed., *Women, Philanthropy, and Social Change: Visions for a Just Society*

Brian O'Connell, *Fifty Years in Public Causes: Stories from a Road Less Traveled*

Pablo Eisenberg, *Challenges for Nonpofits and Philanthropy: The Courage to Change*

Thomas A. Lyson, *Civic Agriculture: Reconnecting Farm, Food, and Community*

Virginia A. Hodgkinson and Michael W. Foley, eds., *The Civil Society Reader*

Henry Milner, *Civic Literacy: How Informed Citizens Make Democracy Work*

Ken Thomson, *From Neighborhood to Nation: The Democratic Foundations of Civil Society*

Bob Edwards, Michael W. Foley, and Mario Diani, eds., *Beyond Tocqueville: Civil Society and the Social Capital Debate in Comparative Perspective*

Phillip H. Round, *By Nature and by Custom Cursed: Transatlantic Civil Discourse and New England Cultural Production, 1620–1660*

Brian O'Connell, *Civil Society: The Underpinnings of American Democracy*

The Internet Generation

Engaged Citizens or Political Dropouts

HENRY MILNER

TUFTS UNIVERSITY PRESS
MEDFORD, MASSACHUSETTS

PUBLISHED BY UNIVERSITY PRESS OF NEW ENGLAND
HANOVER & LONDON

Tufts University Press
Published by University Press of New England
One Court Street, Lebanon NH 03766
www.upne.com

© 2010 Trustees of Tufts College

For permission to reproduce any of the material in this book,
contact Permissions, University Press of New England,
One Court Street, Lebanon NH 03766; or visit www.upne.com

Library of Congress Cataloging-in-Publication Data

Milner, Henry.
The internet generation : engaged citizens or political dropouts / Henry Milner.
    p. cm. — (Civil society, historical and contemporary perspectives)
Includes bibliographical references and index.
ISBN 978-1-58465-858-0 (cloth : alk. paper) — ISBN 978-1-58465-938-9 (pbk. : alk. paper)
1. Political participation. 2. Young adults—Political activity. 3. Youth—Political activity.
4. Internet—Political aspects. 5. Civics—Study and teaching. I. Title.
JF799.M56   2010
323'.0420842—dc22   2009053157

5 4 3 2 1

Contents

Tables

Preface

This book returns to the subject of my last book with the University Press of New England: *Civic Literacy: How Informed Citizens Make Democracy Work*. In the eight years since it was published, much has changed. Two linked aspects that were only secondary features when I was writing at the turn of the century now dominate the landscape: the Internet, and the generation that grew up in its wake.

Civic Literacy, as I wrote at the time, came at the end of an intellectual journey I had taken through the industrial democracies, identifying and trying to understand differences in civic literacy, or the proportion of citizens with the knowledge and skills to effectively exercise their citizenship. I argued that differences in societal efforts at what I termed nonmaterial redistribution explained the substantial differences in levels of political participation, and, thus, in policy outcomes. The societies high in civic literacy had reduced disparities in both material and nonmaterial (intellectual) resources: bringing those on the lower rungs of society to higher levels of knowledge not only augmented their economic opportunities, but also enhanced their capacity to exercise political influence through informed political participation. While the book signaled emerging historical developments, it was primarily comparative. Yet soon after it was published, I came to realize that there was a critical historical—generational—dimension to low levels of civic literacy and political participation. Voter turnout data, complemented by public opinion polling from my own country, Canada, were especially eloquent in this regard, something I found myself frequently asked to explain. As I delved further, it became apparent that incorporating this generational factor into the analysis would mean an additional stage on my intellectual journey.

Several stops along the way took the form of specific research projects, the fruits of which found their way into a number of articles and papers. But it became increasingly clear that to approach the question at the scale and level it required would take another, equally ambitious book. A huge and varied literature touching upon the political engagement of young people, especially in the United States, was emerging; but there are few books on the subject, and none that attempted to incorporate the key dimensions of the issue and do so cross-nationally.

Taking up the challenge of understanding the behavior of this generation entailed revisiting the relationship among civic literacy, political participation. and nonmaterial redistribution. It meant placing not only more emphasis on education, but shifting the emphasis toward civic education and the Internet. Nonmaterial redistribution, for this generation, has become interwoven with disseminating the requisite skills and knowledge via the Internet. And the societal changes these technological developments have brought in their wake have placed the burden of such dissemination increasingly on the shoulders of the school—that is, via civic education. I was not a specialist on either the Internet or civic education.

In the long process of exploring these subjects and integrating them into the wider project, I benefited from the assistance of many people, too many to be listed here. Some names are obvious—for example, younger colleagues in collaboration with whom I wrote some of the papers published in the intervening years. Many of the papers were published under the auspices of an academic or research institute that found the issues worth investigation. I begin by identifying certain individuals associated with these institutes with whom I worked most closely, but this does not do justice to the many others who made the collaborations possible: Geneviève Bouchard and Leslie Seidle at the Institute for Research in Public Policy (IRPP), in Montreal; Andrew Ellis and Maria Gratschew at the International Institute for Democracy and Electoral Assistance (International IDEA), in Stockholm; André Blais, holder of the Chair in Electoral Studies at the Université de Montréal; Svante Ersson and Niklas Eklund in the Department of Political Science at Umeå University, in Sweden; Peter Levine and Mark Hugo Lopez at CIRCLE (the Center for Information and Research on Civic Learning) at Tufts University; Kimmo Grönlund and Lauri Karvonen at DC:E (Democracy: A Citizen Perspective) at Åbo Academi, in Finland; and Miriam Lapp and Alain Pelletier at Elections Canada.

Others helpful at various points through this latest stage of the journey include: Eva Anduiza Perea, Henk Dekker, Michael Delli Carpini, Eugénie Dostie-Goulet, Monroe Eagles, Bernard Fournier, Mark Franklin, Aina Gallego Dobón, Ailsa Henderson, Steven Hill, Paul Howe, Scott Keeter, Andreas Ladner, J. P. Lewis, Peter Loewen, Bob Luskin, Stefan Marschall, Michele Micheletti, Laura Morales, Giorgio Nadig, Chi Nguyen, Richard Niemi, Pippa Norris, Jonna Nurmi, Brenda O'Neill, Murray Print, John Richards, Rob Richie, Larry Rose, Martin Rosema, Andrew Russell, Alan Sears, Kaat Smets, Judith Torney-Purta, Joel Westheimer, Paul Whiteley, and James Youniss.

As far as the content itself is concerned, two anonymous reviewers made a number of useful suggestions, as did Jeanne Ferris, Phyllis Deutsch, and Ann Brash at the University Press of New England. Arthur Milner read the entire typescript: his invaluable contribution cannot be adequately acknowledged. The same is true of Frances Boylston, who has also shared this journey with me. Her insights have found their way onto almost every page of what follows.

MONTREAL, FEBRUARY 2010

PART 1

CITIZENS IN THE MAKING

Why Political Dropouts Matter

The last phrase in the subtitle of this book is provocative: the expression "political dropout" evokes the image of young people who have withdrawn not from the world of education but from the world of politics, but also suggesting that there is some connection between the two. And it conveys a sense of urgency to better understand, and thus address, the phenomenon.

The young people discussed here were under thirty when most of the research on which this book is based was conducted. While there is much to distinguish the world in which they entered adulthood from that of earlier generations, the omnipresence of the Internet is undeniably the most salient factor. The term "Internet generation" is thus more than descriptive; it raises an unavoidable question: does growing up with the Internet foster engaged citizens or political dropouts? Opinion is divided—even about what phrases to use. I chose the term "engaged citizen" because—as we shall see later in this chapter, when we set out the positions of the prominent observers and theorists in this debate—it is favored by those on one side, who view these developments in a positive light.

My concern with political dropouts places me among those who see developments as worrisome. It leads me to stress the informed political participation—that is, the political knowledge and attentiveness, as well as the electoral participation—of the Internet generation, and to look primarily to citizen or civic education to enhance it.

It is only at the end of part 1, in chapters 4 and 5, that we set out facts and figures about the political knowledge and electoral participation of the Internet generation. In chapters 2 and 3, we place the political dropout phenomenon in the context of the fundamental sociological and technological developments that have taken place in the past sixty years. First we consider factors affecting socialization, especially changes in the role of the family; then we proceed to the mass media, beginning with the emergence of television and including an assessment of the effects of the Internet.

Other factors also affect informed political participation, and some, at least in principle, are within the reach of policy or institutional reform. In part 2, we first examine the effects of relevant political institutions, especially those concerned with how elections take place. Then, in part 3, we turn to education, civic education in particular. We outline a pedagogical approach making optimal use of the communications media of the Internet generation, and, in the concluding chapter, set the approach within the framework of the complementary political institutions identified in part 2.

Concrete recommendations draw on examples of complementary institutions and promising practices in certain countries. The perspective here is North American. Other countries such as the United Kingdom— about and from which we have a rich, relevant literature—are brought in to place the North American reality in wider comparative context. The Nordic countries are given special attention, since their experiences appear to provide promising guidelines toward the path to follow.

Green and Apolitical?

People reaching adulthood after 1990 entered a world fundamentally transformed from that of earlier generations. This world has given young people extraordinary technological innovations, but it has another side. In their lifetimes, members of this post–cold war, Internet generation will be confronted with a world drowning in debt and overheated by carbon emissions. Even though most of today's young citizens are aware of the challenges that environmental threats pose, that consciousness has yet to find its way into any kind of comprehensive or effective political program. Instead, concern about the issue is typically manifested in consumption choices or other forms of individual expression. And when it comes to political mobilization and participation, passivity tends to be the rule, a passivity often rationalized by a generalized rejection of politics.[1]

The response to this phenomenon among academic analysts of political participation has been varied. Some see this rejection in positive terms, calling for a redefinition of the very notion of political participation so as to incorporate the individual attitudes and consumption choices of young people. These analysts downplay the role of political parties and other traditional types of political organizations in favor of transnational Internet-based networks, which, it is presumed, add a political dimension to individual actions and attitudes.

In this chapter, we subject this interpretation to critical analysis in light of what we know of this generation. Does following the principle of "think globally, act locally" in fact become one of "bypass governments, act individually"? This cannot be a viable strategy as long as democratically elected governments are driving the wheels of change and, in so doing, responding—however imperfectly—to politically mobilized populations. Despite the highly publicized role of these global networks at international symposiums, the slow progress on climate change, when set against the threat it constitutes, suggests that generations that turn their backs on politics in favor of individual expression will continue to find their priorities at the top of society's wish list—and at the bottom of the "to do" list.[2]

Powerful rich countries—notably the United States and Canada—continue to drag their feet on climate change, pulling down the overall effort. Not coincidentally, in these countries young citizens, with their high levels of political abstention, have little political clout. This generation's failure to bring climate change to the top of the political agenda compares unfavorably with earlier generations' achievements in decolonization and racial and gender equality.

Of course, the issues and the context are not the same: given the economic cost, effective policies to stem climate change are a harder political sell. Moreover, the baby boomers were an especially numerous generation. So we need to make sure that one generation does not place unrealistic expectations on another. Still, we can reasonably ask: why is there no identifiable, youth-based movement to get climate change policies onto the agenda of political parties, interest groups, and governments?

Let us be clear. This is not a handbook for political organizers addressing climate change, but rather a book about the political participation of an emerging generation. The absence of a generation-based, politically sophisticated environmental movement is an acute symptom of a wider phenomenon: the generation reaching maturity is seemingly not prepared to take its full part in the political process. Climate change dramatically brings to light the results of continued low levels of informed political participation by the generation most affected by it, and the fact that even on this most global of issues, there is no avoiding politics.

Paying attention to politics is what this book is about: it explores both the obstacles in the way of increasing informed political participation among young North American citizens to satisfactory levels, and how to overcome those obstacles. Political participation is here understood to encompass a range of activities that, in one way or another, seek to affect the policies of individuals who are—or wish to be—democratically elected, and of the organizations behind them. These include conventional activities like voting and the various activities related to it (party membership, activities in support of candidates and outcomes in election campaigns and referendums, etc.), as well as unconventional activities, such as demonstrations and boycotts, that seek to affect policies.

But opinions vary as to the weight to give to each type of activity and, indeed, how to measure, characterize, and thus interpret the level of political participation in general, and that of young citizens in particular. Not all analysts would agree with our assessment that the current level of youth political participation is unsatisfactory. Nevertheless, it is hard to deny the simple fact that serves as the starting point of this intellectual undertaking: young people in North America and most comparable countries are less attentive to political life, and thus less involved in it, than previous generations. The result is a democratic deficit in political participation, most readily visible in, though not limited to, election turnout.

Tables in chapter 4 set out in detail the trends in voter turnout in the United States, Canada, and Europe over the last few generations. They show, first, that there has been a decline in voter turnout, and, second, that this is largely a generational phenomenon. For example, in the twenty-two countries that participated in the first wave of the European Social Survey (ESS) in 2002, overall turnout was 21 percentage points lower among those aged eighteen to twenty-four than in the rest of the electorate,[3] with the gap increasing to 27 percentage points for first-time voters. The reality over the past twenty years, especially in the advanced democracies, is one of growing abstention among young people. Though people are more likely to vote as they get older, for the most part, the current decline reflects a generational phenomenon.

Young people's failure to vote is a contemporary international phenomenon: even some countries with traditionally high turnout, such as Finland, have not been spared. Of course, not all countries have been uniformly or simultaneously affected. Canada is perhaps not atypical, having experienced especially acute decline during the 1990s, resulting in a youth turnout rate well below 50 percent, comparable to Britain (Phelps 2005),[4] and the United States. But the United States, which saw youth turnout fall earlier than elsewhere, has seen some improvement in recent years. The u.s. reversal of this trend appears to be exceptional and raises a key question to be addressed: does the reversal foretell a long-range change, or is it likely to prove temporary (as seems to be the case in Canada, where a modest improvement in 2004 and 2006 was wiped out in 2008), perhaps simply caused by the Iraq war and the candidacy of Barack Obama.

Voter turnout levels reflect many factors, including the strength of the sense of civic duty to vote. The ESS asked how important it is for a good citizen to vote in elections, and its results show a positive relationship between reported turnout and importance of voting, a relationship that is slightly weaker among new voters. In several countries (Sweden, Denmark, Austria, and Germany), new voters place the highest levels of importance on voting, and it is in those countries that reported turnout is high. In countries (Switzerland, Spain, Portugal, Britain, and Finland) where potential first-time voters place lower levels of importance on voting, turnout tends to be low.

An exception is Norway, where potential first-time voters are lower only in reported voting. This reflects the fact that electoral turnout has been declining somewhat in Norway, but political interest and discussion remain high, and direct, citizen-initiated contact with political institutions, including political parties, has been growing. It would appear that Norway and Denmark, where turnout has remained high and steady, are exceptions that merit investigation, but that also confirm the rule. The rule is a decline in conventional political participation coinciding with the replacement of earlier generations by young people who reached maturity since the 1990s. The rule applies to voting—the simplest, most straightforward expression, or the sine qua non, of political participation in a democracy—but also to other gauges of political participation, including membership in political parties and interest groups (Stolle and Cruz 2005).

Why Informed Political Participation Matters

But why should we be concerned about this decline? Why should we expect that if substantially more young people voted, it would make a difference in political action to confront climate change—or, indeed, in any other matter of importance? The answer lies in our stress on *informed* political participation: little would change if we just augmented the turnout of citizens ignorant of the positions of the parties on the environment by, say, fining nonvoters. Nevertheless, turnout and political knowledge go together. Especially now, as the sense that it is a civic duty to vote diminishes, there is a powerful reciprocal relationship between them. As I have shown elsewhere (Milner 2002a), other things being equal, the level of civic literacy (that is, the proportion of citizens with the minimum level of political knowledge needed to make sense of the political world and thus choose effectively among political alternatives) corresponds to the level of voter turnout.

In my past work, I have shown that the Northern European, especially the Scandinavian, countries are higher in civic literacy than English-speaking ones, and that this correlates with levels of political participation. When we look at who casts the extra votes, we find a simple answer to the question of why we should bother about declining turnout. Countries high in civic literacy achieve informed political participation in particular among those who are elsewhere excluded from the democratic political process; thus, high civic literacy brings their needs and interests to the attention of policymakers and into policy outcomes. High civic literacy is found in societies that practice nonmaterial redistribution, reducing disparities in not only material but also intellectual resources.[5] Bringing those on the lower rungs of society to higher levels of knowledge augments their economic opportunities, and it enhances their capacity to exercise political influence through informed political participation.[6]

By enhancing citizenship skills and knowledge through nonmaterial redistribution, the countries high in civic literacy spread well-being more widely, evidence of which can be found in the various cross-national indicators of life expectancy, infant mortality, and life satisfaction. These factors lie beyond the scope of this book, as, indeed, does the level of environmental consciousness. But I maintain that it would not be difficult to show a positive relationship between environmental outcomes—which can be viewed as a form of redistribution from current to future generations—and the level of informed participation of young citizens.[7]

Protecting the natural environment of future generations, like improving the socioeconomic positions of those low in resources, is a good answer to the question of why bother to try to reduce the democratic deficit by increasing informed political participation. (I use the more unwieldy term "informed political participation" instead of "civic literacy" here, because, more than for earlier generations with a stronger sense of civic duty, for this generation, being politically informed and putting that information into practice are closely associated.)

There is another consideration beyond bringing the needs and interests of those otherwise excluded into the political process. The other case for enhanced political participation is essentialist: political participation is a value in itself, as it is what makes subjects into citizens. For political thinkers from Aristotle to Rousseau and Mill, it is only through citizenship, through participating in the political community, that one's full humanity is realized. Even if the citizen's impetus for participating is to ensure that his or her interests are taken into account, participation effectively entails learning how to place those interests and needs in the context of the interests and needs of the wider community.[8]

Living up to a conception of political participation as civic virtue may be too high an expectation to place upon the contemporary citizen. But maintaining some degree of attentiveness to public affairs should not be too much to expect in the context of appropriate institutions and policies. Such institutions and policies provide ready access to sources of information and foster the requisite skills that facilitate such attentiveness for those low in the needed resources (education, family background, access to the relevant communication media, etc.), especially at an age when habits of attentiveness or inattentiveness are developed.

In parts 2 and 3, we explore the workings of pertinent policies and institutions. We can now turn our attention to the wide contemporary discussion of youth political participation, a discussion that has expanded significantly as concern about democratic deficit has mounted. But despite that expansion, I contend, the informed dimension of youth political participation—namely, political knowledge—receives insufficient attention.

Deliberation, Civil Society, and the Politically Informed Citizen

I am not suggesting that political knowledge has been absent from the discussion. It has gained the attention of several researchers in recent years—as we shall see in chapter 5—and its importance has been clearly signaled by a number of contemporary scholars, including Benjamin Barber[9] and William Galston. As Galston puts it: "Civic knowledge helps citizens understand and promote their interests and increases the consistency of their views across issues and time. It allows them to understand political events and integrate new information into an existing framework, and to alter those views when appropriate. Civic knowledge reduces mistrust of, or alienation from, public life; [and] promotes support for democratic values and political participation."[10]

But knowledge gets less attention in the literature than trust does, in particular the trust said to be generated by participation in voluntary associations and networks. The precursor of this approach is Tocqueville, who documented what he viewed as the positive role of intermediate associations independent of the state. His modern heir, Robert Putnam, conceptualized the process as one of "social capital"—that is, norms and networks based on trust—and shifted the terminological focus from political participation toward "civic engagement."[11] Putnam was a member of the team of American political scientists who wrote *Democracy at Risk*, a report to the American Political Science Association (Macedo et al. 2005). Though not neglecting knowledge, the report stressed trust, social networks, and volunteering (in other words, civic engagement): "Quite simply, when citizens are involved and engaged with others, their lives and our communities are better" (5). Unfortunately, such appealing phraseology invites wishful thinking, specifically the assumption that participating in the activities of voluntary associations induces political involvement.

A recent article tests these claims using survey data from seventeen European countries. While the authors find the expected positive correlation between associational involvement and political action, that correlation is explained not by civic skills and civic-mindedness, but by selection effects: the same people choose both to join associations and to be politically active (Van Der Meer and Van Ingen 2009). Indeed, the very terms "social capital" and "civic engagement" are positively loaded, as noted by Theiss-Morse and Hibbing: "Social capital is an undemanding master . . . social capital is fundamentally about how we conduct our everyday life . . . It does not take years of pushing hard for structural reforms. It does not involve upsetting the political coalitions that have strong stakes in existing institutions . . . Instead, we can mobilize people to do what they would do naturally—join with others in pleasurable activities" (2001, 178); "Belonging to voluntary associations is a woefully inadequate foundation for good citizenship for three primary reasons: People join groups that are homogeneous, not heterogeneous; civic participation does not lead to, and may turn people away from, political participation; and not all groups promote democratic values. Good citizens need to learn that democracy is messy, inefficient, and conflict-ridden. Voluntary associations do not teach these lessons" (2005, 227). Hence, the authors conclude: "The route to enhancing meaningful civic life is not badgering people to become engaged because politics is fun and easy; it is asking people to become engaged because politics is dreary and difficult" (2005, 246).

There is indeed a danger, when stressing the importance of citizen participation, of idealizing the citizen and presenting an overly rosy picture of what is entailed in playing that role. Nevertheless, while we should not "badger" citizens to join the "fun," it is equally inappropriate to ask them to sacrifice themselves to the "dreary" business of politics. Without being blind to the fact that many adult citizens do not possess the basic knowledge and skills of political literacy, we can realistically seek, through institutions and policies explored later in this volume, to encourage citizens to be politically informed, looking for guidelines to comparable societies where this is more frequently the case.

Meaningful—that is, informed—political participation is thus premised on a consistent, solid majority of politically literate adult citizens[12] in the context of appropriate educational and information-dissemination institutions. In making this assertion, I steer clear of the debate over the claim that, despite being uninformed, a citizen can use "heuristics" to make a rational choice (e.g., Lupia 1994); I agree with Delli Carpini, who concludes that this is ultimately a false issue: "[All of the theories] suggesting that effective democracy is possible even if citizens are not fully informed about the details of politics and policy . . . still require some non-trivial level of individual and/or collective knowledge, all of them concede (or imply) that the quality of decisions improves as the amount of information increases" (1999, 30).[13]

Political literacy can be described as a minimal familiarity with the relevant institutions of decision making, combined with a basic knowledge of the key positions on relevant issues and the political actors holding them, issues that will vary over time and the individual's vantage point (age, gender, class, location, etc.). The crucial characteristic is attentiveness to the political world, as illustrated by a recent study of two thousand German citizens. It found that in both the former East Germany and West Germany, controlling for education and income, attentive citizens display significantly higher levels of political knowledge, participate more often in politics, and, unlike the inattentive, feel capable of understanding and influencing political decision making and consider the defense of democracy to be a civic duty (Geissel 2008).

The politically literate citizen is characterized by Schudson (1998) as "monitorial," one who scans the informational environment on a wide variety of issues and may be mobilized around those issues. Political literacy entails a capacity crucial to democracy, that of being able to identify alternative positions on such issues. Citizens with access to only one view are naturally inclined to attribute malevolent motives to those who do not share it, and to follow leaders who make the same attribution. Political censorship is the customary way of achieving this, but a similar result can be attained less harshly via an inattentive citizenry.

A politically literate citizen is not the same thing as a rational, informed deliberator who assembles and weighs the pros and cons of alternative policies to arrive at the optimum outcome. We can realistically envisage the former, but not the latter, as the norm. The reality is that democratic citizens are embedded in relatively safe and agreeable networks of relations, and even voluntary associations, where political disagreement is rare (Mutz 2006). Hibbing and Theiss-Morse cast doubt upon the assumptions of proponents of deliberative democracy: "securing broad-based, meaningful deliberation on contentious issues from ordinary citizens, most of whom have little desire to engage in public policy discussions, is next to impossible" (2002, 228).[14] Here they are on firm ground: it is in fact only when citizens stop becoming "ordinary" that they can be expected to engage in meaningful deliberation on important political issues. The distinction between ordinary and deliberating citizens proved salient recently in Canada, during an effort to take electoral reform out of the hands of legislators, with their vested interests as incumbents, and hand it to the citizens. First in British Columbia in 2005, and then in Ontario in 2007, assemblies of citizens were established to propose a new electoral system to the voters. In both cases, their proposals failed to win sufficient support in a subsequent referendum,[15] at least in part because their content and presentation allowed opponents to play on the fears of ordinary voters. The citizens' assembly members proved insufficiently sensitive to this dimension because, though they had become quasi-experts through an extensive and deliberative educational process, they still saw themselves as representative of ordinary citizens.

These assemblies manifest the tension between democracy as deliberation and democracy as the informed political participation of ordinary citizens. Ordinary citizens as a rule lack access to extraordinary resources, the kind of resources allocated via the citizens' assembly deliberation process to the chosen few. The assemblies were, in part, established in response to the efforts of what might be termed the deliberation lobby, whose goal is to enhance and encourage citizen deliberation and incorporate it into the process of political decision making. The assemblies are structured as "deliberative spaces," characterized by face-to-face and online discussion groups that promise to bring the public into contact and potential partnership with decision makers in setting agendas and designing policies, implementing them, and monitoring their outcomes (see Lukensmeyer and Torres 2006, 9). The latter function especially, in the form of democratic audits and the like, is seen to render decision makers accountable. Hence the appeal of deliberative participation to local, regional, and national governments and to international bodies like the United Nations, the European Union, and the World Bank. Warren notes that in response to citizens' expectations of having their voices heard, "decision-makers increasingly find themselves with legislative mandates inadequate for carrying out their responsibilities. They look to new and old participative mechanisms to involve citizens in decision-making: referendums, deliberative polling, town hall meetings, participatory budgeting, citizen juries, citizen assemblies, neighborhood councils and the like, to gain legitimacy for their policies" (2008, 4).

But to whom are these mechanisms accountable? Assuming the mantle of democracy, their advocates redefine democracy as "citizen governance," which entails, as characterized by Susan Phillips, "decentralizing control from governments to civil society . . . [and] the creation of new institutions and policy frameworks that enhance dialogue and collaboration" (2006, 3). Of the hundreds, if not thousands, of groups in the United States that comprise this lobby, typical is the National Coalition for Dialogue & Deliberation, which brings together and supports "people, organizations, and resources in ways that expand the power of discussion to benefit society." Its ambitious mission is to "advance participative change methods, leveraging the power of over 60 approaches being used to transform whole organizations and communities as they tackle 21st century challenges, address critical needs at local and global levels, expand the reach of the methods around the world, design significant field research projects, invent new tools, techniques, and applications, incorporate technology to leverage existing methods, connect with others to form joint ventures, innovate educational programs and courses, craft a common language, and articulate a platform for this body of work."[16]

All of this is commendable, but how legitimate are the claims of democracy from a mechanism that makes no mention of parties or elections, the standard means by which the ordinary citizen enters the political process? Indeed, the language betrays a disregard for the situation of the ordinary citizen. Unlike the citizens' assemblies, which had the financial and organizational capacity to recruit and educate ordinary citizens, most of these various deliberative projects and experiences do not, and hence favor citizens with superior resources, an "aristocracy of intellectuals,"[17] and exclude the rest. According to Sanders:

> As these mechanisms proliferate, democracy is increasingly seen to take place here rather than within formal representative institutions. Such activities are based on individuals and groups on behalf of any number of interests, identities, and ideals, the representativeness of which are usually untested. Were they to be tested, we would see that many of these forms of participation, being based on self-selection, favor those with greater resources, and can thus increase political inequality. The loudest voices are heard over those of the less organized, less educated, for example when it comes to decisions over the location of institutions to help the disadvantaged but generate opposition in local communities. (1997, 347)

To state the point crudely, to make them function meaningfully, those involved in the various forms of deliberative participation must either comprise an elite or, indirectly, create one. This is not because ordinary citizens are incapable of deliberation, or cannot benefit from it,[18] but because they need information and skills not normally at their disposal. The fact that deliberative experiences can make useful contributions to policy does not in itself make them an expression of democracy. They lack the basic attribute of traditional elected political bodies: however flawed the electoral process may be, elected bodies are accountable to the majority of ordinary citizens.

Civil Society in Europe

Proponents of deliberative democracy can exacerbate these flaws by, in effect, using them to rationalize abstention from informed participation in electoral politics. We see this process in the currently fashionable European notion of a so-called civil society as an improvement on political society. While in the Anglo-American world, the distinction between state and society has a long pedigree, Europe has retained the classical notion of the state as an inherent feature of society. When the state was challenged by the New Left in the 1970s and the New Right in the 1980s, a new expression was needed for relationships which excluded both the traditional state (the bugbear of the right) and the market (the bugbear of the left). So Europe discovered civil society, defined by the European Union as the sum of non-governmental, non-profit making organizations, networks and voluntary associations, sometimes also referred to as a third sector—the first and second sectors being those governed by the logic of the state and the market.

Incorporation of the notion of a European civil society in this way could serve to buttress the European Union's claim to democratic legitimacy, a claim which rests unsteadily on the bureaucracy in Brussels and the European Parliament in Strasbourg. The July 2001 White Paper on European Governance embraced an agenda of strengthening civil society, and of bringing it into the process of policy consultation. The process intensified around the effort to draft and adopt a treaty establishing a constitution for Europe. Article I-46 of the draft treaty recognized the need for EU institutions to regularly engage in open dialogue and consultation with civil society. Moreover, the convention which drew up the treaty created a forum—a network of organizations representing sectors of civil society, such as the business world, nongovernmental organizations, and academia—to receive input from civil society groups beyond the political representatives, especially including young people.[19]

The forum was envisaged as the embodiment of deliberative democracy, a community based on the voluntary consent of participating individuals. It would allow deliberation free of the constraints and influences of particular interests, and thus would potentially be able to transcend the traditional politics of negotiation and compromise and to produce a vision of the common welfare. A specific target was the neocorporatist alliance of business, labor, and government that characterized much of Europe since World War II. Rejecting the neocorporatist system and embracing civil society were spokespersons for groups and organizations identified with emerging postmaterialistic causes including the environment, international peace, and feminism—groups that deemed themselves excluded from the neocorporatist arrangements. They proclaimed themselves to be opening and occupying what they called action spaces within civil society (see Saha, Print, and Edwards 2005). The nation-state, around which these postwar arrangements were structured, was thus part of the problem, and civil society, which transcended it, was the solution.[20]

Promoting civil society in this way served to deflect attention from the simple fact that democracy in the European Union was running a deficit at its core: the European Parliament. Even in countries with high civic literacy, many people who vote in national elections sit on the sidelines when it comes to electing representatives to the European Parliament. In Sweden, for example, over 80 percent voted in the most recent (2006) national elections, but only 45 percent turned out in June 2009 to elect their representatives to Strasbourg. Yet the Scandinavians display a high level of knowledge of Europe, unusually positive attitudes toward people from other European countries, and fluency in major European languages. The Eurobarometer surveys show a consistent suspicion in Sweden, Denmark, and Finland toward deepening European integration. The ambivalence, I suggest, is based on an informed appreciation of the dangers to democracy presented by a central institutional apparatus with significant powers and responsibilities accountable to the citizens of Europe, who are represented via the European Parliament. In reality, intelligently exercising such citizenship entails understanding the cultural, ideological, and institutional context in which representatives of other member states act,[21] with political knowledge of one's own state as a poor guide. In other words, the value of experience, skills, and knowledge gained as an informed participant in national politics is dwarfed by that acquired from connection to European civil society via multi-national group networks—which is limited to an unrepresentative elite.

Thus it should come as no surprise that most Europeans, especially in the postmaterialistic Nordic countries, are skeptical of such shortcuts to democratic accountability via civil society. In a study using data from the 2004 European Social Survey, Hooghe and Dejaeghere find that while in the United States, postmaterialistic attitudes tend to comprise a rejection of political parties and other traditional political institutions, this is not so in the Scandinavian context: "The group of citizens that most closely corresponds to the notion of postmodern citizens identified by various authors still belongs to parties and trade unions . . . [and feels] quite well integrated into the political system" (2007, 270). Similarly, as noted above, when average voter turnout in Norway declined in the 1990s by almost 10 percent, it paralleled an increase in citizen-initiated activities taking place via conventional modes of political participation (Aars and Strømsnes 2007; Listhaug and Grønflaten 2007). And while 37 percent of Finns strongly agreed and 32 percent somewhat agreed that more referendums should be used when important political questions are decided, Bengtsson and Mattila conclude:

> [It is not,] as the post-material wing appears to believe, the young, knowledgeable, interested and politically enthusiastic citizens that favour more direct public involvement in politics . . . The expectation about support for a greater public involvement among the politically interested, resource- and skilful citizens does not get any support whatsoever. On the contrary attitudes in favour of a greater use of referendums in the future are negatively connected with such factors as education and knowledge about political matters. (2008, 9)[22]

In sum, in the most politically sophisticated modern societies, the connection between democracy and representative political institutions has not been severed: civil society offers no shortcut.

Ultimately, the question of whether measures to extend public deliberation reduce the democratic deficit or weaken the already shaky foundations of our democratic institutions is answered by the place given to citizens at the margins of political literacy. We noted earlier that countries high in civic literacy, through mechanisms of nonmaterial redistribution, extend effective citizenship to many people whose counterparts are excluded in countries with low civic literacy. There is no reason to expect a parallel effect from an expansion of deliberative exercises. Combining the voices of representatives of groups and organizations identified with emerging causes with the voices of traditional business and labor organizations to create consultative bodies can have beneficial results. However, reducing the democratic deficit is not one of them, since such mechanisms give those with advantageous social and educational backgrounds access to channels of influence not available to ordinary citizens.

Political Dropouts or Unconventional Participants

Encouraging further circumvention of traditional democratic forms in the name of extending democracy to the people (seen in opposition to elected politicians and officials) will not reduce the democratic deficit where young people are concerned—despite the fact that such demands are often made in their name. In the discussion surrounding youth political participation and engagement, this argument tends to take a different, less institutional form. The issues parallel those raised in the debate over transcending traditional political institutions via civil society (see Milner 2002b), but in somewhat more individualistic terms. Issues are most often couched in terms of whether unconventional forms of political participation are replacing declining conventional forms—which, as we have seen, have been declining over the past two decades in most countries, coinciding with the arrival of the Internet generation.

It is possible, of course, to interpret this development as natural, a matter of keeping up with the times: "maybe formal participation mechanisms and traditional political organizations have been necessary during the development phase of mass democracies, but in contemporary societies they have lost much of their relevance" (Stolle and Hooghe 2004). Such thinking is influenced especially by the portrayal of these developments by Ronald Inglehart as natural in the postmaterial world, of which the emerging generations are the avant-garde.

Data accumulated by Inglehart (1997), as well as by Pippa Norris (2002), are often cited by those who contend that reduced legitimacy for traditional democratic institutions, as manifested in declining voter turnout and interest in and attentiveness to party politics among young people, is counterbalanced by participatory attitudes and repertoires of unconventional political participation. Norris specifically refers to civil society in her redefinition of political participation as "any dimensions of activity that are either designed directly to influence government agencies and the policy process, or indirectly to impact civil society, or which attempt to alter systematic patterns of social behavior" (2002, 4). Such a definition includes illegal political protests; activities implemented by associations, organizations, and networks; and those aimed at influencing actors other than elected representatives.

In a later work, Norris draws on data from the first round of the European Social Survey[23] about political acts that respondents in fifteen nations reported having done during the previous twelve months, breaking the respondents down by age: younger citizens (aged eighteen to twenty-nine); the middle-aged (thirty to fifty-nine); and older citizens (sixty and over). She identifies "a significant age gap . . . in all the citizen-oriented repertoires of action, including voting, contacting, donating money, party membership and party work, [that] contrary to the thesis of . . . young people's apathy, compared with the older group, young people were 8 percent more likely to have signed a petition, 7 percent more likely to have bought a product for political reasons, and 6% more likely to have demonstrated" (2003, 11).

But do the data in fact constitute a refutation of "the thesis of young people's apathy"? First of all, the difference between those under 30 and those over 60 in 2002 to report resorting to unconventional, cause-oriented activity is far too small to suggest that unconventional participation is substituting for conventional forms. Fifty percent of the young Europeans claimed to vote, and no more than 28 percent reported having participated in any cause-oriented activity. From what we know generally from the literature,[24] we have no reason to assume that a significant number among the 28 percent are nonvoters. Hence, when we compare the generations' engagement in *any* form of political participation, traditional or unconventional, we have no basis for assuming that adding the cause-oriented activists to the citizen-oriented activists meaningfully reduces the overall gap between the 50 percent of those under thirty and the 80 percent of those over thirty who reported voting in the previous election.

To be fair, Norris does not explicitly claim that such a substitution is taking place. Inglehart goes further, however, associating the arrival of recent generations with an overall rise in elite-challenging behavior, drawing evidence from the World Values Survey data. The problem is that the wvs asks about participation not over twelve months, like the ess, but over the respondent's lifetime. Hence Inglehart cannot, as he does, use the wvs data to support his 1977 prediction "that these newer forms of [elite-challenging] participation have become increasingly widespread" (Inglehart and Catterberg, 2002, 303–4). This is because the way the wvs poses its questions—"have you ever taken part" in such activities?—means that the variation in responses over time reflects generational replacement more than anything else, especially when the key group is the extremely large boomer generation. Because of this, the rising proportion of positive responses in succeeding waves found by Inglehart reflects only the fact that boomers, more of whom took part in such an activity at least once (typically during the radical 1960s and 1970s), count increasingly in the overall totals as the previous genera-tions die off: the increase tells us nothing about the choices of recent generations. Moreover, Norris's conclusion, we should remind ourselves, compares those under thirty with those over sixty, rather than with the generations in between—generations whose members, at least when they were younger, were likely to take part in similar levels of cause-oriented activities.

When we try to find broad evidence that unconventional forms of political participation are substituting for traditional ones, we seldom succeed. An analysis of the results of a survey of fourteen-year-olds in the iea (International Association for the Evaluation of Educational Achievement) study of twenty-four nations found "no overall shift in post-materialist societies from voting to more active, issue-specific forms of participation. Rather ... except in the usa, teenagers in the most post-materialist countries, such as the Nordic countries, predict [for themselves] the least diversified range of activism" (Amnå, Munck, and Zetterberg 2004, 35). Overall, the data suggest that in certain countries, a measure of substitution is taking place among a small group of well-educated young citizens. However, as Gallego Dobón notes, it is the concentration rather than the substitution hypothesis that "is more ap-propriate in regard to poorly educated citizens who are increasingly withdrawing from political activity, while most highly educated persons find ways to make their voices heard" (2007, 1).

Similarly, generalizing from cross-national data, Gidengil, Blais, Nevitte, and Nadeau conclude that "the affluent and the highly educated are the most likely to sign petitions, join in boycotts, and attend lawful demonstrations, just as they are more likely to vote, to become members of political parties, and to join interest groups" (2004, 142).[25] Yet the fact that data on conventional and unconventional forms of participation fail to substantiate the substitution hypothesis has by no means ended the debate. This is because some observers have adopted a methodology that might be termed subjective. Political participation is extended beyond repertoires of organized action to individual consumer choices and expressed attitudes. Norris opens the door to this redefinition by including boycotts and what she calls buycotts (purchasing certain products and services for political reasons) as forms of political participation, and by adopting a definition which, as noted above, includes efforts "indirectly to impact civil society, or . . . alter systematic patterns of social behavior." But she leaves unanswered the question of whether such activities are consciously part of a coordinated effort. To the extent that this is the case, including boycotts is uncontroversial. But this criterion is implicitly or explicitly rejected by other observers, who include choices made by a consumer as a statement with regard to business or government practices—for example, in relation to the environment or the production of healthy foods (e.g., Micheletti, Føllesdal, and Stolle 2004).

A parallel tendency, especially among younger British observers, is to associate political participation with certain attitudes expressed in youth surveys. For example, the British Electoral Commission found young nonvoters disproportionately inclined to state that they did not vote because it made little difference who won the election, and that "no one party stands for me." Seizing on these responses, O'Toole, Marsh, and Jones conclude that "young people are far from being apathetic," since "politics is something that is done to them, not something they can influence" (2003, 359). In a similar vein, the authors of another British survey found that 71 percent of their respondents agreed with the statement "there aren't enough opportunities for young people like me to influence political parties" and concluded that young people are "sufficiently interested in political affairs to dispel the myth that they are apathetic and politically lazy" (Henn and Weinstein 2003).[26] The problem with using such survey data is that when respondents are given the choice between blaming others or, in effect, admitting to being "apathetic and politically lazy," the result is predictable.[27]

A similar problem has crept into the recent work of Russell Dalton, the respected American student of democratic participation. Dalton

(2006) extends Norris's notion of cause-oriented political participation to what he terms "engaged citizenship," which he distinguishes from "citizen duty."[28] Rather than centered on actions, Dalton's criteria for engaged citizenship, like those of the British observers, are in large part a matter of expressed attitudes. Critics of young people, he asserts, have missed the good news about young Americans, manifested in repertoires of attitudes associated with such things as forming one's opinion, supporting the worse off, understanding others, and being active in voluntary associations. Against the bad news of young people's being lower on the various measures of citizen duty then older generations, he presents "good news" in the guise of data showing them often to be more likely to express such attitudes.[29]

We have borrowed Dalton's term of "engaged citizens" for the subtitle of this book because, as he elaborates it, it downplays the existence of political dropouts. The problem is that an attitude, however commendable, is not in itself a form of political participation. By conflating the two, Dalton is sending out a misleading message: encourage expression of the right attitudes, and you are promoting the political participation of young people. Encouraging expression of an appropriate attitude, as in the case of the questions posed by the British observers of youth political participation, invites respondents to place themselves in a positive light, at no cost to themselves. Young American respondents cannot help but suspect that answering positively about "forming one's opinion," "supporting the worse off," "understanding others," and "being active in voluntary associations" places them in a positive light. They live in an educational environment replete with powerful institutional incentives for expressing an interest in being active in voluntary associations and other good causes that support the worse off and promote tolerance. Indeed, the voluntary nature of such participation is dubious, given the fact that in many schools and colleges, such activity is obligatory. A recent study of young people in four American high schools found "a single theme about the meaning of civic engagement [that] appeared repeatedly: 'resume padding' . . . Young people of all class strata, races, and ethnic backgrounds told us that they needed 'something' to put on their resumes, and this was so whether their goal was . . . a state school with quasi-open admission . . . or a highly competitive private school" (Friedland and Morimoto 2006, 32).[30]

Conclusions by Dalton and others who rely on the high levels of positive responses to questions that sound out attitudes of this kind are intrinsically unreliable. Even when these attitudes are genuine, it is questionable to assert that they constitute a form of political participation. While not addressing young people in particular, Theiss-Morse and Hibbing's (2005) critique of what they perceive to be a conception of political participation based on social capital is pertinent here. To paraphrase them, young citizens need to learn that democracy is not an expression of appropriate feelings, unrelated to efforts to confront the messy realities of political life.

Political Knowledge as Key

In a survey, one can express attitudes one does not hold and report votes one has not cast, or voluntary activities never carried out, but one cannot demonstrate knowledge one does not have. Political knowledge questions provide an objective measure impervious to norms and institutionalized incentives. Unfortunately, it is rare for those who defend cause-oriented repertoires, engaged citizenship, or political consumerism to pose the question—let alone pose questions—of political knowledge. But by not including such questions in surveys of attitudes and reported repertoires of political activities, especially unconventional ones, those scholars are in effect inviting the same kinds of distortions pointed to by students of the relationship between surveys of public opinion and knowledge. Althaus (2003), for example, recites chapter and verse about how not incorporating the political knowledge dimension into attitudinal surveys results in failure to distinguish meaningful opinions held by respondents from artifacts of the interview process.

Studies of political participation that exclude the information dimension—as many still do—can suppose that abstention from participation in traditional politics is a form of protest, and that young nonvoters must be practicing a different kind of politics, one inaccessible or even incomprehensible to older generations. The above-noted British instances of taking at face value young nonvoters' justification—the parties are "all the same" or "none stand for me"—were not accompanied by an effort to test whether the response was based on at least a minimal knowledge of what the parties actually do stand for. In the same vein, it would be useful if, alongside Dalton's criteria for engaged versus dutiful citizenship, there were questions testing whether the young people who express positive attitudes toward "supporting the worse off" have some idea of which parties and candidates favor policies supporting the worse off, as well as some knowledge of the measures the parties plan to employ, or have employed, when in power.[31] Had he done this, as we shall see from data presented in chapter 5, he might have come to rather different conclusions.

It is not surprising that such questions are still infrequently asked. Political scientists do not like to point fingers, lest they appear to be judging their fellow citizens. Hence positive expressions of "interest in politics" in surveys are taken at face value, without probing whether that interest was actually invested in any efforts to gain relevant information. Does it mean anything at all to claim to be interested in something that one pays no attention to? The problem is well illustrated by a simple American experiment that varied the order in which the political interest and political knowledge questions were presented. It found that while 75.9 percent of respondents reported an interest in politics, this figure dropped to 57.4 percent when respondents to the survey were first asked political knowledge questions (Schwarz and Schumer 1997).

This is not a matter of semantics. By incorporating the knowledge dimension into our surveys, we can distinguish political participants (including engaged, cause-oriented citizens, and even political consumers) from political dropouts. Political dropouts are young citizens so inattentive to the political world around them that they lack the minimal knowledge needed to distinguish and thus choose among parties or candidates. In most established democratic countries, these citizens constitute an important phenomenon, despite the fact that they are part of a generation that is better educated on average than previous ones. Though they may express positive attitudes toward citizenship when invited to, and even assert a willingness to vote when asked about it, political dropouts lack the knowledge and skills to do so in any meaningful way.

More likely than not, as we shall see in chapters 4 and 5, political dropouts are not to be found among those who respond to surveys in the first place, and there is good reason to believe that this is a large and growing, even if mostly invisible, segment of society. Conversely, a smaller group of young people who do not participate politically but who do pay attention to politics is likely to be overrepresented in our surveys compared to the first group, and thus in our policy responses. This is unfortunate since, if they are paying attention, it is fair to assume that many of these young people will eventually decide to participate in politics, when the political situation changes either objectively or in terms of their own interests.

This is not the case with political dropouts. They are the prime target of our investigation here, as they ought to be of our policy initiatives, if we wish to boost the informed political participation of young citizens. The core challenge we face can be characterized as the identification of policies that could prevent young people from becoming political dropouts by helping them to develop the habits of political attentiveness. We should not be misled by dubious survey data and glowing depictions of engaged citizenship or cause-oriented repertoires that minimize the phenomenon and underestimate the challenge. We need to rely instead on indicators that place political knowledge and attentiveness front and center. And having thus identified the dimensions of the problem of potential political dropouts, we need to develop public policy responses that target this group in particular.

Why Bother with Political Dropouts?

Here we are brought full circle back to the fundamental reason for being concerned about the number of politically literate citizens: the needs and interests of those unable to participate effectively in political life fall to the bottom of the political agenda. Moreover, the needs and interests of young people are not identical to those of their elders. Wattenberg (2003, 170) uses data from the National Election Studies to show important generational differences. Americans under thirty are significantly more liberal on abortion and gender equality, as well as on government intervention in and spending on education, health, and especially the environment. Indeed, in a very real sense, the interests of young people are nothing less than those of the future of the planet, and to the extent that they drop out, those interests will lose effective political expression.

As younger generations replace older ones, the increasing proportion of political dropouts threatens the very principle of informed active consent by a majority of citizens which underlies democracy. The test facing democratic nations is thus whether the majority of members of the emerging generations will be attentive to the political world and will be able to participate politically as informed citizens. However sympathetic their attitudes, those who lack the knowledge and skills to do so undermine the foundations of our way of life.

It is not, simply, that the majority of citizens should cast ballots. Low turnout is better understood as a symptom of the problem than as the problem itself. If it were the problem, compulsory voting would be a simple solution. But, as we shall see in chapter 6, there is no evidence that those who vote just to avoid fines become more attentive and thus informed citizens. And not all votes count equally. Institutions that invite symbolic rather than meaningful participation, as in the case of the European Parliament, can be counterproductive. It is time to heed the voices of the many Europeans who cast informed votes in national elections but stay home for European Parliament elections:[32] Either a way must be found to offer Europe-focused choices that are meaningful to the voters, or the selection of delegates to Strasbourg should be left to the members of elected national parliaments.

Outline of the Remaining Chapters

The next two chapters elaborate on the factors that have shaped the current generation's orientation to informed political participation. Chapter 2 begins with the emergence of political dropouts when the labor market began to exclude from secure employment a large number of young people who lacked the necessary degree of literacy and numeracy. Chapter 3 goes on to identify the factors that distinguish from its predecessors the generation that reached maturity with the revolutionary transformation of communications technology in the final decade of the twentieth century. These chapters explore how the traditional forms of political socialization and media consumption have given way in the face of these forces. Family and neighborhood influence and the sense of a civic duty to vote have become less compelling, placing additional burdens on the schools.

A young person whose primary peer group is linked electronically more easily bypasses not only traditional information gatekeepers and authorities, but also sources of information and skills relevant to becoming an effective citizen. As the sense of civic duty to vote declines, political knowledge and attentiveness become more important—just as the traditional sources of political knowledge come under increased challenge.

The final two chapters of part 1 elaborate how these wider historical forces express themselves in quantifiable indicators of informed political participation. Chapter 4 sets out the contours of what we out know about historical and cross-national trends in voting turnout and related forms of political participation generally, and for young people in particular. It establishes that in most of the mature industrial democracies, young people nowadays vote, and think it important to vote, at lower levels than did their parents and grandparents when they were young, and that unconventional political activity is not filling the gap left by the decline in conventional forms of participation. Chapter 5 turns to the informed part of informed political participation, setting out in comparative perspective what we know about the evolution of knowledge of politics and public affairs, and the link between levels of youth voting and political knowledge.

The cross-national data in these chapters opens the door to part 2's focus on the institutional context in which individuals act. The approach elaborates on the author's previous comparative work, which identified institutional and policy frameworks characteristic of the countries high in civic literacy, and applies its findings to emerging generations. Civic literacy is not a reflection of individual capacity, which does not vary depending on whether a society is high or low in civic literacy; it is a reflection of whether that capacity is enhanced by the institutional arrangements particular to that society. Institutions affect the supply— and hence the cost to the individual—of political knowledge, and thus of informed political participation. As a rule, the more intelligible the relevant institutions, the more the institutions are able to simplify the relationship between citizens' actions and political outcomes, and the more citizens are capable of informed political participation.

Modern democratic societies are placed on a continuum according to how conducive their institutional arrangements are to fostering informed political participation. On one pole for most dimensions is the United States, which lacks a central electoral authority to check partisanship in the electoral process, and which is hamstrung by a constitution that limits the regulatory role of public agencies in the dissemination of political information. On the opposite pole are often found the Northern European countries that are high in civic literacy, which are characterized by institutions conducive to policy initiatives that promote informed political participation. Typically, Canada falls in between, though it is closer to the United States.

The discussion takes up the question posed at the end of part 1 as to the meaning of the recent rebound in political participation and attentiveness by young Americans. Absent political institutional reforms, the likelihood is that they will prove to be short-lived.

Chapter 6 starts from the relationship between nonmaterial redistribution and informed political participation, proceeding to the effects of institutions. Other things being equal, it is argued, countries that disperse power—between executive and legislative, between two legislative chambers, or between national and regional governments—are, by making the relationship between actions and outcomes more complex, reducing the potential for citizens' awareness of that relationship. The chapter also explores the potential of deliberative polls, focus groups, and citizens' assemblies.

The bedrock of informed democratic participation is voting, and the institutions most directly concerned are those that set the rules of participation in elections. Chapter 7 examines the effects of alternate electoral systems. At the core lie electoral systems based on PR—proportional representation, or the principle of proportionality between representation in the legislature and popular support. Under PR, citizens, including young citizens, can more readily find parties that stand for policies and principles that they support. Moreover, PR parties have an incentive to inform people even in regions where they are weak. Under PR, a marginally informed voter can identify with a political party and use that identification as a guide through the complexities of issues and actors at various levels of political activity over time and over space.

Chapter 8 continues with an analysis of the effects of other mechanisms related to elections most relevant to the participation of young citizens. The first is fixed election dates. It is argued that fixed election dates make it easier to plan election-related public and school events—seminars, adult education activities, information campaigns, and the like—to raise awareness, interest, and involvement, and, potentially, turnout. The second is voting age. Chapter 8 examines the contention that instead of first being able to vote between the ages of eighteen and twenty, when young people are starting to establish their own social networks, the voting age should be younger, when more people are still under the influence of parents and traditional social networks. The chapter concludes that reducing the age to sixteen could be counted on to get more young people to the polls only if voting were reinforced in the school setting. This sets the stage for part 3's discussion of policies to promote informed youth political participation and prevent political dropouts in and through the school system.

Various approaches are delineated in the context of complementary electoral and information-dissemination institutions. Chapter 9 critically examines voluntary community service as a strategy for boosting informed political participation. Too often, it is argued, such service learning serves to depoliticize, instilling a conception of citizenship devoid of political parties, ideological differences, and competing interests. The relationship between classroom and community should be one of integrating, rather than escaping, political life. Contrast is drawn between North America and Europe, where, generally speaking, there is less emphasis on voluntary community service and more on involvement with partisan issues, and where party politics is less in opposition to civic engagement.

This approach is developed in chapter 10, which sets out to identify guidelines for an effective approach to civic education, beginning with activities in the school but outside the classroom, and then turning to the civics courses themselves. The approach brings to bear the concern with making the environment of young people rich in political information, targeting especially those who lack access to such an environment on their own, and doing so during their compulsory schooling at an age as close as possible to their reaching voting age. The emphasis is less on increasing political knowledge than on fostering habits of attentiveness to public affairs. Doing so requires harnessing the potential of the communications networks of the Internet generation to break down the barriers between the political world and the world of the young adult, complemented by government programs in education, media support, political party financing, information dissemination, and the like. The approach is made concrete by simulations, in particular a press conference, in which students take on the role of journalists, with an invited political figure presenting his or her views—or those of a political party—before the students. In preparation, the students carry out research about the issue and the guest; after the event, they report on it in a mass medium in which they are comfortable.

The concluding chapter attempts to weave all the various threads together. It marks the trail to be followed, identifying both possible agents and pitfalls, promising directions and uncertainties. A concrete example of how the approach to civic education is linked to institutional reforms is found in PR elections ensuring that even small, principle-based parties have an available stock of elected representatives to present their positions in the classroom.

The book ends with a call for more targeted research, and also for action. We do not know enough to know exactly how to act; but we know enough to know that inaction is unacceptable.

2

Political Socialization, Social Class, and Technological Transformation

I n the previous chapter, we introduced an approach based on political knowledge to the question of youth political participation—an approach that targets potential political dropouts. In this chapter, we shall try to deepen our understanding of the phenomenon by looking at changes that distinguish the generations reaching maturity in recent years from those that came before. The latest stage, the subject matter of the next chapter, ushers in the revolutionary transformation of communications technology at the end of the twentieth century. Here, we are concerned with the earlier and broader developments that shaped the conditions under which recent generations reached political maturity, the process that specialists label political socialization. Political socialization is "the process by which new generations are inducted into political culture, learning the knowledge, values, and attitudes that contribute to support of the political system" (Gimpel, Lay, and Schuknecht 2003, 13).

The intensity of the ongoing debates about declining youth political participation noted in the previous chapter tells us that something new is happening. One indication is the revival of interest in political socialization as a field of research.

Whatever Happened to Political Socialization?

The intellectual origins of political socialization research lie in debates about teaching civic education. In the 1930s, in the United States, academic emphasis began to shift toward empirical investigations into the development of citizenship orientations. At the time, a main concern of political scientists was to weaken the appeal of machine politics, especially among the growing immigrant population, which meant downplaying the need for active political participation and stressing patriotism, obedience to the law, and respect for government. In his investigation into the qualities of citizenship being taught in different nations, Charles Merriam noted that the idea that citizens should be able to exercise judgment about political issues was missing. His work, combined with that of John Dewey, proved influential in making critical thinking a skill that American civic education would seek to develop—not only in the school, but also in newspapers, radio, and film (Owen 2004).

The development of political socialization as an accepted subfield reflected the postwar shift in the focus of political science research toward political behavior, and to an understanding that political behavior was learned behavior. Hence the political life of individuals could be understood in the same way as other developmental processes (see, e.g., Hyman 1959). Political socialization tended to be viewed as a natural maturation process in which healthy attitudes toward democracy and participation were developed. As Torney-Purta notes:

> It appealed specifically to political scientists who sought to trace partisanship from generation to generation, and the various sources of support for the political system. Most of this research posited a straightforward model of process. Socialization agents (families, schools, other authority figures) acting to further their own interests and those of society attempted to inculcate certain values, attitudes, knowledge, or behaviors. Youth then assimilated or incorporated this knowledge or these attitudes . . . If political learning was inadequate, ineffective socialization agents were responsible . . . Rare was the researcher who argued that the young person might resist the socialization message. (2000, 88)

However, it gradually emerged that the assumption that political lessons learned early in life persisted was in fact little supported by empirical testing of the relationship between childhood political learning and adult political attitudes and behaviors (Sears 1990). This raised doubts about the value of studying children's perceptions, which had been the common procedure in the 1960s and 1970s (Dudley and Gitelson 2002), resulting in fewer and fewer social scientists' seeing youth as an interesting population to study. Torney-Purta notes that "the field was thus left to the developmental and educational psychologists, the result of which was a greater emphasis on children rather than adolescents and, especially, young adults, who served further to distance political science research from the field" (2000, 88–89). What had still been an important facet of political science in the 1960s and into the 1970s was now relegated to the sidelines.

It soon became difficult to locate a literature that provides systematic insight into the political socialization of the young. In retrospect, the absence reflected a change in the context in which political socialization takes place. For the generation reaching maturity in Western countries, these were decades of extraordinary psychological and social change. The lesson, as Niemi and Hepburn (1995) note, was that rather than assuming that what one learned as a child, largely unaltered, had a significant influence on one's political orientation later in life, the focus shifted toward adolescence as the key period for the development of identity, both personal and collective.

As attention shifted toward the group aged from about fourteen through to the mid-twenties, a different vocabulary, one suited to portraying a youth subculture, was required. Moreover, it was no longer possible to conceive of political socialization as the development of healthy attitudes toward democracy and participation; one could also be socialized to political apathy and cynicism, and against democratic participation. Thus the new research focus had to take in, for example, a home or media environment in which politicians are disparaged as crooks, exposure to media focusing on political scandal, or a peer environment that regards caring about issues and engaging in politics as not cool.

Work such as that of Niemi and Hepburn both signaled and encouraged empirical investigations of the political participation and civic engagement of young people. As studies in the United States in the 1980s and elsewhere in the 1990s exposed evidence of the declining political involvement of young people, an interest emerged among some scholars in combining research and practice in an effort to increase civic competence among young people. A new dynamic began to break the vicious circle of a lack of interesting research results, leading in turn to a lack of interest by researchers in political socialization. As various national studies revealed a generation-based decline in traditional forms of democratic participation, and the norms underlying them, governments in many parts of the democratic world were spurred to action—at least, the form of action that saw the creation of commissions to investigate the phenomenon—which in turn generated findings raising further concerns about the decline. This was a virtuous circle, at least as far as research was concerned.

Few of the newly activated researchers into the phenomenon identified the field in which they were operating as political socialization. Indeed, many of those working on relevant issues consciously rejected the terminology and its conformist connotations. Though not entirely suitable, given that it traditionally refers to a legal relationship to the state, the term "citizenship" is probably the one that today best characterizes this literature. Citizenship is more neutral a term than political socialization, leaving room for a critical social-movement form of citizenship. Whatever the terminology, the challenge is to combine the various strands. As Owen puts it: "Civic education and political socialization scholarship have left a legacy of stock citizenship constructs. These include the citizen as loyal subject and patriot, the citizen as voter, and the citizen as enlightened community participant . . . More complicated times call for more nuanced approaches to political socialization and learning" (2004, 6).

Comparing the Generations

With the change in terminology came a change of emphasis and focus. Political socialization suggests stability, a process essential to a given society's continuity. But a new political generation can also act as the driving force of changes in political culture. New generations are malleable, the products of changing conditions characterizing the historical period in which they reached adulthood. In the emerging literature, recent generations began to be referred to in more specific terms. While authors vary in attributing dates and names, the most commonly accepted terminology identifies four political generations among those 15 and over today (given national differentials in the rate of diffusion of change, we use American dates and terminology): the preboomers; the boomers, born between the end of World War II and the late 1950s; Generation X, born from the mid-1960s and the 1970s; and the most recent, born beginning at the end of the 1970s—sometimes called Generation Y or Generation Next, or the Internet generation, the term we use here.

These generations are marked to varying degrees by the social transformation that they experienced, at least in part: from an industrial to postindustrial (or material to postmaterial) society based on technological advances, especially in the communications media—a society characterized by relative peace and prosperity, a better educated citizenry, suburbanization, the movement of women into the paid labor force, and the disruption of family ties. Observers differ in the importance they accord to the various factors. Some, like Wattenberg (2007), stress the new media environment. Others, often adopting Inglehart's notion of advancing postmaterialism, see the security, material prosperity, and increased education of recent generations as underpinning a new set of values.[1] A somewhat different perspective emerges when the phenomenon is understood as one of delayed maturity, manifested concretely in the fact that young people now remain at home longer than previous generations did.[2] In Boyte and Kari's (1996) terms, this generation, in contrast to previous ones, experienced an extended adolescence at least for middle-class children, one which had little place for civic-minded activity. It produced a kind of marketplace democracy, in which young citizens were consumers rather than producers of civic life, more prone to criticize government from the outside and abstain from involvement than to attempt to change it through civic engagement.[3]

Soule (2001) stresses the fact that those born after 1978 were—at least until September 11, 2001—raised in a time of relative peace and prosperity. This, she suggests, is part of the explanation for their developing a political ethos characterized by declining political engagement. Comparing the values of this generation with those of U.S. college students in the late 1960s, she notes that developing a meaningful philosophy of life, which once ranked highest among college freshmen's values, plummeted, while being very well off financially jumped to the top.[4]

Twenge (2006) contrasts the individualism of the baby boomers—who, lacking guidance from the past, as individuals had to reinvent their way of thinking—with the generations that followed, including what she calls "Generation Me," which entered a world where things had already changed and soaked it up. Howe (2008) builds upon this approach, starting from the emergence of adolescence as a discrete stage in the life cycle—which took place in the early years of the twentieth century, since youth as a social category did not exist before the Industrial Revolution. Universal education consolidated the process. And as compulsory schooling expanded, the period of youth gradually lengthened to include secondary and then postsecondary education. The emergence of adolescence as a discrete stage of life led to a greater societal focus on adolescents' experience, characterized by exploring one's identity and delaying adulthood and the responsibilities that go with it. "Adolescent

dispositions became more deeply entrenched, constituting an important wellspring of social change, and planting the seeds of new values
and attitudes that slowly matured into the social and political landscape"
(Howe 2008, 3).

There is no shortage of data comparing the preboomers and boomers with the generations that followed. The most comprehensive international study of young people, that of Torney-Purta, Schwille, and
Amadeo, reported that "countries find themselves with increasing numbers of adolescents who are disengaged from the political system" (1999,
14). Wattenberg (2003, 164) sets out the data for generational differences
in expressed interest in politics, showing that those aged eighteen to
thirty were only marginally below their elders in the latter 1960s, but
that the gap was over 20 percentage points in 2000. More recently, Wattenberg reported that among those under thirty, the proportion who rejected the idea that "it doesn't matter much to me whether I vote" in U.S.
national election surveys went from an average of 91 percent between
1952 and 1960 to 87 percent between 1972 and 1980, and 70 percent between 2000 and 2002 (2007, 133). Another American survey found that
only 38 percent (as opposed to 50 percent to 66 percent for older generations) of those aged fifteen to twenty-five stated that citizenship entails
special obligations, while for 58 percent simply being a good person was
enough (Andolina, Keeter, Zukin, and Jenkins 2002). In 2000, only 28.1
percent of incoming freshmen believed that keeping up to date with
political affairs was essential or very important, a number that declined
in 2008 to 26.7 percent. The high, attained in 1966, was 57.8 percent
(Bennett and Bennett 2001).

As the twenty-first century began, Delli Carpini summarized the
existing American literature, providing a rather disturbing picture of
what he termed the civic disengagement of America's youth. Whether
compared with older Americans or with younger Americans from earlier eras, young adults were less likely to feel a sense of identity, pride, or
obligation associated with citizenship; read a newspaper or watch the
news on television; register or vote; or participate in community organizations designed to address public problems through collective action
or the formal policy process. Significantly less likely than older adults
to think their participation in politics would make a difference, young
people also expressed declining interest in serving in appointed or
elected government positions or in pursuing careers in teaching, public

law, or the nonprofit sector (Delli Carpini 2000, 341–43). (Note that these numbers predate changes in the United States brought on by the Iraq war and the Obama campaign, which raises the question—to which we turn in later chapters—whether developments in the United States in 2004 and 2008 herald a rebound in informed political participation.)

Similarly, the 2000 Canadian Election Study (CES) reported that while overall 75 percent strongly agreed that it is every citizen's duty to vote in federal elections, and 32 percent said that they would feel very guilty if they did not vote in a federal election, these numbers declined to 55 percent and 18 percent for young Canadians (Blais, Gidengil, Nevitte, and Nadeau 2002). Similar results were reported in the 2006 CES, with 40 percent of Canadians under thirty feeling no guilt at all about not voting, compared to 21 percent for those over thirty, and 62 percent compared to 93 percent believing that every citizen has a duty to vote (Archer and Wesley 2006, 29). This decline needs to be kept in mind when we look at the impact of political knowledge in chapter 5. Far more members of earlier generations with marginal levels of political knowledge vote out of a sense of civic duty than do young people. For example, in the United Kingdom, 63 percent of those who claimed they were "not at all interested in news about the election" cast a vote nevertheless; but among those aged eighteen to twenty-four, the proportion plummeted to 16 percent (Electoral Commission 2002, 29).

The Impact of Social Class

Starting in the 1950s in North America, and somewhat later in developed countries elsewhere in the world, changing economic conditions resulted in increasingly precarious financial trajectories over the life span, greater ambiguity as to the social markers of adulthood, and, on balance, a lowering of young people's social status. The most striking technological development was the decline of smokestack industries, a process accelerated by globalization. Delayed adulthood became mandatory rather than optional thanks to the precarious market for low-skilled workers, as blue-collar jobs moved to developing countries or became obsolete due to technology. The result was that a growing number of young people with low levels of literacy and numeracy—who, in earlier times, would have had relatively secure employment—were excluded from the labor market. These were largely young men, as young women were encouraged to stay in school and proved especially suited to fill jobs in the expanding service sector.

This was a dramatic change. Just a decade earlier, many women had left the labor market that they had entered during World War II, and young men willing and able to work could reasonably assume that their lives would satisfactorily fulfill the basic needs of adult citizens, allowing them to support their families and communities. But their younger siblings and, especially, their sons faced a changing situation, marked by earnings instability, a wage gap with older workers, and the prospect of temporary and lower quality jobs with fewer benefits. Simultaneously, the transitions on the way to adulthood—leaving school, leaving parents' home, entering the work force, entering conjugal relationships and having children—were lengthening (Clark 2007; Côté and Bynner 2008). Thus delayed with respect to work, parenthood, and financial independence, young people could not be counted on to take up a citizen's responsibilities, including that of voting. In Paakkunainen's words: "When political identities and the mobilization of collectives (classes, regions, nations and religions) are disintegrating and the political arenas are becoming bureaucratized, it is not easy to speak about traditional citizenship with social rights and national political movements and elections" (2000, 3; see also Hébert 2008). [5]

Moreover, the transformation took place in the context of geopolitical mutation. The democratic world seemed solid and stable in the decades following World War II, before the onset of globalization and the demise of the Soviet empire. The resulting end of conscription in most countries eliminated for many young men a key rite of passage into adulthood. During the same period, the mass media were skillfully projecting the image of a high-consumption middle class as the norm to which everyone inevitably aspired. The combination of these various factors meant that, both objectively and subjectively, a large number of young men lacked what their counterparts in earlier generations had had—namely, the economic and educational resources to regard themselves as full citizens-to-be.[6] Excluded from social citizenship, they become prospective political dropouts.

There are many manifestations of the political dropout phenomenon. While recent levels of voter turnout among young women are hardly inspiring, the real drop from 1960s and 1970s levels took place among young males. The American Citizen Participation Study of Sidney Verba and his colleagues (see Verba, Schlozman, and Burns 2005) revealed in stark terms the effect of socioeconomic status, especially parental level of education, an effect we have good reason to believe is stronger now than in the recent past. For example, a Canadian study compared political knowledge data from 1956 Canadian Gallup polls and the 2000 Canadian Election Study, finding that age differences were significantly more important in 2000, especially among those with no more than a high-school education. The young today "know less about politics and . . . their impoverished knowledge is more likely to affect whether or not they vote" (Howe 2003, 81).[7]

Especially in the United States, class and race are intertwined. For example, Levinson finds a significant civic achievement gap along what she identifies as the four dimensions of civic engagement (knowledge, skills, attitudes, and behaviors) between poor, minority, and immigrant citizens, on the one hand, and wealthy, white, and native-born citizens, on the other hand. According to her data:

> In the presidential election of 2004 . . . Hispanic and Asian voting-age citizens voted at a rate only two-thirds that of eligible whites . . . while people living in families with incomes under $15,000 voted at barely half the rate of those living in families with incomes over $75,000 . . . Reliable analyses of political participation, as measured by membership in political parties, campaign donations, campaign volunteering, participation in protests, contacting an elected official, and so forth, show vast disparities linked with both class and race . . . People who earn over $75,000 annually are politically active at up to six times the rate of people who earn under $15,000.[8]

Gimpel and Lay (2006) report on an elaborate American study that identified young people most at risk of nonparticipation. These include African Americans, Latinos, the poor, people living in single-parent households, the children of the foreign-born, women, people with low educational aspirations, people living in environments with low voter turnout or little political competition, the nonreligious, people who are not attentive to news media, and students who avoid or are not exposed to discussions of politics, or who dislike their government-related courses or feel unfairly treated by school authorities. For the respondents who display more than a few of these risk factors, the likelihood of nonparticipation in adulthood is exceedingly high, while for those who report only two or three factors, there is a chance that the presence of positive forces in their environment may neutralize or overcome the ones that diminish participatory impulses.

As we shall see below, the workings of such a positive, counterbalancing force explains why civics courses have a more significant effect on the political knowledge and skills of African American students than on those of other students (Langton and Jennings 1968; Jennings and Niemi 1974). A similar effect can be attributed to mobilizing forces, especially the civil rights movement. Using data from the 1960s and 1970s, Wolfinger and Rosenstone (1980, 60) found that political participation increased from age 18 to 65 only marginally for the best educated, but significantly (from 20 percent to over 50 percent) among the least well educated Americans. Rosenstone and Hansen attribute this phenomenon to political mobilization:

> When political leaders offset the costs of political involvement—when they provide information, subsidize participation, occasion the provision of social rewards—they make it possible for people who have few resources of their own to participate . . . During the 1950s when the political parties mobilized whites more than blacks and registration laws systematically excluded blacks (particularly in the South), the racial disparities in citizen participation were immense. During the 1960s and into the 1970s, in contrast . . . , the political parties reached out to blacks, and the racial inequalities in political participation narrowed. During the 1980s, finally, political mobilization declined, and progress toward equal representation in the political community stalled (1993, 242–44).[9]

We know of the traditional capacity of social democratic and labor parties in Europe to mobilize their supporters. In the United States, in the absence of class-based political organizations and strong trade unions, the above-described mobilizing activities—which had boosted not only the proportion of citizens who voted, but also the relative proportion of the lower classes among voters—proved predictably temporary, as turnout dropped in the 1970s.[10] The timing suggests that when the mobilizing activities of the civil rights movement receded, the full impact of the underlying changes in industrial structure came to be felt in the form of political abstention among the poor, the young, and the nonwhite—the emergence of political dropouts. History will tell us if the mobilization around the Iraq war and the Obama campaign follows a similar trajectory.

Though class bias in political participation is a significant phenomenon that spares none,[11] it is clear that the least affected societies are those that have developed mechanisms to adjust institutions and policies in order to reduce entrenched inequality. The data from the 2002 European Social Survey displayed in chapter 4 are suggestive. Among Western Europe countries without compulsory voting, both absolutely and in comparison to older citizens, voting among young Danes, Swedes, Dutch, Germans, and Austrians is high, while it is low among British, Irish, Swiss, Spanish, and Portuguese youth.[12] Compared to the latter countries, the former have paid more attention to redistribution of both material and nonmaterial resources.[13] The more laissez-faire approach of the latter countries, to which we can add the United States and Canada, excludes a larger proportion of people from informed political participation, which makes it less likely that policies needed to improve their chances to attain those resources will be implemented, leading to further abstention on their part, and so on—a classic vicious circle.

This is confirmed by a recent study using results of the Political Action Study from 1973 to 1976, updated by more recent surveys.[14] Gallego Dobón (2007) compares, by level of education, the proportion of completely politically inactive people in the three generations that were adults in the mid-1970s with those in comparable generations in the 2004 survey. In both periods, inactivity, which rose in the interval, is concentrated among the poorly educated and is higher in the United States and United Kingdom than in the continental European countries in the survey. (The proportion of completely politically inactive persons goes from 35 percent to 40 percent in the United Kingdom; 20 to 35 in the United States; 29 to 36 in Sweden; 20 to 29 in Finland; and 10 to 16 in Germany.)

In consequence, the class dimension will loom especially large in our approach to civic education in part 3—the approach of targeting potential political dropouts before they have dropped out of school, and aiming civic education at those who need it most. In the past, more traditional approaches to civic education seem to have better served the needs of potential political dropouts, especially African Americans, which is a development parallel to the mobilization efforts around civil rights described above. Though no significant overall effect of civic education on political participation or political knowledge was found, "on several measures the effect was to move the Negro youths—especially those from less-educated families—to a position more congruent with the White youths and more in consonance with the usual goals of civic education in the United States" (Langton and Jennings 1968, 866). In the words of Comber, since "educational improvements have greater effects on minority race/ethnicity students than on non-Hispanic white students . . . civic education may be a means of equalizing the distribution of skills needed to politically participate" (2006, 27–28). Yet this potential has not been realized, according to recent studies (Brayboy, Castagno, and Maughan 2007; Campbell 2007). It seems that the emphasis on critical thinking skills and the movement away from traditional political participation, and toward more apolitical civic engagement, have been accompanied by reduced efforts to instill fundamental knowledge about government and politics—knowledge empowering to those lowest in resources.[15] As Lee Hamilton, noted scholar and former member of Congress, puts it: "The very teenagers who most need opportunities for civic learning . . . tend never to be included in . . . experiences that would develop their civic skills."[16]

Institutions of Political Socialization

But we are getting ahead of ourselves: these aspects of the current political socialization literature are explored in subsequent chapters. A preliminary question arises here: how have the roles of the main socializing agents—the family, the peer group, the school, and the media—evolved during this period? Some current studies attempt to rank these agents. Edwards, Saha, and Print (2005) listed twelve possible agents in a young person's environment and asked young Australians: "where do you get your information about voting in elections?"[17] The family received the highest score, followed closely by television, newspapers, teachers, and radio. In contrast, another study found that Dutch teenagers placed the school ahead of television and parents as their primary source of political information (Dekker 2007). Overall, results confirm the important role that the school must play to complement the role of the family, especially where the family lacks the requisite resources. In this final part of this chapter, we briefly summarize what the literature—largely American—tells us about the impact of these institutions on political socialization, and the complex interactions among them.

The School

The importance placed on the school varies with time and place. If political socialization seems to be taking place as a natural social process, experts and officials tend to look to the family and the community. When the process appears to be wavering, the focus tends to be on the media as prime suspect, and as fostering political socialization climbs higher on the agenda of governments, the onus falls increasingly on the school to correct matters.

In the classic American literature (Hyman 1959; Greenstein 1960, 1965; Easton and Dennis 1969; Easton and Hess 1962), the school is complementary to the family in preparing children for democratic citizenship, reinforcing the political socialization that takes place at home. A change came with a wide-ranging study of what 12,000 schoolchildren and their teachers thought about political and social institutions, which concluded that the school played no less an important role in political socialization than the family (Hess and Torney 1967). But just how socialization took place in school was unclear. A study by Langton and Jennings found the link between the number of civic education classes and variables such as knowledge, interest, or political discussion to be weak, constituting only a "minor source of political socialization" (1968, 863).

It was only later that attention focused on a second finding in this article, and in a subsequent book (Jennings and Niemi 1974)—that, as noted above, there were significant effects of civic education in the African American subsample. The explanation was straightforward: because these children had a very low base level of political knowledge, their educational experiences tended to reduce the gap between them and children from the majority group. Little attention was given to this citizenship gap at the time, however, as racial equality activists tended to dismiss political socialization through civic education as a reinforcing agent of existing power relationships through what they called the hidden curriculum (see, e.g., Merelman 1980).

Like more conservative observers who describe political socialization as functional, these radical critics tended to regard young civics students as passive receptacles of values and norms. Yet the empirical literature, limited though it was, did not support this view. In a survey, Ehman (1980) found the school curriculum to be effective in transmitting knowledge, but far less so in influencing attitudes, which was more a matter of social status, student participation in school activities, and the school's organizational environment.

Such findings marked the beginning of a shift in attention toward political knowledge—and the classroom. Niemi is a key figure in this refocusing, as signaled in his article with Hepburn cited earlier. While his earlier writings tended to discourage interest in political socialization, his more recent research (Niemi and Junn 1998) has revealed positive, significant, and persistent effects of civic education on political knowledge. Along with the work of Torney-Purta, among others, it has rekindled interest in political socialization in and beyond the school. Nonetheless, as we shall see in part 3, we have not made much progress over the last thirty years in identifying the real effects of civic education. We still lack a cumulative body of knowledge.

The Family

The family forms the center of the child's universe and thus of his or her basic understanding of the world, including the world of politics and democratic participation. In the classic literature on political socialization (e.g., Dennis 1973; Jaros 1973), it is during adolescence, when teenagers develop a life outside the home, that influences beyond the family gain importance, as the school becomes the prime locus of efforts by adolescents to win approval, admiration, and respect, and the media start to have significant impact on their lives.

Values, attitudes, and behavior are transmitted from parents to children. Studies have shown substantial parent-offspring similarities when it comes to concrete, observable measures such as voting behavior, identification with the Left or the Right, and party affiliation, as well as participation in political and civic activities such as voluntary organizations (Jennings and Niemi 1974; Youniss et al. 2002). Yet much remains unclear about how intergenerational transfer of political or civic attitudes and behaviors takes place. For one thing, children do not seem to have a clear knowledge of their parents' values (Westholm 1999).

Gender appears to be an important mediating factor. Wernli (2007) found that boys are more influenced than girls by their fathers' political orientation. A Canadian survey found that a politically active mother can have a role-model effect on her daughter's political interest, knowledge, and degree of political participation, and that her influence typically outweighs that of a politically active father (Gidengil, O'Neill, and Young 2008). Conversely, an Australian study found that adolescents—especially girls, who report obtaining more information from their parents about voting than boys do—discuss politics with male family members significantly more than with female family members, and that where participants reported discussing politics with female family members, there was a tendency for male family members to be unavailable (Edwards, Saha, and Print 2005). This finding corresponds to that of another Canadian study, which found that receiving a daily newspaper at home, taking a civics course, or having a member of the family involved in a political party has a substantial positive effect on young women's political knowledge, but no discernible effect on young men's (Thomas and Young 2006).

Recently, some scholars have begun to conceptualize political socialization in the family as a more complex process, during which external influences enter via the child as well as the parent: adolescents, thus, are seen not as passive recipients of socializing influences, but as active agents in their own civic development (McDevitt and Chafee 2002). Such a trickle-up influence typically takes place when a child—stimulated, say, by a civics course discussion—initiates the discussion and prompts the parent to seek further political information, perhaps through the media, in order to reassert his or her role in the family. This mechanism sheds some light, according to the authors, on the especially powerful impact of civic education on children in low-income homes, whose parents have few resources for providing political information and skills: parents who had little exposure to politics in their own youth are afforded "a second chance at citizenship" by their children's exposure to the school intervention.[18]

A parallel insight emerges from a study that investigated the effect of divorce on voter turnout in the United States. Noting that various factors related to the family, such as parents' education (positively) and early parenthood (negatively), affect turnout, Sandell and Plutzer (2005) hypothesized that divorce, which often uproots families from their communities, would also affect it.[19] More specifically, turnout could be affected by a reduction in the number of opportunities for political discussion after divorce and possibly—given that lowered educational attainment is a strong predictor of nonvoting—the economic hardship associated with divorce that may lead some children to abandon plans to attend college.

A related study (Pacheco and Plutzer 2007) using a nationally representative, twelve-year panel survey found that, for whites, early parenthood
leads to increased risk of dropping out of high school, and that inter-
rupting high school had major negative impacts on later voting turnout,
even when the student eventually returned to earn a diploma.

To test the hypotheses, Sandell and Plutzer used data from the 1988
National Education Longitudinal Survey of eighth graders from the National Center for Education Statistics, and interviewed a random subset
of children and parents in 1990, 1992, 1994, and 2000.[20] Among white
youth whose parents were married in 1988, divorce lowered parental
voter turnout by 9 percent and decreased discussion of current events
by 8 percent (as well as diminishing annual income by roughly $10,000
and doubling the probability of moving). As expected, holding parental
education, family income, sex, and parent-child communications constant, divorce decreased voter participation by roughly 10 percent. While
lower family incomes and lower educational attainment contributed
to the very real impact of divorce on the participation of young white
citizens, what contributed most was the effect of divorce on parental
political participation, current events discussions, and residential mobility. Remarkably, no such effect on turnout was found among African
Americans, and the effect was much weaker for Hispanics. A clue to the
explanation for this lies in the finding that divorce actually bolsters stability among African Americans.

In sum, while the effects of the family are complex, a fragile family
situation, whatever its causes, weakens political socialization. When the
family appeared strong, levels of political participation appeared solid.
The changes described above from an industrial to a postindustrial society weakened the traditional family especially in those segments of society most dependent on traditional blue-collar jobs. In the case of
hard-hit African American families, maintaining a modicum of stability
depended largely on women's finding stable employment, particularly in
the expanding care sector. But women's arrival in large numbers in the
labor market had an overall destabilizing effect. Along with changes in
the media discussed in chapter 3, it reduced the time spent by young
people with their parents, especially over meals, when most discussions
related to politics take place. This was felt less in families with well-
educated, high-income parents who had the resources to counter the
impact of these developments on their children.[21]

The breakdown of the family means more political dropouts. Since the family cannot be repaired by public policy, the onus falls on the public school to pick up the slack. It is also frequently contended that even in intact families, there is increased cultural and intellectual distance between the generations. While there is nothing new about parents and adolescent children operating in different cultural networks, the distance between them has apparently grown over recent generations due to many factors, especially the changes in communications technology. A description of how this affects political participation is offered by Archer and Wesley, based on Canadian survey data: "Due to advances in technology or changes in parenting styles, the 'duties' and 'obligations' of yesterday's children have all but disappeared in many of today's households . . . Broad trends in socialization . . . may be instilling a different set of core values in our youth, teaching them that voting—like doing the dishes—is something that simply 'gets done,' without much effort or concern on their part" (2006, 13).

Peer Groups and Voluntary Associations

If the family today faces greater obstacles in carrying out its traditional political socialization role, this may be even more true of another traditional agent of socialization and transmission of politically relevant information. This is the peer group, composed of young people who are close in age, physical location, and interests. But—as of course is not the case with parents—the young person can choose his or her peers, which makes the peer group much less amenable to research into its role in political socialization.[22] While some scholars suggest that young people are today pushed into more—perhaps too many more—organized activities by their parents than was the case with previous generations, these activities are now less likely to involve adolescent schoolmates who share extracurricular interests. Jennings and Stoker (2002), combining Jennings's earlier data with more recent data from 1997, find a significant decline of extracurricular activities among American high-school seniors since 1982, and, compared to 1962, a drop in organizational memberships of more than 50 percent.

One interesting study provides insight into the relationships between peer group behavior, political socialization, and race in the United States. Roland Fryer asked a large number of public-school students to name their friends and—considering only children who named each other to be friends—found that the number of friends correlated positively with academic grades for white children, but negatively for black ones.[23] On the whole, however, such efforts at studying peers' attitudes directly are exceptions; studies typically use as indicators of peer influence adolescents' own reports of their peers' behavior and attitudes, since tracking down and questioning the peers is difficult and expensive. This is problematic since individuals tend to believe that their peers think as they do, and such studies thus generally overestimate peer influence (Kandel 1985). Nevertheless, they do provide us with an idea of the changing role of the peer group in political socialization.

We can break down these changes into the physical and the virtual. It has long been understood that community attachment is an important factor in political socialization (e.g., Verba and Nie 1972). Franklin (2005) identifies the mobilizing effect of social contacts, suggesting that there is a powerful effect of length of residence among new cohorts when it comes to political participation, due to the importance of living in a locale long enough become known to politically oriented groups and individuals. Complementing this claim, Pacheco (2008) shows that adolescents who resided in politically competitive locales have higher turnout years later than those who lived in uncompetitive ones. And a comparative U.S. and U.K. study concluded that communities sharing sociological and political characteristics have a similar causal impact on the development of adolescents' levels of political tolerance, civic virtue, and sense of efficacy as citizens (Benz, Conover, and Searing 2008).

We can thus expect this effect to be reduced as the increased mobility fostered by new patterns of urban transportation and population movement results, overall, in young people's encountering greater diversity in their environment than did previous generations. As Putnam puts it, "the most certain prediction that we can make about almost any modern society is that it will be more diverse a generation from now than today" (2007, 137). And the key effect of greater diversity, he concluded from a survey of more than 30,000 individuals in forty-one communities in the United States in 2000, was heightened distrust of one's neighbors.[24]

It is thus fair to conclude that while diverse urban settings can give rise to peer groups rich in the resources that contribute to political involvement, that potential is less likely to be realized than in more homogeneous settings. Moreover, and we cannot overstate this point at least insofar as it concerns the United States,[25] racial diversity is interwoven with class. Overall, since the 1960s the United States has experienced both increasing economic inequality and residential economic segregation, with a resulting decline of voter participation in segregated, low-income neighborhoods (Widestrom 2008).[26]

A good empirical illustration of how the class-diversity connection affects young people is set out in a recent paper by Lay (2006), which compares rural and urban environments. Lay notes that poverty and its various social effects are found in both small towns and urban neighborhoods, except that the poor are less isolated in the former; she hypothesizes that small towns foster forms of social interaction that have relatively positive outcomes related to political knowledge.[27] Her study examines the interactions of parental income with both the number of people per square mile and the proportion of the community's residents who make less than $15,000 per year, as well as the influence of students' reported political discussions with family members and friends.

As expected, low-income, African American, and female students are less politically knowledgeable; but lower-income students in more-urban areas have lower scores than their counterparts in smaller towns. (This is also true of African American students, though their numbers were few in the small towns.) The explanation, Lay suggests, lies in the fact that social interaction within smaller towns help young people learn about politics and government. For every additional day a week that a respondent from a small town discusses politics with others, his or her political knowledge score increases by an average of 1.2 points, but no such relationship is found in the urban neighborhoods. Smaller communities are characterized by "relationships that have formed through kinship and friendship ties that have developed over long periods of time . . . Social interaction within smaller towns, in the form of political discussions, is also an important mechanism helping young people learn about politics and government. Informal ties can flourish in small towns, where residents often meet" (Lay 2006, 334–35).

Communities such as these, which can mitigate the effects of class upon citizenship, are demographically in decline. Hence geography provides little ground for optimism. But what of virtual ties that transcend geography, resulting from the spread of new communications technology? Until recently, people with low incomes could not afford access to high-speed Internet, but increasingly this is no longer the case. Can we expect that the Internet will make it possible for a significant number of young people from communities weak in social capital to participate in discussions with effects parallel to those in small towns?

There is good reason to be cautious in our expectations of electronic peer groups. Changes in information technology make it possible for young persons with the necessary skills and resources to create virtual peer groups. But these are detached from a community framed by geographical and political boundaries, and thus unsuited for supplying the community-based information and skills relevant to becoming an effective citizen. Though by definition partial, the knowledge we have about the online networks used by young people (as elaborated in chapter 3) suggests that, unlike the neighborhood-based physical ones, virtual peer groups cannot, as a rule, be seen as agencies of political socialization. We cannot expect them to meet expectations that voluntary groups will stimulate youth civic engagement.

In chapter 1, we noted the unrealistic expectations placed upon civil society groups. Especially when linked through dense and overlapping horizontal social networks, appropriate voluntary associations are expected to teach young people what it means to be part of a community and to work with others, thus fostering good citizenship—that is, the values and behavior essential for democracy (Putnam 1993, 2000; Flanagan 2003)—though there is some concern that associations may encourage an in-group mentality, causing bonding rather than bridging, in Putnam's (2000) words. Yet it is hard to find strong effects of organizational involvement on social capital at the individual level even in face-to-face groups (Dekker and van de Broeck 1998; Mayer 2002).[28] One problem is that empirical analysis of the results of participation in voluntary associations is affected by expectations arising out of cultural norms. The study of American high-school students cited in chapter 1 found that common to all kinds of reported engagement was "the need to demonstrate service for external and instrumental reasons." It concluded, further, that such activities did not lie at the core of the "lifeworld" of the students:

> [It is doubtful that] these phenomena ... begin to address the core life-
> world issues in which young people are ensnared: the paucity of viable
> career paths, the enormous pressure to succeed or risk slipping backward,

the sense of being an object of constant marketing campaigns, the diffi-culty of building social and cultural community within the high school where one can be oneself. [Their] lifeworld environment . . . includes the omnipresent status system of high school, and the equally omnipresent and related media pressure to consume, both the latest products of the media system itself and consumer goods that demonstrate status . . . This intersection shapes both the space for deciding what kinds of "civic" activi-ties to engage in and their meaning. (Friedland and Morimoto 2006, 32)

The Media

It is in this context that the real and potential effects of electronic peer groups and online networks should be regarded. Indeed, as the above quote suggests, these groups and networks cannot be separated from the final set of institutions concerned with political socialization, the communications media. Media content frames much of the communi-cation in the peer networks through which socialization takes place, networks that both replace and complement those of family and school.

As we shall see in the next chapter, the generational differences in media use are well documented, especially in the United States. First the multichannel, remote-controlled television universe and then the Inter-net radically transformed the patterns of media use, especially among young people. One aspect is germane to the discussion in this chapter. The new media have complicated the potential socializing role of par-ents and teachers by magnifying the gap between them and their chil-dren and students. A decade ago, Barnhurst concluded from his study of college-age youth in Spain and the United States that "much of what passes for political news on television and in the papers—because it simply doesn't have meaning within the localities where they live—never reaches these young citizens" (1998, 215). Although less powerful than the morning paper at the breakfast table, television still has the poten-tial, realized in certain European countries, to contribute to the family's political socializing role through the institution of the evening news. The individual-focused interactivity of Internet-based communication leaves less such room.

Does this result in what Bauerlein (2008) describes, an Internet-based youth culture that has engendered a brazen disregard of books and reading? As Bauerlein sees it, instead of using their reading to learn and grow through books, young people exchange gossip about each other and pop-culture icons, fearful of falling behind and not being cool. Never sticking to a subject that requires effort to grasp, they become disconnected from culture, history, and context, cut off from the cultural transmission provided by parents, teachers, and other adults.

Perhaps he is being alarmist. Ease of access to the high-speed Internet also augments the potential of parents and teachers to bring information to the attention of the young people. Do we have any reason to believe that this a potential can be realized? To begin to answer this question, we must look more carefully and deeply at the changes in media technology.

3

The Revolution in Information Technology

In the first chapter, we introduced a way to approach the question of youth political participation based on political knowledge. In this chapter, we look at changes over time in the information media, the prime agency through which political knowledge is disseminated. In chapter 2, we noted that the information media, along with other agents of political socialization, form the context in which young people develop their political orientations—or fail to do so. But we noted further that the media are more than a communications tool: their content is intricately linked to the development of an adolescent's personal identity. In a media-saturated culture, adolescents' choices among communication media are not only objective responses to technological change, but also a means of self-expression—of choices in clothing, entertainment icons, etc.—that stake out who one is and associates with, and where, if at all, one fits.

In this chapter, we explore the objective side, tracing the evolution of media technology. The Internet and digitalization-based ICT (information and communications technology) revolution is the latest stage in a series of transformations, going back to the invention of the radio. We will not go back quite that far, since we are concerned with changes that affected those generations still active today. These changes take place in the context of the structural change from an industrial to a postindustrial society which, as set out in chapter 2, denied a significant number of members of the emerging generations the economic and educational resources to regard themselves as full citizens-to-be.

The profound changes, especially among young men who lacked the necessary levels of literacy and numeracy for employment, that marked the progression from industrial to postindustrial society were first signaled at the beginning of the 1960s. Yet looking back on this period from the vantage point of the early years of a new century, we can see something not evident to the prophets of postindustrial society: the most significant and most indelible accelerating aspect of this transformation has proven to be in the area of information and communications technology.

Technological Change and Media Use

From Newspapers to Television

Several distinct stages of media use can be discerned, though the time and manner in which they arrived differed, depending on the institutional arrangements in different countries. As with so many aspects of development in industrialized regions, the United States is at one end of a continuum, and Northern Europe at the other. (Canada lies, as usual, closer to the United States—hence the frequent references to North America.) The roots of the difference in this case can be traced to the arrival of radio early in the twentieth century. In the United States, it took a commercial form; the state became significantly involved elsewhere, including in the other English-speaking countries, where the BBC served as a model. In the early days of radio, the adult-education function of the medium overshadowed its mass entertainment role. This is especially true of Scandinavia, where even today the educational function remains significant (see, e.g., Hultén 2003). This U.S.-European distinction also applies to state subsidies to newspapers (Milner 2002a, chapter 8). We need to keep these differences in mind in exploring the stages of development, since we rely in good part on American data and sources.

The generation that emerged into adulthood with the advent of radio is gone, but the preboomers who reached maturity before the use of television are still with us. Although they listened to radio, in countries with high literacy levels, the primary source of information was newspapers. Radio tended to supplement rather than substitute for newspapers in informing the public—which proved not to be the case with television, a medium that soon competed directly with newspapers for an audience used to getting information visually. In the United States, the proportion of respondents who reported reading newspapers daily declined steadily, from 76 percent in 1957 to 41 percent in 2004. But generations tend to hold onto the habits developed in their formative years. While only 20 percent of those born after 1973 read newspapers daily, the proportion

TABLE 3.1

Self-reported daily newspaper readership

COUNTRY	YOUTH (PERCENT)	AGE OF YOUTH	ADULTS (PERCENT)	PAGE*
Norway	81.0	13–19	86.0	290
Sweden	77.0	15–24	88.0	340
Denmark	76.6	16–24	79.7	124
Finland	72.0	15–24	87.0	145
Austria	69.5	14–29	75.2	56
Switzerland	68.1	16–24	74.8	345
Netherlands	58.0	15–24	71.4	265
Germany	53.6	14–19	76.2	155
Greece	52.0	18–24	54.6	159
Belgium	50.7	15–24	47.4	68
Hungary	49.2	15–24	52.6	171
Canada	44.9	18–24	54.1	88
Spain	41.7	16–24	39.7	330
Italy	40.2	18–24	39.3	196
United States	40.0	18–24	54.0	375
France	36.3	14–19	45.3	147
United Kingdom	35.7	15–24	32.8	324

SOURCE: *Derived from *World Press Trends* (Paris: World Association of Newspapers, 2004).

goes up steadily by generation, with different generations reporting quite consistent levels of newspaper reading throughout this period (Wattenberg 2007, 14–16). Yet even for generations reporting high levels of newpaper reading, television became the primary source of news. Habits of media use were changing in the 1970s and 1980s,[1] so that by the end of the latter decade, only 21 percent of Americans chose newspapers as the most credible news source, compared to 55 percent for television (Hepburn 1990).[2]

Lauf (2001) reports a parallel generational development taking place in Europe. However, there are still important differences, as we can see in table 3.1, when we compare levels of newspaper reading in North America and Europe. We see the Germanic and Scandinavian countries on one side of a dividing line, and the United States, the United Kingdom, Canada, and Southern European countries on the other side. The contrast is magnified, as far as the United States and Canada are concerned, when we limit the comparison to young people. (Indeed, it would likely be greater were the ages standardized, since the North American sample is on average older than the European one.)[3]

What effect does this transformation have on political knowledge and attentiveness? Using American data, Prior (2007, 90) argues that the initial impact of the advent of television on political knowledge (and, thus, probably on political participation) was a positive one for the sizable segment of the population that did not read newspapers but that, though looking for entertainment on television and faced with a lack of choice, did not turn off the television when the news came on. But, as we shall see in the next section, the arrival of choice made this effect short-lived.

While the debate continues, the weight of evidence is that the change from newspapers to television—especially commercial television—lowered overall levels of political knowledge.[4] Postman (1986) reminds us that every time a newspaper includes a feature that will attract a specialized group, it can assume it is increasing its circulation at least a little; this is not the case with television news. Television's critics persuasively argue that the generations raised on commercial television have a reduced capacity to make distinctions—between information and entertainment, between news and gossip, between fact and wishful thinking.[5]

Of course, public television, which followed on the heels of public radio, played an important informative role in many countries during the first decades of television, and in some countries, it is still an important force—though it has been fighting a losing battle in the 500-channel universe. Numerous studies have shown that public television, on average, does a better job of informing people than commercial television,[6] and the presence of public television helps to explain differences in political knowledge and participation (Milner 2002a, 101–4).[7]

Linked to the replacement of newspaper reading by commercial television watching is the decline in television news watching, from its peak in the late 1960s. Among Americans born between 1923 and 1942, those watching network TV news daily declined from 68 percent to 49 percent between 1967 and 2004, although the latter number is still a great deal higher than the sad 8 percent figure for 2004 for those born between 1983 and 1986 (Wattenberg 2007, 38).[8] Moreover, in an effort to stop the hemorrhaging of viewers for American television news, providers have downplayed politics in their coverage and emphasized entertainment-oriented, soft news (Patterson 2000).[9] In Northern Europe, in contrast, the greater continued presence of public television seems to have dampened the tendency to abandon watching TV news,[10] and to have kept commercial broadcasters from going soft.

The Remote Control Device

So far, we have treated the advent of television as one development. It is more appropriate, however, to understand the television era as falling into two distinct periods based on the availability of choice—that is, before and after the widespread introduction of the remote control, and the more or less simultaneous expansion of viewing options through cable and, later, satellite transmission. The relationship of viewers to television in the era before the remote control can be understood as closer to their relationship to newspapers, while the remote-controlled television (RCT) is closer to the online computer in its relationship to the user.

Prior (2007, 126) argues that the choice presented by cable fundamentally altered the effect of TV watching on political knowledge and political participation. His data show that the political knowledge of respondents without access to cable or Internet is unrelated to their degree of preference for entertainment. For those with access to cable television (via the RCT), however, moving from low preference for entertainment to a high one corresponds to a drop of 20 percentage points in political knowledge. Entertainment seekers could now easily avoid exposure to information. Observers have found that pre-RCT generations developed TV watching habits that made them close to if not quite captive audiences for the network news telecast. Many television watchers were thus exposed to coverage of political news and events because they simply did not wish to switch the channel (Bellamy and Walker 1996). The result, it is argued, was significant learning even if interest in politics was not always present (Morris and Forgette 2004).

The combination of the RCT, videocassettes, and the personal channel repertoires that cable and satellite providers offered subscribers resulted in a situation that allowed viewers, with minimal or no effort, to

avoid political news. The consequence, notes Prior (2007), was a deeper
political knowledge gap between those who pursue news and those who
avoid it, a gap that could only grow with the arrival of a far more powerful range of avoidance devices. The fundamental shift in information
dissemination was from an externally imposed order (within which, in a
democratic society, the individual can exercise choice) to one in which
the content is internally selected, ordered, and, potentially, created. The
former is characteristic of the linear logic of the newspaper, but also traditional radio and television, especially where the public media play an
important role. It is the onset of the RCT and multichannel universe that
marks the transition to the world now associated with the digitalization
of content and the integration of personal and media communication.[11]

Digitalization and the Internet: Competing Interpretations

The RCT sets the stage for the revolution in information and communications technology (ICT), with the arrival of three closely related phe-
nomena: the home computer, digitalization, and the high-speed Internet.
What makes this latest transformation in ICT revolutionary is its comprehensive and multidimensional character. The arrival of television and
then the RCT constituted important changes in information technology,
but not in communications technology—that is, two-way information
exchange. With current ICT, however, we have a simultaneous and integrated transformation of the medium of communication and the nature
of the content. To conceive of an equivalent, we would have to imagine
that the telephone and the television were invented simultaneously, and
developed together. Even this analogy does not do justice to the change
heralded by the arrival of the high-speed Internet and the digitalization
of media content, since the content is not merely sound, as in the telephone, or text, graphics, pictures, or video, but all of them together—
and at much higher resolution. With the RCT, you can easily leave a
boring program—perhaps a news show—for another program; with the
Internet, you have the constant option of easily switching to a less boring form of media content.

Given the complexity and recentness of the transformation, there
is no consensus about its effects. For every observer who is persuaded
that the unlimited information available through the Internet will foster
an increase in political communication and political knowledge, and,

therefore in political participation, there is another who fears that its effect will be to reinforce the participation gap between the politically engaged and the dropouts, to widen the digital divide. Still others, like me, are ambivalent: one can readily imagine that both sides are right, and there will be an increase both in political communication and knowledge and in the gap between the engaged and the dropouts. Hence, although a fairly wide consensus has emerged about the overall negative impact on informed political participation of the replacement of print by multichannel, remote-controlled television, any overall verdict on the Internet will have to await the return of a jury that has barely begun to deliberate.

A case in point. A survey conducted early in 2007 of some 1,200 Internet specialists, many "hand-picked due to their positions as stakeholders in the development of the Internet or . . . reached through the leadership listservs of top technology organizations," asked respondents if they thought people would be more tolerant of others in 2020 than they are today:

> Some 56 percent of the expert respondents disagreed with a scenario positing that social tolerance will advance significantly by then, saying communication networks also expand the potential for hate, bigotry, and terrorism. Some 32 percnt predicted tolerance will grow. A number . . . indicated that the divide between the tolerant and intolerant could possibly be deepened because of information-sharing tactics people use on the Internet.[12]

It is still not clear what effect the Internet has had on television consumption, even among young people. A survey of students at a large public university in the United States tentatively concluded that "even when computer skills and Internet access become more widespread in the general population, use of the World Wide Web as a news source seems unlikely to diminish substantially use of traditional news media" (Althaus and Tewksbury 2000, 25). Though the Internet adds an entire new set of simple-to-access media choices, these cannot be counted on to crowd out television.

The clearest effect of the onset of ICT seems to have been on print. Looking at U.S. data, we can see that the biggest drop in reported regular newspaper reading was not in the heyday of television, but in the 1990s, the decade when the Internet emerged and readership declined from approximately 50 percent to 40 percent (Wattenberg 2007,14). And it was only in the next decade that the Internet—especially with its replacement of paid classified ads in newspapers by free, interactive listings on sites such as craigslist.org—began to seriously undermine the newspapers' revenue stream,[13] leading to layoffs and even some closures.[14] At one level, then, this completes the shift from primarily externally ordered, "objective" content to internally ordered, "subjective" content witnessed in the replacement of newspapers by remote controlled, multichannel television.

But that is not the whole story. The Internet is also a print medium. One of its effects has been to transform the very nature of print journalism. Old-style reporters are giving way to the "mojos," mobile journalists who have smart phones, laptops, and digital audio recorders and cameras, but no office and no landline telephone. They send their material electronically, directly to their newspaper's website—material that may also find its way into print in the hard copy of the newspaper, if it still has one. The text can be readily complemented by pictures, graphics, and videos, even sound. The original source of that content can be a report prepared by a *New York Times* or BBC News journalist. But it can also be one of many other things—blogs, podcasts, and so on—produced under a very different cost structure.

A number of observers take a very pessimistic view of where these trends will lead. For example, Keen argues that the supposed democratization of the Web has in fact been the opposite, that the Internet, which was supposed to replace the dictatorship of experts in the old media with podcasts and streamed videos, is in reality just another dictatorship: one of idiots. These unaccountable blogs and so-called news sites, Keen contends, are often just fronts for public relations machines, or other forces with hidden agendas. Once dismantled, the institutions sustaining professional media can never be put back together. A politician refuses calls from representatives of the press and TV news at his peril. When they are gone, asks Keen, who will hold politicians to account (2007; see also Jacoby 2008)? Or, as another observer puts it, "if newspapers go bust there will be nobody covering city hall ... corruption will rise [and] legislation will more easily be captured by vested interests."[15] Not all are convinced. There's nothing to worry about, reply optimists like Colville (see also Tapscott 2008), for whom "the Internet will bring a far greater openness to politics":

The power of search will enforce consistency and depth in both policy and communication of policy. And the tone of debate will, at least in many cases, remain lively, anti-establishment and original. For the activist and the citizen, the internet will increasingly be used to hold politicians to account and to enable like-minded groups . . . to develop potent single-issue campaigns . . . For policy development, the internet will bring greater scrutiny; and greater access to official government data could revolutionise the way policy-making works . . . The most subtle, but perhaps most powerful, change, will be to the public's mindset. As we grow used to the instant availability of information online, we will no longer tolerate delay and obfuscation in getting similar information from government. The individual, and not the state, will be the master in the digital age. (Colville 2008, i–ii)

Such polar opposite views can coexist because the facts are contradictory or incomplete. For example, we do not know the effects of switching from print on paper to print on the screen. Some research suggests that such a shift may be more significant than it appears. For example, an experiment in which subjects read either the print or online version of *The New York Times* for a week found online readers less likely to follow the cues of news editors and producers, which meant that they read fewer public affairs stories (Althaus and Tewksbury 2002).

In October 2007, in its report titled "To Read or Not to Read," the U.S. National Endowment for the Arts linked low scores on national reading tests among young people with the decline in reading for pleasure. While time spent on the Internet by children has exploded,[16] the study did not find evidence that this had enhanced reading achievement. But others have found evidence suggesting that Internet access improves scores on standardized reading tests and school grades among low-income students (Jackson et al. 2006). In sum, the jury is still out on Bauerlein's claim that the Internet has caused young people to turn their backs on reading.[17]

It is plausible that the addition of information received through the Internet to that disseminated by the press, television, and radio results in a decline in the average quality of news coverage. For example, one study compared campaign coverage of candidates in the 2007 Australian election in traditional media and various Internet sources, finding the latter more skewed toward the major candidates and parties: "Far from re-ordering old hierarchies, the Internet news may have made the election a less even contest" (Goot 2008, 99). On the other hand, the addition of Internet sources has undeniably resulted in an explosion in the quantity of accessible information. Hence, it is commonly supposed that while average quality of information may decline in the short term, heightened competition among so many sources will result in good quality's winning out over time. But that presumes that good, professional news reporting can find a reliable market—which was far from certain even when the print media were profitable. If information is free, ask observers like Keen, what are the incentives for providing good, accurate information about public affairs? Can we expect a generation that expects to be able to download its music and other media content at no charge to pay for professional news reporting? No one has yet come up with a formula under which third parties replace the income that print newspapers once received from readers, as well as advertisers.

Even if they are able to survive, professional news sources must compete in a market where consumers of information are increasingly flooded with content produced by amateurs. How, for example, will young consumers be able to distinguish the electronic sources that strive for fair and accurate reporting from those that model themselves on Fox News, which consciously blurs the line between news and opinion? Newspapers know that they can be sued for libel for printing false information; the sanctions on bloggers posting the same information on the Internet are far less certain.

It is, thus, hard not to fear that as the Internet generation becomes freed from the gatekeepers of the professional media, it will increasingly be unable to distinguish the "facts" that many conspiracy theorists purvey on the Web from real facts. How justified is this fear?

The Quality of Information on New Media

One Finnish study (Carlson 2008) shows that YouTube uploads (see below) intensify negative aspects as they are circulated and get picked up by media. And a *New York Times* article reports: "Donald J. Leu . . . asked 48 students [at the University of Connecticut] to look at a spoof Web site . . . about a mythical species known as the 'Pacific Northwest tree octopus.' Nearly 90 percent of them . . . deemed the site a reliable source."[18] In a similar vein, a 2008 *Economist* article describes how easy

THE REVOLUTION IN INFORMATION TECHNOLOGY // 63

it is to propagate hatred and lies through messages "amplified with blogs, online maps and text messaging;[19] as a campaign migrates from medium to medium, fresh layers of falsehood can be created":

> During the crisis that engulfed Kenya . . . it was often blog posts and mobile-phone messages that gave the signal for fresh attacks. Participants in recent anti-American marches in South Korea were mobilized by on-line petitions, forums and blogs, some of which promoted a crazy theory about Koreans having a genetic vulnerability to mad-cow disease . . . In Russia, a nationalist blogger published names and contact details of students from the Caucasus attending Russia's top universities, attaching a video-clip of dark-skinned teenagers beating up ethnic Russians. Russian nationalist blogs reposted the story—creating a nightmare for the students who were targeted.[20]

It clearly does not take much effort to spread falsehoods, as this news story during the 2008 U.S. presidential campaign illustrates:

> Sen. Barack Obama, born in Hawaii, is a Christian family man with a track record of public service. But [there is] another version of the Democratic candidate's background, one that is entirely false: Barack Obama, born in Africa, is a possibly gay Muslim racist who refuses to recite the Pledge of Allegiance . . . Born on the Internet, the rumors now meander freely across the flatlands of northwest Ohio . . . When people on College Street [in Findlay, Ohio] started hearing rumors about Obama—who looked different from other politicians and often talked about change—they easily believed the nasty stories about an outsider.[21]

Fortunately, while it may not have convinced the residents of Findlay, the Obama campaign had the resources, electronic and otherwise, to bring the truth to a large enough number of Ohioans and Americans. But can we expect that resources can and will be marshaled to counter other such nasty rumors? In principle, yes: it is far easier to check facts in newspaper stories than in television reports, and even easier to verify ICT information. Since digital media files persist over time in ways that analog files of the same types do not, they can be indexed, stored, and readily used in comparing information. The Internet thus provides easy means of testing claims, making every consumer of information a potential fact checker through Google, Wikipedia, etc. Access to the high-speed Internet brings information costs toward the heretofore mythical zero built into economists' model of the market. There can be no doubt that many, including professional researchers like the author of this book, benefit greatly from easy access to limitless information.[22] And the generation born after this medium naturally develops a level of savvy with it that earlier generations cannot aspire to.

However, the storing and ready accessibility of digitalized information is a two-edged sword, due especially to the unequal distribution of the pertinent skills. In seeking information from the Internet, users leave traces of data that sophisticated online companies can follow, which enables them to target users with advertising tailored to their tastes andproclivities. And files—sometimes bogus—can follow individuals through their lives, reappearing at inopportune moments. Young people, even those increasingly sophisticated about the Internet's potential uses and abuses, run the risk of having their normal youthful experiments becoming embedded into digital media.[23]

An example of the positive, if largely unrealized, potential of this technology to facilitate informed political participation is discussed in chapter 6—namely, voting advice applications (VAAs), which provide the voter with an electronic, objective, and individualized way to compare her or his policy preferences with those of the candidates and parties. Among the most effective is the Swiss VAA, called smartvote. According to its designers, although smartvote has broken through to young people, it is still predominantly used by those who need it least: better-educated, higher-income males (Ladner, Nadig, and Fivaz 2009). The overall implication is clear. We cannot at this point count on the average citizen—for whom a potential information cost of zero is one matter, but its realization another—to be sufficiently motivated to check assumptions against facts, even if the user-friendliness and reliability of Internet information sources like Wikipedia are increasing. The Internet makes it even easier than television does to emulate the prototypical talk-radio listener, selecting sources that skew information so as to reinforce assumptions and prejudices. As a study cited by Sunstein (2007) reveals, political bloggers rarely highlight opposing opinions—of 1,400 blogs surveyed, 91 percent of the links were to like-minded sites.[24]

What can we expect of the generation that has grown up online? Does the Internet even have the potential of serving as a universal source of political information? We know that political information accounts for a small fraction of information sought and provided on the Web. A

TABLE 3.2

Media use

COUNTRY	AGE GROUP	DOES NOT READ NEWS ON THE INTERNET (%)	DOES NOT WATCH NATIONAL NEWS ON TELEVISION (%)	DOES NOT READ NEWSPAPERS (%)
United States	15–25	41.3	20.0	26.6
	26 and up	49.2	13.5	21.5
Canada	15–25	44.6	17.0	20.7
	26 and up	58.5	8.5	13.7

study of hits in March 2007 found that 2.9 percent of Web traffic went to media sites, and a tiny 0.12 percent to political sites identified with a political purpose. Broken down by age, the study revealed that Americans aged eighteen to thirty-four accounted for 43 percent of all Web traffic, but only 32 percent of visits to news sites and 22 percent of visits to political sites (Hindman 2009, 61, 68).

In a recent comparative study (discussed in detail in chapter 5), a representative sample of Americans and Canadians aged fifteen to twenty-five, and a smaller sample of those twenty-six and older, answered the same questions testing their political knowledge (Milner 2007). They were also asked how many days each week they read newspapers, watched TV news, and read news on the Internet. Table 3.2 displays the breakdown of those answering "none." It shows that in 2007, young people were using the Internet more (and television and newspapers less) than their elders, but the Internet was still far from a universal source of political information

Nevertheless, as we shall explore in chapter 5, the media-related activity with the strongest correlation with political knowledge, irrespective of age, country, or gender, turned out to be reading news on the Internet, with newspaper reading a strong second, and TV news watching quite a bit weaker.[25] This corresponds to the conclusion of an analysis of U.S. data on civic engagement and political participation: that reading online news tends to lead to an increase in the level of interest in politics, as well as increases in political knowledge and political discussion (Mossberger, Tolbert, and McNeal 2008).[26] Hence, in the context of the inevitable decline in newspaper reading, the potential of the Internet

as a source of political information for young people cannot be left un-
explored and unexploited.

Our existing knowledge of its effect on the informed political participation of young people is spotty. A study using results of the Maxwell
Poll on Citizenship and Inequality found that moderate and occasional
users of the Internet are more likely than nonusers to participate politically, but that—as with television—the effect apparently reverses for frequent users, who are generally less likely be involved in outside activities
(Reeher 2006). This suggests a parallel to Prior's above-noted finding of
the effects of the widened choice provided by cable television: increased
Internet access may widen the gap in informed political participation
between people looking for news and those looking for other things.
Suggestive in this regard is a survey of eighteen- to twenty-five-year-olds
by Kidd and Phillips (2007), which found that the effect of the Internet
as an information source on participation was significantly positive only
when it took the form of irregular e-mails with information about important issues. This insight corresponds to an unexpected finding in an
experiment by Sherr (2005), in which the young participants learned
less from the more youthful and dynamic websites that they preferred
than from the standard sites, more of whose information they retained.[27]

A recent Spanish study (Gallego Dobón and Jorba 2008) delved more
deeply into this question, asking if the Internet could also have an effect
comparable to television in the days before cable, when entertainment
watchers stayed tuned to the same TV channel and thus accidentally became politically informed when the news came on. The researchers were
unable to find evidence of a similar accidental effect on political knowledge from the use of e-mail servers and other websites that contain
news portals, or to the uninvited receipt of electronic correspondence
with political content. Yet they did find that, controlling for education,
Internet use raised political knowledge more among those who described
themselves as politically uninterested than it did among the politically
interested, suggesting that in some unknown manner, Internet use com-
pensates for low interest in politics.

Such findings suggest that daunting obstacles remain to the Internet's becoming a source of political information for as wide a segment
of the population as newspapers and television reached in their heydays.
As access to the high-speed Internet approaches levels of access to multichannel television (see below), the digital divide is increasingly based on

skills. More than watching the news on television, effectively using the Internet as a source of public affairs information requires a certain level of skill. With increasing dependence on digital information and tools, citizens are expected to exercise independent, informed judgment to make use of the information and tools, but the skills involved in those judgments are unequally distributed. This unequal distribution, as in other domains, reflects class differences. But does age also have an effect? Is the gap smaller for the Internet generation? And are there important cross-national differences, based on efforts to narrow the gap by nonmaterial redistribution of such knowledge and skills—as was argued to be the case with civic literacy? For answers, we must first get a better understanding of Web 2.0, which allows Internet users to be producers as well as consumers of content.

A Web of Netizens?

As Drotner notes: "Like 300 million other kids around the globe, every Dane under the age of 20 knows that the protagonist of *The Little Mermaid* is Ariel, a feisty redhead who manages to shape her fate and fortune" (2007, 167). We now have a commercial culture that appropriates and transforms existing elements in ways imperceptible to those born into it—in this case, the derivation of an animated movie from a fairy tale by Denmark's most famous author, Hans Christian Andersen. Yet this seemingly passive process has an active side, taking such appropriation into a further dimension: "Disney's figures, like many other media elements, are routinely appropriated by children in their own, increasingly digitized, media productions, from simple drawings to blogs, screen dumps, and home pages" (ibid.). According to one recent study (Jenkins 2006), roughly one-third of those who use the Internet have shared content that they produced; but another study, which explored the extent to which young adults create and share video, music, writing and artistic photography online, found this activity still largely confined to a relatively small minority of young adults with well-educated parents (Hargittai and Walejko 2008).

One popular characterization of this development sees the Internet as a participatory Web, having moved into a new phase called Web 2.0., defined as a "user-driven platform" providing "an architecture of participation: the Web shifts from a publishing medium to a platform for social participation and interaction based around social networking activities" (Carlson 2008). As such, it raises the practical possibility of a generation's practicing netizenship,[28] effective citizenship through interactive communication and the distribution and sharing of political content. But this is far from being realized, especially when we look at readership. In a careful study of blogs and other sites on which American citizens post their views on political matters, Hindman concludes that "the disparities in the readership of online views are orders of magnitude more unequal than the disparities we are used to in voting, volunteer work, and even political fundraising" (2009, 17). But there is inequality on the posting side as well. As suggested earlier, a fundamental obstacle to Web 2.0's living up to its potential is no longer that of universal access per se. In 2004, three out of four Americans under the age of eighteen had access to a computer, which, on average, they used for thirty minutes every day.[29] As we can see in table 3.3, Internet access in EU countries is uneven, but the Northern European countries with high civic literacy were above 80 percent in 2008. Indeed, on 15 October 2009, Finland became the first country in the world to make broadband Internet access a legal right.[30]

In the comparative U.S.-Canada survey cited above (Milner 2007), only 8 percent of the young American respondents and 10 percent of the young Canadians reported never using the Internet. As the cost of high-speed access declines, the physical capacity to retrieve and exchange digital content—in the form of text, sounds, still and moving pictures, and various types of graphics—anytime, anywhere, and with anyone becomes standard. But it is standard only for those with the requisite skills. Eszter Hargittai[31] found that many Internet users could not complete simple online tasks, such as finding a political candidate's website.[32] Beyond e-mailing and texting, netizenship requires the ability to maneuver effectively through blogs, podcasts, social networking services, digital petitions, and wikis. Informed choices must be made about joining online communities, message boards, etc. And skills must be upgraded to keep up with new forms of expression.[33]

Closing this skill-based digital divide will entail attaining an ICT literacy akin to—and including—print literacy. Yet we should remember that universal effective print literacy has yet to be attained in North America, where over 20 percent of adults are not functionally literate—a situation quite different from that in the Northern European countries with high civic literacy, where state agencies are directly involved in

TABLE 3.3

Home Internet access in Europe, 2008

COUNTRY	PERCENT
Austria	69
Belgium	64
Bulgaria	25
Cyprus	43
Czech Republic	46
Denmark	82
Estonia	58
Finland	72
France	62
Germany	75
Greece	31
Hungary	48
Iceland	88
Ireland	63
Italy	47
Latvia	53
Lithuania	51
Luxembourg	80
Malta	59
Netherlands	86
Norway	84
Poland	48
Portugal	46
Romania	30
Slovakia	58
Slovenia	59
Spain	51
Sweden	84
United Kingdom	71

promoting adult literacy and appear to be initiating parallel efforts to promote literacy and access for new media. In North America, such efforts are largely in the hands of private foundations, some of which have poured large sums of money into new initiatives to teach young people the skills to express themselves through digital media links.

In a sense, the outcome of the debate between pessimists and optimists over the capacity of the new ICT media to foster a generation of netizens hinges on the potential effectiveness of these initiatives to close the new digital divide. The evidence is contradictory, and opinions vary. Optimists like Krueger (2002) argue that, given equalized access, the Internet shows the genuine potential to bring individuals into the political process. But more pessimistic observers interpret the data to show that online activities reinforce established patterns of inequality between participants and dropouts (see Gibson, Lusoli, and Ward 2005). The Spanish study cited above, which surveyed 3,700 respondents, supports this interpretation, having found that the low political participation and political knowledge of people with lower levels of education and income is magnified through online participation (Anduiza Perea et al. 2008; Anduiza Perea et al. 2009; Gallego Dobón and Jorba 2008). Similarly, surveying Australians aged eighteen to thirty-four, Vromen (2008) shows that Internet use facilitates participation by the already politically engaged, but exacerbates the digital divide due to geography, education level, income level, and occupational classification.[34]

Using evidence from the 2005 Oxford Internet Survey, Di Gennaro and Dutton (2006) found that Internet experience and proficiency had a significant impact on whether one becomes politically engaged online, but that online political participation reinforced—and in some cases exacerbated—existing social inequalities in offline political participation. A parallel finding emerges from an interesting case study (Kavanaugh et al. 2008) of local political participation recently conducted in a Virginia community with a mature computer network (the Blacksburg Electronic Village): "Though these communication technologies add voices from engaged segments of the population, voices from passive-apathetic and apathetic groups largely remain silent . . . If we are to broaden enfranchisement, it seems powerful social and technological interventions remain needed." At this point, then, the online computer is no more a technological fix to the problem of political dropouts than it is to school dropouts.[35]

Political Mobilization on the Internet

Although netizenship as a generalized state of affairs has yet to be attained, netizen networks have mushroomed on the Internet, which creates an extraordinary new space for political interaction and organization. In the above-cited article, Vromen describes how information sharing and organizing on the Internet facilitates young Australians' involvement in activist and community groups. Offering a variety of interactive resources, such sites often seek not only to encourage young people's interest, but also to convey young people's views and concerns to policymakers and enhance two-way communication between them (Xenos and Bennett 2007).[36] Some function specifically as means of social networking. For example, on Essembly.com, young people can find others with similar political interests, vote on posted resolutions, and engage in online discussion of political issues.

There are many targeted social networking sites, but they are dwarfed as forums for political organizing by the social network Facebook. Originally, political organizing on Facebook was confined to unconventional forms of involvement, but the network's success[37] soon attracted the attention of mainstream political parties, which increasingly use Facebook and similar social networks for recruitment purposes (Schifferes and Lusoli 2007).

One specific activity that takes place via these networks is online petitioning. Some insight into this activity is provided by a study that analyzed online petitions hosted on the Petitions Online website, focusing on petitions about entertainment and the media (one of eight categories into which the site classifies its petitions). The 14,395 such petitions with over ten signatures in the month of November 2006 roughly equalled the number of petitions in the other seven categories combined (those categories are environment; technology and business; religion; and politics and government divided into international, national, state, and local levels). A careful study of a large sample of the 14,395 petitions, with a median of 143 signatures, reveals that these typically focus on products and industries associated with youth culture, and often represent consumers' objections to decisions about the scheduling (or canceling) of entertainment programs or events (Earl and Schussman 2008).

There is some skepticism as to the commitment of the signers of petitions that require minimal effort to circulate.[38] Yet some are clearly effective in getting results, when they address matters that are important to young people. For example, "a petition signed by just 592 fans of a canceled program was submitted, and shortly after the submission of the petition, the program was brought back" (Earl and Schussman 2008, 81). A question of greater concern here is whether these matters can be considered political. We are once again confronted with issues raised in the discussion of political consumerism in chapter 1. Earl and Schussman respond to the question of whether such creative uses of digital technologies by young people are expanding the boundaries of politics and public issues. They suggest that protests in online gaming communities, sharing music files, or fans' petitioning of music companies may constitute political behavior to the extent that the communication skills and actions in these areas of online life are being transferred to more familiar political realms, such as voting and public protest. In the same vein, Calenda and Mosca (2007) argue that this is in fact happening, since the Internet is perceived by young people as the appropriate medium for discussing political matters, via new and more creative forms of communication and participation. Yet the evidence is spotty. In carrying out "sophisticated electronic content analysis," Wilhelm found that "political forums do not provide virtual sounding boards for signaling and thematising issues to be processed by the political system" (1999, 175).

In sum, while Internet idealists (e.g., Trippi 2004) envisage a universal electronic public sphere for debate and deliberation, this characterization is contested by other scholars as, at best, "premature [since] the web does not lead to objectively measurable changes in political involvement or information" (Scheufele and Nisbet 2002, 68). Though younger citizens seem to increasingly expect e-engagement possibilities and are encouraged to make use of e-services from government, a survey of their usage suggests that only those already interested take advantage of these opportunities (Gibson and Ward 2008).

The question thus remains, to what extent do Internet-based social networking sites such as Facebook, in transcending the social limits of the geographic community and bypassing traditional information gatekeepers and authorities, also provide forums for communicating, organizing, and socializing for young people without face-to-face contact? So far, cross-national research suggest that the hopes of the creators of youth-oriented civic and political sites that the Internet would reengage the young in the public sphere have not been realized (Livingstone and

Dahlgren 2007).[39] Even optimists (e.g., Ferguson 2007) thus insist on the necessity of profound educational and political change in order to fulfill the potential of information and communications technology.

The Internet and Political Campaigns: The Obama Effect

Overall, then, the literature suggests that the Internet has not yet lived up to its potential as an instrument of youth political involvement. But the literature predates the Obama campaign, which has been heralded as ushering in a new era in online (and offline) youth civic engagement and two-way communication between citizens and political decision makers. An important step in this direction came in 2006, when You-Tube created YouChoose, a section of the site devoted to showing videos from political candidates. Seven of the sixteen main American presidential aspirants in 2008 announced their candidacies on YouTube.

> As the campaign season wore on, many candidates . . . uploaded ads and permitted freewheeling—sometimes ferocious—discussion of them . . . Candidates virtually forfeited control over the context of their videos and allowed them to be embedded, critiqued, recut and satirized . . . Some candidates also discovered, to their surprise, that they could upload vanity videos (or ones that seemed fairly parody-proof) and supporters would circulate them on social networks, amateurs would use them to make ads and they would get influential, focused advertising for nothing. Early on, the musician will.i.am used film of an Obama speech to make his "Yes We Can" music video. That video, in multiple versions, has become the most-watched political entry on the site, having been seen around 15 million times. (The campaign's upload of the actual "Yes We Can" speech has fewer than two million views.)[40]

The Obama campaign perfected techniques developed by various politically motivated organizations—including, among those left of center, MoveOn, the Huffington Post, Daily Kos, and Democratic Underground. Only the last, however, takes the grass-roots approach perfected at the other side of the spectrum, by the right-leaning website Free Republic, which developed discussion lists connected by participants to "a plethora of state message boards organizing real-time, boots-on-the-ground political action . . . a do-it-yourself kit for spreading messages and connecting them with local, face-to-face activism." This approach was very successfully emulated by the Obama campaign, which used its website to disseminate tools for grass-roots organizing and made its campaign infrastructure infinitely expandable, as groups were cloned over and over, learning from and copying one another. [41]

Obama was able to come from virtually nowhere to wrest the Democratic nomination from the seemingly invincible Clinton machine, and to win the presidency convincingly. While his extraordinary oratorical skills are not to be denied, the electronic mobilization of support, making use of an e-mail list of some thirteen million names, played a key role.[42] In the primaries, Obama racked up huge majorities in college towns—especially in states that require greater efforts at participation by having caucuses select delegates to the party conventions—through the use of sophisticated electronic mobilization techniques that capitalized on the candidate's attractiveness.

It remains to be seen if this approach can be replicated: no candidate in the 2006 mid-term U.S. elections achieved anything similar.[43] It could be that there is something unique in the Obama phenomenon in 2008, which raises a more prosaic question: for how many young supporters was Obama in effect the celebrity of the moment? A political figure can become hot under extraordinary circumstances, but as a rule, politicians are at a disadvantage on the electronic playing field. Their world is less engaging than competing worlds that are only a click of the computer mouse away. In the real political world, one is a mere citizen; in a video game, one is a player; and on Facebook, one is a bright star in a constellation. Many young people apparently happily shared virtual space with Obama—but will they do so indefinitely, or in other campaigns?

Aware of the challenge, the Obama organization moved immediately to try to convert the campaign's success with social networking technologies into a tool for good governance: "to remake the tools of factional organization as instruments of broad, cross-partisan and respectful public engagement."[44] The challenge will be immense in the context of the inevitable disappointments of governing, especially given the difficult economic circumstances that face the Obama administration.[45]

Conclusion

If our analysis is right, the critical question now is, how many of those electronically touched by the Obama phenomenon gained real and lasting political knowledge and, in the process, developed habits of attentiveness to public affairs—habits they might otherwise never have developed? If that number is large, then we are seeing the harbinger of a more informed and attentive public, and a firmer basis of civic engagement. But we need to be wary. Noting that in the twentieth century, civic engagement tended to take place within formal organizations that one had to join and pay dues to, as well as complying with their rules and the decisions of their leaders, while with the new forms of online engagement, membership is provisional and not clearly defined, governance is horizontal, and the actual act of participation is often individualized and performed alone, Levine asks:

> Is it possible to overcome collective-action problems through loose, voluntary networks? For example, in an online group in which people use pseudonyms and can easily exit, can members be persuaded to take disciplined and costly steps, equivalent to going on strike in a traditional union? We see a "tragedy of the commons" online in the form of unsolicited e-mail, viruses, and other destructive behavior.[46] Can self-organizing online groups handle such behavior? . . . Can online organizing translate reliably into offline activity when the latter is necessary? (2007, 94–95)

The Internet has transformed the world of information and communication, but we still must ask, will the emerging generations be able to participate politically as informed citizens? Those lacking the skills to make sense of what is happening in the political world cannot be counted on to participate meaningfully. New technologies provide new ways of paying attention and participating, but they require not only access to their networks, but the skill to use them effectively. There is reason to expect that new digital technologies will boost civic literacy—the proportion of citizens with the knowledge and skills to be effective citizens—but also will exacerbate class-based gaps in such knowledge and skills. We do not yet know enough to assert which effect will be the stronger, but we do know enough to assert that, whatever the case turns out to be, we have no choice in the matter.

We do not know if the Obama phenomenon will leave young Americans meaningfully higher in their level of informed political participation. But we do know that during the presidential primary season in 2008, 40 percent of American adults stated that they looked for political information on the Internet, 9 percentage points higher than in the 2004 primary season, and that by the end of the campaign, the Internet had displaced newspapers as the second source—after television—for national and international news. Moreover, among young people, the Internet had come to rival television as the leading source.[47]

For good or bad, as a way of becoming informed and communicating about politics and public affairs, the Internet is here to stay. To have any hope of succeeding, any strategy for dealing with political dropouts must involve the Internet.

4

Political Participation

DO YOUNG PEOPLE STILL VOTE?

I t's time to get to the numbers: just how many young people vote? We have established that nowadays, for the most part, they turn out to vote at lower levels than did their parents and grandparents when they were young. While emerging generations appear to be more comfortable with less conventional forms, unconventional political activity is not filling the gap left by the decline in conventional forms of participation among younger citizens. Where substitution is taking place, as was suggested in chapter 1, it is among a small group of well-educated young citizens, not among the less educated—that is, the potential political dropouts. Moreover, in looking at the only apparent case of such substitution, Norway, we found voting being replaced less by protest behavior than by more direct, citizen-initiated activity that targets conventional parties and government agencies.

Measuring and Comparing Turnout: Why and How

Voting is a visible act, readily identifiable and quantifiable—an act for which we have objective as well as subjective measures. People who normally do not vote are highly unlikely to take part in more active forms of politics.[1] Moreover, these more active forms of participation are, as a rule, limited to a minority of the population. For conventional forms of participation, this is clearly illustrated in table 4.1, which shows that though declining since the 1970s, average voter turnout is still about four times the average for other forms of conventional participation.[2]

A similar relationship appears when we compare turnout to unconventional forms. An analysis of the results of the 2003 European Social Survey (Milner 2009a) found that, respectively, 23.3, 14.5, and 8.5 percent of respondents reported having signed petitions, taken part in boycotts, and participated in demonstrations in the previous twelve months.

TABLE 4.1

Conventional political participation (percent)

COUNTRY	VOTE IN LAST GENERAL ELECTIONS		ATTEND MEETING OR RALLY		CONTACT A POLITICIAN		BELONG TO A POLITICAL PARTY	
	1970s	2004	1970s	2004	1970s	2004	1970s	2004
Austria	95	91	19	10	12	15	23	22
Germany	92	88	22	9	11	9	11	4
Italy	92	89	20	NA	18	12	18	3
Finland	87	77	19	6	12	8	11	9
Netherlands	82	80	6	6	14	9	7	10
United Kingdom	77	70	9	3	12	9	8	10
United States	71	63	18	13	28	22	21	42
Switzerland	59	60	17	14	15	11	13	9

SOURCE: Gallego 2007, 6. Data are derived from the Political Action Study and International Social Survey Program. Recent data for Italy are from the first wave of the European Social Survey.

In sum, alternate forms of political participation cannot expect to engage even a quarter of the potential participants, while elections can reasonably expect participation by three-quarters. If civic engagement is not to be restricted to a minority, political participation must be something open to and, under normal circumstances, practiced by the majority of the population. Under such circumstances in advanced democratic societies, voter turnout is the still the best thermometer we have to measure the health of the body politic.

In addition, voter turnout is an objective indicator than can be operationalized for the purposes of international comparison. For political science, it provides the bedrock of relevant data, comparable to gross domestic product for economists, allowing for meaningful comparative research. Comparison is the sine qua non of meaningful analysis, allowing us to subject alternative approaches to the test of whether outcomes meet expectations. When it comes to political participation, as we noted, critics of studies using turnout and other conventional forms of participation have failed to produce a practical alternative indicator; their repertoire of reported unconventional forms of participation and conducive attitudes is not applicable to effective cross-national research.

Voter turnout, for all its limitations, does meet the necessary conditions. Ideally, we would like to be able to use comparable turnout data for a variety of legislative and administrative offices, but because of the un-availability of some of these data,[3] cross-national research concentrates on voting for candidates for national legislative office.

When we compute the average turnout in legislative elections in industrial democracies in the decades since World War II, we can see a pattern of overall decline since the end of the 1980s, following a stable period of consistently solid average turnout in the 1960s and 1970s (Ellis, Pammett, Gratschew, and Thiessen 2007). Using data on parliamentary turnout levels in the European countries and Canada, Siaroff (2007) calculated decade averages at 82 percent for both the 1970s and 1980s, declining to 76 percent in the 1990s, and 71 percent in the first half of the 2000s.[4] When combined in table 4.1 with data on other forms of conventional political participation in the last quarter of the twentieth century in seven European countries and the United States, we see that the decline in turnout for general elections is strikingly parallel to the shrinking membership of political parties.[5] But significant differences remain: for example, compared to North Americans, the Europeans are high in voting (except for the Swiss), and low in reported contacting politicians.

The relationship between voting and these other forms of partici-pation, to cite the Canadian authors of a book on citizens, is "striking" (Gidengil, Blais, Nevitte, and Nadeau 2004, 172). In the thirteen-nation European study on citizenship, involvement, and democracy, the find-ings lead unequivocally in the same direction: citizens in every country failed to see a trade-off between the different modes of participation. Teorell, Torcal, and Montero note: "It is not the case, as is commonly held, that some citizens continue to use the traditional channels of par-ticipation, such as contacting officials and working for a political party, whereas others favor the less conventional modes such as protest or consumer participation. On the contrary, activists within one mode of activity tend to be activists within the others as well" (2007, 334).

Recorded Turnout versus Telephone and Internet Surveys

A brief digression on the use of surveys to measure turnout is in order at this point. Table 4.1 is based on the percentage of registered voters who showed up to vote. Survey data is used instead when we need to link casting a vote with information concerning an individual's attributes, attitudes, and reported actions. It is also used when we wish to break down the aggregate turnout into subcategories, including the one of interest to us: age.[6] Here we need to take into account overreporting, which is often assumed to average approximately 10 percent but which can fluctuate a great deal.[7] Overreporting is, in part, due to the fact that in a survey, an individual can report votes that he or she has not cast—either because of a memory lapse or as a conscious lie.

Analyzing European Voter Project data for six countries that have carried out national election studies regularly for a long period (Denmark, Germany, the Netherlands, Norway, Sweden, and the United Kingdom), Gallego Dobón points out that "over-reporting has grown in some countries at the same rate as turnout has declined." Comparing elections before and after 1985, "in the Netherlands electoral participation has dropped by five per cent in the period observed, but according to survey estimates it has not decreased but rather risen by two per cent . . . In Denmark the official decline is three per cent, but the over-reporting has grown by exactly the same amount, and thus, according to survey data, turnout is completely stable in this country . . . In Germany and Sweden over-reporting rates have doubled between the two periods observed" (Gallego Dobón 2009, 29).

Table 4.3 (below) illustrates the discrepancy by setting side by side the results of the 2002 European Social Survey with actual recorded figures compiled by International IDEA for the election closest in time to the survey. Differences are often substantial, averaging around 10 percentage points, but countries tend to rank high or low on both measures. Still, the discrepancy varies quite a bit. For example, while Denmark is highest on the survey data, Belgium—with its compulsory system—has the highest actual turnout. The association between votes reported and votes cast can also be problematic when the aim is to compare age groups even in the same country, since we cannot assume the bias attributable to these factors to be equally strong among the groups. Consider Pammett and LeDuc's (2003, 20) estimate of a 22.4 percent turnout for first-time electors in the 2000 Canadian election, which gave impetus to a Elections Canada study (discussed below)—the results of which confirmed, as many had suspected, that the 22.4 percent was too low. This was likely due, at least in part, to Pammett and LeDuc's applying a statistical correction on the rate of turnout to account for overreporting,[8] which turned out to be too high for young people because, given their low sense of civic duty to vote, they tend to overreport less than older citizens.

There is another dimension to overreporting. As survey response rates decline—an almost universal trend—voters are more likely to be successfully contacted than abstainers. This will inflate the level of reported turnout over real turnout, especially for those countries with the lowest survey response rates.[9] This is less the case for door-to-door surveys; but given the cost, these are increasingly rare. The problem of low response rates is even more acute in telephone surveys. For young people, this is compounded by the fact that increasing numbers of them do not own a landline phone.[10] Combined with the fact that young people are the most likely to be available online, there is a shift among researchers, especially those polling young people, toward Internet surveys. Apart from being quicker and less expensive, Internet polls also lessen the risk of providing unintended cues about appropriate answers, since there is no voice contact as in telephone polls, or eye contact as in door-to-door ones.

Among the most reputable providers of Internet surveys is a company called Knowledge Networks, which uses what it calls its Knowledge-Panel, made up of more than 50,000 participants solicited through random telephone calls. Those who agree to take surveys are sent e-mail three to four times a month, inviting them to participate in research on the company's website.[11] For the Cooperative Congressional Election Study in the United States, Polimetrix, another company, has developed an even more sophisticated system that uses a sophisticated weighing technique to make the random sample of opt-in respondents resemble the general population as closely as possible.

This is not the place to explore the relative merits of these methodologies. It is clear that as Internet use increases, and response rates to telephone polls decline, the trend toward sophisticated Internet polling will only accelerate, and online pollsters will, as Knowledge Networks claims it already does, increasingly overcome the problem of the professional respondent and other hazards of opt-in online panels. But we are not there yet, especially in Canada, where respondents to Internet surveys are typically drawn from a list of e-mail addresses of people who, in another context, had indicated an interest in participating in them.

Hence we must be wary of claims made based on polling such opt-in samples. For example, reporting on a survey that D-Code (which describes itself as "an organization that aims to engage youth in the political process") conducted in January 2006, its founder, Robert Barnard, debunked "the myth that [those aged fifteen to thirty-four] are disengaged, by stressing the large number of respondents who reported sending e-mails about a cause or signing an online petition."[12]

The Hazards of Using Intention to Vote Surveys

When it comes to young people, an additional dimension adds to the complexity of measuring reported turnout since, depending on the age criterion, some or all may have been ineligible to vote at the time of the most recent election. Hence surveys often test willingness to vote, with questions like "I would have voted if I were eligible," or "I plan to vote in the future." In contrast to a question asking whether or not one actually voted (for which there is an objectively correct answer), these are purely hypothetical questions, which often elicit little more than an attitude. Adolescents for whom the first vote is still far off are especially prone to answer based on cultural expectations, which vary cross-nationally. This helps explain the great variation in table 4.2.

As might have been expected, we cannot meaningfully predict actual turnout figures from the responses to such hypothetical questions. The large disparities between the numbers in table 4.2 with actual turnout figures—especially in countries like Greece, Poland, Portugal, and Spain and for younger voters—in table 4.3 confirm that "willingness to vote . . . does not seem to be inspired politically, but rather reflects a more general attitude, in which adolescents simply echo the kind of values that are being portrayed as socially desirable by either their parents or the school environment, a general willingness to accept adult norms" (Hooghe and Kavadias 2005, 29).

Comparing Youth Turnout: Europe

With these caveats in mind, we can proceed to set out what we know about voter turnout among young people in postindustrial societies, and its relationship to the overall decline. The first important cross-national initiative analyzing this development was undertaken by the International

TABLE 4.2

Fourteen-year-olds' willingness to vote in future (percent)

COUNTRY	YES	NO	DON'T KNOW
Australia	74.4	12.7	9.2
Belgium	61.2	28.1	9.0
Bulgaria	50.9	36.2	10.7
Chile	69.6	24.2	6.1
Columbia	84.5	12.8	2.7
Cyprus	93.8	4.8	1.3
Czech Republic	45.6	37.9	16.4
Denmark	81.0	8.0	10.1
England	71.5	17.6	6.6
Estonia	61.1	28.3	10.0
Finland	81.0	12.6	6.1
Germany	63.0	30.3	6.5
Greece	81.9	12.8	5.2
Hong Kong	71.3	17.6	9.0
Hungary	90.4	9.0	0.5
Italy	70.6	17.2	12.2
Latvia	63.9	25.6	9.8
Lithuania	67.2	17.0	15.5
Norway	80.6	12.0	7.0
Poland	83.6	11.4	4.4
Portugal	83.5	11.9	3.8
Romania	76.3	16.7	6.9
Russia	76.1	16.8	7.0
Slovak Republic	90.5	6.6	2.8
Slovenia	78.8	15.5	5.6
Sweden	65.8	22.2	11.6
Switzerland	59.0	31.9	8.8
United States	78.2	14.3	6.2
Mean	73.6	18.2	7.4

SOURCE: Hooghe and Kavadias 2005, based on the 1999 IEA Civic Education Study (see chapter 9). Entries are percents of respondents who said, that once they reached adulthood, they were likely or very likely to participate in national elections (yes); or unlikely or very unlikely to do so (no); those who did not respond were considered not sure (don't know). A few respondents were entered in two categories, or in no categories, so the total in the three columns may be slightly higher or lower than 100 percent.

Institute for Democracy and Electoral Assistance (International IDEA), which published a report titled *Youth Voter Participation* (1999). The report investigated the political activity of young people in fifteen Western European countries, using national election survey data. The average turnout level in the early 1990s for voters between eighteen and twenty-nine years old was 12 percentage points below the participation rate of those over thirty, though there were important differences—with the discrepancies in Finland, France, Ireland, Portugal, and Switzerland well above the average.

The most important methodologically consistent study for our purposes is the European Social Survey (ESS), the first round of which took place in 2000–2003 in some twenty new and old European democracies. Table 4.3 presents the results from this comparative survey on indicators related to political participation.

The ESS asked: "Some people don't vote nowadays for one reason or another. Did you vote in the last [country] national election in [month/year]?" Using weighing techniques to compensate for the discrepancy between reported voting and actual turnout rates, Fieldhouse, Tranmer, and Russell (2007) found that overall turnout in the twenty-two European countries in elections between 1999 and 2002 averaged 70 percent, but only 51 percent for electors under the age of twenty-five. In no country did turnout for young people exceed the overall turnout rate. In general, greater cross-national variation was found among younger voters than older ones, with Greece, Norway, Slovenia, and Spain the countries where the age disparity is greatest. As might have been expected, Belgium, which has compulsory voting, has the highest turnout; Switzerland, whose unique constitution results in only a loose connection between the composition of the executive branch and election outcomes, has the lowest. In explaining the results, the authors stress the fact that there were greater differences in the impact of being young in countries where turnout was lower (Fieldhouse, Tranmer, and Russell 2007, 804).[13]

But how have these patterns evolved over time? A study by Smets (forthcoming) assembles turnout data for the United States, Canada, and eight European countries from the 1960s and early 1970s up to the early 2000s, and breaks them down into two age categories, over and under thirty-five.[14] She found that all countries except Denmark had seen some overall turnout decline, but that the gap between the two age groups has clearly been widening in Canada, Denmark, Norway, the United Kingdom, and the United States, but not in Finland,[15] Germany, Italy, the Netherlands, and Sweden. Overall, this fits the expectations generated from the ESS data: the impact of being young is stronger where turnout is lower. Denmark is the exception, but its turnout rates have remained so high that it is hard to imagine any other evolution. Finland is somewhat more surprising, given the relatively high level of overall decline, but the cutoff age of thirty-five may mean that the dropout effects of the high youth unemployment beginning in the mid-1990s is not reflected in the turnout figures, which end in 2003.

Another ESS question asked how important respondents felt voting was as part of being a good citizen, using an eleven-point scale from extremely unimportant to extremely important. As we can see in the last two columns of table 4.3, the differences between all respondents and first-time voters was fairly small. There is a strong positive cross-national relationship between reported turnout and importance of voting, which is slightly weaker among new voters. But there are important cross-national differences. These emerge especially when we consider only those who said that voting was very important. We can see that in several of these countries (Austria, Denmark, Germany, Luxembourg, and Sweden), where new voters place the highest levels of importance on voting, the reported vote is high; among those countries (Portugal, Spain, Switzerland, and the United Kingdom) where new voters place the lowest levels of importance on voting, it is low. Finland fits in here as well, given that it shows an especially steep generational drop in both indicators, which fits the supposition set out in the previous paragraph.

Norway's numbers, showing an age-based gap only in reported voting side and not in importance of voting, fit the above-noted replacement of voting by other forms of conventional participation. With 54.5 percent of eighteen- to twenty-year-olds turning out in 2001 and 55.3 percent in 2005 (compared to 75.5 and 77.4 percent for all eligible voters), Norway's young citizens contributed significantly to the decline in voter participation.[16] But instead of dropping out, many were becoming involved in other forms of political participation, especially direct citizen-initiated contact with political institutions, including political parties.

We learned in chapter 2 that a higher share of earlier generations with marginal levels of political knowledge voted out of a sense of civic duty than is the case today, an extreme case being the United Kingdom —where only 16 percent of those aged eighteen to twenty-four who "were

TABLE 4.3

Voting behavior and attitudes toward voting (percent)

COUNTRY	TURNOUT C. 2000	REPORTED VOTE (ALL)	REPORTED VOTE (BORN SINCE 1980*)	VERY IMPORTANT TO VOTE (ALL)	IMPORTANT TO VOTE (ALL)	IMPORTANT TO VOTE BORN SINCE 1980*
Austria	84.3	88.46	74.6	39.5	8.07	7.46
Belgium	93.0	85.23	53.5	18.1	6.56	6.38
Czech Republic	57.9	65.93	61.4	17.6	6.16	5.88
Denmark	87.1	93.67	78.9	52.0	8.87	8.09
Finland	69.7	81.70	54.5	25.7	7.59	5.97
Germany	79.1	85.30	72.8	32.1	7.55	7.06
Greece	75.0	90.56	59.8	39.0	8.12	7.60
Hungary	73.5	80.93	69.2	45.8	8.26	7.94
Ireland	62.6	75.87	41.8	31.6	7.70	7.23
Israel	67.8	78.66	38.4	NA	7.98	7.13
Italy	81.4	89.45	76.4	29.9	7.51	6.69
Luxembourg	86.5	64.74	12.8	48.5	8.00	7.27
Netherlands	80.0	86.33	74.8	19.5	7.48	6.89
Norway	75.0	83.66	50.0	32.8	8.19	7.48

Poland	46.2	66.16	48.2	31.2	7.65	6.95
Portugal	62.8	72.49	41.3	26.7	7.13	6.40
Slovenia	70.4	80.21	42.0	22.1	6.74	5.89
Spain	68.7	77.67	27.4	15.6	6.43	5.02
Sweden	80.1	86.96	81.4	45.5	8.38	8.12
Switzerland	45.4	68.98	17.6	22.0	7.37	6.66
United Kingdom	59.4	72.35	41.0	27.0	7.16	6.51

SOURCE: Data from the first round of the European Social Survey and International IDEA survey (see Milner and Ersson 2009).

*Indicates first-time voters (excluding those too young to vote in the previous election).

not at all interested in news about the election" reported casting a vote. The reported 41 percent turnout (based on the ESS survey) for young U.K. citizens (in table 4.3) corresponds to recorded turnout figures (39 percent in 2001, and 37 percent in 2005). The largest decline in the turnout of young people took place in 1997, a drop of almost 30 percentage points from 1992 (Phelps 2005).

Analyses of ESS data show a similar trend in certain other European countries,[17] while data comparable to those in the ESS suggest parallel North American patterns. The pattern has been one in which the United Kingdom and Canada joined other countries with traditionally low turnout—Japan, Switzerland, and the United States—at the bottom. For Canadians, who as a matter of course use U.S. figures as a yardstick, 2004 marked an important milestone, given that real turnout in Canada dipped below that in the United States,[18] a trend that increased in 2008.

Comparing Youth Turnout: North America

In the United States, as in Canada and the United Kingdom, turnout decline is primarily due to the fact that young citizens behave differently than previous generations—though in the United States, this change occurred earlier. In the United States, unlike in Canada and the United Kingdom, the middle of the first decade of the twenty-first century witnessed a rebound in turnout, due in good part to a sudden surge of young voters. In comparing the rates, we need to keep in mind that U.S. turnout is measured against potential rather than registered voters, which makes a great difference: voters must personally register in the United States, while in Canada and the United Kingdom, and generally in other democratic countries, eligible citizens are automatically registered by the authorities. Nevertheless, recent political developments combined with certain administrative improvements (discussed in part 3) have made it significantly easier to register in the United States, and 72 percent of potential U.S. voters were registered to vote in 2004.[19]

In 2004, as we can see in table 4.4, overall turnout rose to 55.3 percent, due especially to those aged eighteen to twenty-four, among whom turnout jumped by more than 9 percentage points from 2000—and jumped again to 48.5 in 2008. Note that the numbers in the two columns are not strictly comparable, since the youth vote is based on reported votes from a sample. Using a similar methodology for the left-hand

TABLE 4.4

Turnout in u.s. national elections, 1960–2008

YEAR	TURNOUT OF VOTING-AGE POPULATION (%)	TURNOUT OF 18–24 YEAR-OLDS (%)
2008	56.8[a]	48.5[b]
2004[c]	55.3	41.9[d]
2000	51.3	32.3
1996	49.1	32.4
1992	55.1	42.8
1988	50.1	36.2
1984	53.1	40.8
1980	52.6	39.9
1976	53.6	42.2
1972	55.2	49.6
1968	60.8	50.4

SOURCE:

[a]2008 election results (http://elections.gmu.edu/Turnout_2008G.html).

[b]"Young Voters in the 2008 Presidential Election, Center for Information and Research on Civic Learning and Engagement (CIRCLE) Fact Sheet (http://www.civicyouth.org/PopUps/FactSheets/FS_08_exit_polls.pdf, accessed 14 October 2009).

[c]Prior to 1972, data are for those 21–24 years old, except for Georgia and Kentucky (18–24), Hawaii (20–24), and Alaska (19–24).

[d]u.s. Census Bureau, Current Population Surveys, for 1968 to 2004.

column, overall turnout for 2004 rises to 64 percent. The overall trend is quite clear, however: a steady decrease in turnout from 1972[20] until 2000 (except for a large spike in 1992, when a viable third-party candidate was on the ballot), followed by a rebound in turnout in 2004 that continued in 2008.

The rise in youth voting, like the rise in overall turnout, was due to additional nonwhite voters—especially African Americans—the reported turnout for whom "surged from 60.3 in 2004 to 65.2 percent in 2008 . . . turnout by African Americans under 30 increased by 9 percentage points, which accounts for the entire increase in youth turnout."[21] The turnout of young white Americans did not change from 2004, indicating that the Obama movement did not mobilize potential political dropouts among them. There was, of course, a more active form of mobilization that did take place, as is evident in data from the Democratic Party's presidential primaries and caucuses. More than 6.5 million young people under the age of thirty are estimated to have participated in 2008, a dramatic increase over 2004, with participation by those aged seventeen to twenty-nine as a percentage of the total in the Democratic Party primaries estimated to have risen from a median of 9 percent to 14 percent.[22] An analysis by the Center for Information and Research on Civic Learning and Engagement (CIRCLE) of participation in the "super Tuesday" primaries showed that almost 80 percent of this group had been to college.[23] Overall, while only one in fourteen eligible young voters with no college experience participated in the primaries, one in four college-educated young people did so. This latter figure is quite impressive when set against the fact that in 2000, only 17.6 percent of first-year college students surveyed thought that influencing the political structure was essential or very important (Bennett and Bennett 2001). Table 4.4 goes back only to 1968, but we know from data from the U.S. Federal Election Commission that the 61 percent turnout in that year corresponded fairly well to the rate that prevailed through the 1950s and 1960s. Change begins in earnest, then, with a steady decrease in turnout from 1972, the first election in which eighteen-year-olds could vote, until 2000, followed by a sharp reversal in turnout that began in 2004.

Neighboring Canada underwent an equally precipitous decline in turnout some fifteen years after the United States, beginning at the end of the 1980s, and despite a blip in 2006, has had no meaningful recent upturn—the Iraq war has not been as significant in Canada, and of course that country did not experience the Obama phenomenon. As we can see in table 4.5, the turnout of registered voters in 1988 was 75.3 percent, a number not far from the average of the previous thirty years, dropping fairly steadily to 60.9 percent in 2008.

Official voting results in Canada do not divulge whether particular voters actually turned up, so the voting turnout rate for cohorts has been estimated from opinion surveys. The fact that young Canadians traditionally have a lower turnout than older ones[24] does not explain the decline in turnout among recent generations. Instead, we must look to differences in generational patterns of turnout. In the 1960s, about 70 percent of the members of a new cohort would vote in the first election in which they were eligible to participate; by 2004, it was only slightly over 30 percent. At least two-thirds of new voters cast a ballot in the

1960s; by 2004, it was about one-third (Blais and Loewen 2009, 12). Canadian Election Study survey data suggest that the 14 percentage point drop in turnout between the 1993 and 2000 elections is almost entirely due to the behavior of those born since 1967—that is, those first eligible to vote in the 1988 or subsequent elections (Gidengil, Blais, Nevitte, and Nadeau 2004).

Out of concern for the plummeting youth turnout rate indicated in these survey results, Elections Canada developed a number of programs encouraging young people to vote (discussed in chapter 8). In order to test the effectiveness of these interventions, it simultaneously instituted a new methodology for measuring turnout, using a very large sample of electors identified by age.[25] Based on the application of this method to the election results in 2004 and 2006, it estimated (see table 4.6) that turnout rose by 6.8 percentage points for youth aged eighteen to twenty-four. Most interesting, and indeed unexpected, was the gap between first-time voters and others younger than twenty-five, who had been eligible to vote in the previous election. The first group's turnout was only 2.6 percentage points higher, while the latter's was a hefty 9.9 percentage points over the same age group in 2004.

A methodological change that took place in 2006 may have resulted in the overrepresentation of college students among those aged eighteen to twenty-four in the voter sample.[26] If so, this could explain the unexpected boost in the turnout of those under twenty-five who had been eligible to vote in the previous election. We would expect that discrepancy between college students and those the same age no longer in school to increase as the educational discrepancy between them grows. If this is so, then the contribution of young people to the overall rise from 60.9 percent to 64.7 percent in the recorded vote is less than estimated.

In any case, the question has proven moot since Elections Canada reported in February 2010 that the turnout among eighteen to twenty-five year olds in the 2008 federal election reverted to the 2004 rate of 37 percent. As might have been expected, young citizens contributed their share to the overall drop of percentage points from 2006.

Clues from Scandinavia

The United States, with its post-2000 rebound in voter turnout, is quite exceptional.[27] External events, specifically the war in Iraq, explain the

TABLE 4.5

Voter turnout at Canadian federal elections, 1945–2008 (percent)

DATE OF ELECTION	TURNOUT
11 June 1945	75.3
27 June 1949	73.8
10 August 1953	67.5
10 June 1957	74.1
31 March 1958	79.4
18 June 1962	79.0
18 February 1980	69.3
4 September 1984	75.3
21 November 1988	75.3
25 October 1993	69.6
2 June 1997	67.0
27 November 2000	61.2
28 June 2004	60.9
23 January 2006	64.7
14 October 2008	58.8

SOURCE: Reports of the Chief Electoral Officer, 1921–2008 (http://www.elections.ca/content
.asp?section=pas&document=turnout&lang=e).

U.S. rebound in 2004 and 2006, with the Obama phenomenon contributing by adding new African American voters in 2008.[28] But external events do not explain why, say, turnout declined little in Sweden, not at all in Denmark, but a great deal in the United Kingdom and Canada. Other factors are at work that inhibit the emergence of political dropouts, factors linked to cross-national differences in institutions and policies to be explored in parts 2 and 3. Underlying our exploration is the contention that societies with high civic literacy, like Denmark and Sweden, are best equipped to promote informed youth political participation. In this chapter, we have focused on the participation side; in chapter 5 the focus will be the informed side.

Before closing this chapter and addressing the political knowledge dimension, we need to place our approach in the context of the standard interpretations and relevant findings in the literature on political knowledge.

TABLE 4.6

Estimated turnout by age in 2006 and 2004 Canadian general elections

| COHORT | TURNOUT (PERCENT OF ELIGIBLE VOTERS WHO CAST BALLOTS) | | DIFFERENCE (PERCENTAGE POINTS) |
	2006	2004	
First-time voters	42.2	39.6	2.6
Previously eligible to vote, under 25	44.2	34.3	9.9
18–24	43.8	37.0	6.8
25–34	49.8	44.0	5.7
35–44	61.6	54.5	7.1
45–54	70.0	66.0	4.0
55–64	75.4	72.9	2.4
65–74	77.5	75.5	2.0
75+	61.6	63.9	−2.3

SOURCE: Elections Canada.

* Significant at a 95% confidence level.

The most important recent comparative work investigating turnout decline and its underlying causes is undoubtedly Franklin's (2004) analysis of trends in twenty-two democracies. At the core of his argument are two suppositions. The first is that what ultimately matters is the character—or, more specifically, the competitiveness—of elections, which is largely the consequence of the workings of electoral and related political institutions. The second, following Plutzer (2002), is that voting is to an important extent habitual, and that therefore the circumstances surrounding the earliest opportunity to vote are especially important, since young people have not at that point developed habits of voting or nonvoting. One corollary of this second assumption is that the lowering of the voting age from twenty-one to eighteen has been an important factor in explaining turnout decline. Franklin's argument, reviewed more fully when we discuss changing the voting age in part 2, is that those aged eighteen to twenty are typically in transition from their family and school environment and therefore more likely to develop the habit of nonvoting. Franklin's numbers show a general pattern of turnout decline corresponding to the period after the voting age was lowered to eighteen —for example, in the United States starting in 1972—but this was not the case in Canada, where the voting age was lowered to eighteen one year before the u.s. change.

Combining the two arguments, Franklin contends that changes in turnout can best be explained by the habits of behavior developed by a given cohort in response to the character of the first elections in which they are eligible to vote. The initial response is immediate, but the effect is lasting. The explanation for historical turnout decline thus lies in the gradual replacement of older cohorts with developed voting habits by younger cohorts newly eligible to vote, and set in their nonvoting ways. Franklin's analysis helps explain not only the general decline since 1972 in the United States, but also the turnout blip in the 1992 presidential election, when Ross Perot's candidacy brought increased competitiveness.

Applied to Canada, Franklin's analysis points to the fact that the cohorts first eligible to vote in federal elections in the 1990s came of age in a period of low competitiveness, during which the split opposition virtually guaranteed the election of a Liberal government. The analysis is also compatible with the results in 2004 and 2006 reported above, when competitiveness returned with the reuniting of the Conservatives. The poor October 2008 election results do not fit, however, though one might argue that the decline fits the "character of election" explanation in that the Canadian campaign was overshadowed by the dramatic American presidential campaign.

Competitiveness, however, does not explain the higher turnout in the u.s. 2004 and 2008 elections, the outcomes of which were more predictable than for the 2000 cliffhanger. Clearly, factors other than the character of early election experiences must be added to the mix to fully explain the generational aspects of this phenomenon. Despite Franklin's best efforts, we will need to take into account differences not only in national institutions, but also in political culture. In table 4.3, we saw that in Denmark and Sweden, where civic literacy is high, new voters place the highest levels of importance on voting and report high turnout. These numbers are reinforced by the voting intentions reported in a second round of the IEA Civic Education Study cited in table 4.2, this time of those aged sixteen to eighteen. A study using its data for students in that age group in their last year of upper secondary academic programs in Denmark, Norway, and Sweden found that:

More or less all Scandinavian students regard voting in general elections as the most effective way to operate politically. Somewhat surprisingly, given the generally low interest in political party membership, working in political parties is ranked as the second most effective mode of action ... Swedes stand out as the most passive, while Danes in general anticipate participating the most actively, regardless as to mode. Norwegians foresee somewhat more often joining of political parties ... Young Danes simply seem to be more interested in politics, and discuss politics with their peers, parents and teachers to a greater extent. However, Norwegians and Swedes report that they more frequently read newspaper reports about domestic affairs, and nearly every Scandinavian student sometimes or often follows political developments on the television news. (Amnå, Ekman, and Almgren 2007, 70)

In a large survey carried out by the Swedish National Board for Youth Affairs in 2007,[29] Swedes aged sixteen to twenty-nine differed from those thirty or older on whether every citizen should "get to know how decisions are made and how the country is governed" (42 percent; 55 percent). But they effectively agreed on the need to "get involved in politics" (56 percent; 61 percent). Both groups (83 percent) rejected the idea that political decisions are "so complicated that it is best that only experts decide," while the young were actually less concerned about "the gap between established politicians and common citizens" (53 percent; 74 percent).[30] Compared to North Americans, Scandinavians are less inclined to eschew politics and information about it. In this regard, Finland, as we noted, is the Nordic exception: as shown in table 4.3, young Finns are low in the importance they accord to voting. Moreover, Finns do not display the high level of trust in their national legislature and other political institutions that is generally characteristic of Sweden, Norway, and especially Denmark (Grönlund and Setälä 2004).

This is not the place to explain Finnish exceptionalism (see Milner 2009a), but two facts stand out. First, Finland has experienced a political dropout phenomenon more typical of the Anglo-American countries: only about a third of the young people who left school early—a proportion, we should note, that is far lower than in the many comparable societies with far higher school dropout rates—turned out in the 1999 election; the rest are highly likely to become "chronic abstainers" (Martikainen 2000). This phenomenon emerged later in Finland than elsewhere and is linked to the country's having experienced an especially severe economic crisis in the 1990s, one that was compounded by the loss of its large Soviet market and that led to extremely high, un-Scandinavian levels of youth unemployment. And while Finland's high-tech, export-driven economy rebounded by the end of the decade, it was a jobless growth as far as many young people who had left school early were concerned. This tends to distinguish Finland from its Nordic cousins—with whom it otherwise shares a great deal, especially policies affecting material and nonmaterial redistribution, making it among the most egalitarian of countries, with a politically knowledgeable citizenry, as we shall see in chapter 5.

Because the labor-market problems were not accompanied by any overall trend toward greater inequality, we would expect Finland to be in a good position to tackle the political dropout problem. This is especially the case since Finland is one of the countries that have most fully addressed the digital divide.

In the case of Finland, abstention levels have stabilized in the last decade. Much remains uncertain, but it seems reasonable to predict that if it is able to maintain a reasonable economic performance in these hard times and thus find ways to bring down youth unemployment, youth abstention should decline, bringing Finland's turnout levels closer to those of its Nordic cousins.

But there is another dimension to Finland's distinctiveness in the Nordic context—namely, its political institutions. While not quite as unique as those of the United States, Finnish political institutions stand out among those of the other Northern European countries. As we shall see in chapter 6, political institutions that insufficiently enhance the intelligibility of politics and public affairs by producing oversized rainbow-coalition governments help account for Finland's unexpectedly low levels of political participation. These place a particular challenge on Finland, and make it an especially interesting test case for observers of ongoing trends in political participation.

Yet it is the United States that is the real test case: the first decade of the new century saw a reverse in the trend toward youth abstention. Will it continue? So much is tied to the Obama phenomenon, something in many ways historically and cross-nationally sui generis. The theoretical contributions offered here are thus not especially helpful in answering this question. How much bounce there is in the American rebound depends on the resilience of a remarkable and perhaps one-of-a-kind phenomenon.

5

The Political Knowledge
of Emerging Generations

etting the Internet generation to participate politically entails,
first and foremost, instilling in them the habit of paying attention
to public affairs. The data presented in chapter 4 that show declining turnout to be due largely to this generation's electoral abstention
are worrying enough with regard to the future legitimacy of democracy.
Even more worrying is the likelihood that the data reflect a decline in
political attentiveness among emerging generations: compulsory voting
is a simple policy remedy for low turnout, but there is no equivalent
solution for lack of attentiveness.

Moreover, the level of voter turnout cannot serve as a cross-national
indicator of political attentiveness. Unfortunately neither can the various
usual suspects—attitudinal indicators of political interest or efficacy—
which are subject to the distortions due to social desirability. The American experiment cited in chapter 1 illustrates this point all too clearly.
Just posing political knowledge questions at the beginning of a survey
will significantly reduce the number of subjects who report interest in
politics. The data on media use set out in chapter 3 give us a useful, if
incomplete, basis for comparing political attentiveness cross-nationally.
But at the individual level, questions about attentiveness to public affairs
in the media are as subject to the distortions of social desirability as are
questions of political interest.

In order to test whether that interest is actually invested in efforts
to gain political information, we need to place political knowledge front
and center. What evidence is there that the drop in voting and related
forms of political participation since the early 1990s reflects a generational decline in political knowledge? Such evidence can help us answer
the question posed at the end of the last chapter: was the rebound in
turnout recently witnessed in the United States more than a blip? While
it is too early to expect to find political knowledge data to evaluate that

rebound, this chapter will place the question in historical and cross-national context. I do not claim that political knowledge causes electoral participation; this is not something we can readily prove from existing data. But this does not mean that the two are not linked. There is an overwhelming amount of data in support of the "near universal agreement" (Junn 1995, 9) that politically informed people are more likely to vote than those who are not informed, and that voters are likely to be more informed than nonvoters.

Comparing Political Knowledge

In reviewing the philosophical debate about the meaning of democratic citizenship in chapter 1, we arrived at what might be termed a strong definition of a democratic citizen. It is built upon a key assumption underlying representative democracy: that those entitled to select representatives have sufficient information and skill to compare political parties' commitments to their own preferences, and weigh the credibility of the commitments in light of the parties' records. A citizen with such information and skill can reasonably be expected to participate in various forms of political activity.

Various empirical studies link declines in voter turnout, membership in and identification with parties, and trust of politicians and political institutions with declines in levels of political knowledge. Numerous studies show that otherwise similar citizens develop significantly different political orientations if they are better informed.[1] Delli Carpini and Keeter (1996) show that people with higher political knowledge can link their personal interests with appropriate public issues, and therefore can select the right person as their representative and can judge officials on the responsibilities they carry in the political system; in contrast, people with lower political knowledge tend to judge officials on their characters and images. Political knowledge increases support for democratic values and political participation (Claes and Hooghe 2008), and dampens the fear of immigrants (Popkin and Dimock 1999).

The empirical literature linking political knowledge and political participation relies on plain, inconsistent indicators of political knowledge or ignorance. Yet the literature still shows a positive relationship with voting and other forms of political participation for virtually every indicator of political knowledge used in the research. For example, a simple

test[2] used data from the huge Roper Social Capital Community Benchmark Survey of 2000, controlling for education, sex, race, marital status,
religion, and group membership.[3] The test showed a strong correlation
between the ability to name the two senators of one's state and having
voted in the 1996 election. Respondents who knew the names of both
U.S. Senators were about 3.5 times more likely than those who did not
to have voted. Moreover, that knowledge had nearly four times the impact in boosting voter turnout in the younger and less educated population than among older and more educated eligible voters.[4] In the study
comparing young Americans and Canadians discussed later in this chapter (Milner 2007), controlling for gender, language, and education, we
found a clear association between political knowledge and reported voting, as well as other forms of conventional and unconventional political
participation.

In looking at the data, we need to keep in mind that being politically
informed is not only a reflection of individual characteristics, it is also a
product of the intelligibility of political institutions and the effectiveness
of policies designed to enhance the dissemination of pertinent information. We shall see in part 2 how electoral institutions in particular affect
the accessibility and intelligibility of political information.

The lack of consistent, comparable indicators of political knowledge
can be seen in the questionnaires used by the two main cross-national
surveys concerned with political participation. No political knowledge
questions are included in the European Social Survey,[5] while participants
in the Comparative Study of Electoral Systems (CSES) are expected to
include three or more political knowledge questions of their choice
(see below). The only cross-national surveys with common questions are
those that test knowledge about international events and processes (e.g.,
the National Geographic–Roper Geographic Literacy Survey discussed
below) and the Eurobarometer surveys, which focus on EU-level institutions.[6] Such surveys are useful, but their questions do little more than
touch upon national political issues, actors, and institutions, areas that
would help us compare and explain differences in political participation.

Despite the limitations of the existing cross-national political knowledge data, I was able to show that countries whose citizens were knowledgeable about such events and institutions also had high turnout (Milner
2002a). Given the limitations of the available data, as the proxy for political knowledge, I used indicators from two international surveys. The

TABLE 5.1

Percent correct answers to political knowledge questions

	FINLAND	CANADA
Can name the minister of finance (Finland) or one cabinet minister (Canada)	67	33
Can name the second largest party	52	57
Understands income tax progressivity	52	40
Can name permanent members of U.N. Security Council	52	43
Knows who is eligible to vote	73	56
Average of five questions	60	46

first was a simple study of knowledge of the United Nations. The second, the International Adult Literacy Study (IALS),[7] was not about political knowledge per se. It tested reading comprehension, on the premise that individuals who lack the capacity to understand the relevant material are very unlikely to acquire the minimal level of political information needed to be an effective citizen in an advanced democracy. This did indeed turn out to be the case. Countries with the highest percentage of functionally illiterate citizens—that is, those who scored in the lowest category in the prose reading test of the IALS[8]—also scored poorly on average in a simple comparative test of knowledge of the United Nations, and vice versa.[9] The countries that did well are those with high civic literacy, which are concentrated in Northern Europe; the countries that did poorly are those with low civic literacy, which are concentrated in the English-speaking world.

Since 2002, despite the large number of studies in which political knowledge is a factor, there have been few international studies that take us much further in comparing political knowledge.[10] A step in this direction can be found in table 5.1, which compares Finnish respondents' average scores on multiple-choice political knowledge questions with the scores of Canadians in a recent North American study (Milner 2007, discussed below). Given institutional differences (there are three large parties in Finland, making it harder to identify the second largest party than it is in Canada), the figures tend to underestimate the overall superior level of political knowledge in Finland.[11]

Age, Education, and Political Knowledge

Turning to the political knowledge of young people, cross-national data from the CSES confirms that, at all levels of education, younger citizens are less knowledgeable about political matters than their elders. For those who did not complete secondary education, the average score on the three or more political knowledge questions used in CSES surveys was just over 40 percent for those aged eighteen to thirty-five, just under 50 percent for those aged thirty-five to fifty-five, and 53 percent for those aged fifty-five and over. Broken down by educational attainment, the age-based disparity is unchanged for those who completed secondary or vocational school. When we look at those who completed college, the disparity is roughly halved, with the youngest group averaging 65 percent.[12] A study that surveyed over 2,500 citizens in Norway and Denmark—both countries with high civic literacy—tested knowledge of local political actors and institutions, and substantive policy issues. It found that "older people . . . display higher levels of political knowledge, regardless of their educational attainment" (Rose 2002, 6).[13]

Wattenberg (2008, 79) examined U.S. data, finding that younger people score worse on all sorts of political knowledge questions. Moreover, based on the average score on eight similar political knowledge questions asked in the 1964 and 2000 National Election Studies, he calculates that the political knowledge gap between young and old, controlling for education, has risen steadily from 6 percentage points in the 1960s to 28 percentage points in the 2000s (Wattenberg 2003, 167). A parallel picture emerges when levels of knowledge are compared over time. A Pew Research Center study in April 2007 included nine questions comparable to questions asked in the late 1980s and early 1990s. In 2007, 69 percent of the respondents correctly named Dick Cheney as the vice president, while in 1989, 74 percent were able to name the much less powerful Dan Quayle. Only 66 percent could name their state's governor in 2007, compared to 74 in 1989.[14]

A somewhat similar exercise was carried out in Canada by Howe (2001), who compared responses to questions testing knowledge about political leaders in the 2000 Canadian Election Study to two Gallop polls from 1956.[15] Age differences turn out to be important in both periods, but significantly more so in 2000. The mean percentile in political knowledge of the youngest age group (twenty-one to twenty-nine years old) in

1956 was 5.4 points below the mean, whereas it was 14.3 points below the mean for the same group in 2000. Howe concludes: "Not only are the young less informed about politics today than they were forty-five years ago, they are also more likely to allow this condition to influence at least one important element of political behavior, the decision to vote or not to vote.[16] In this, they are quite different from older Canadians, especially those fifty and over, whose behavioral habits mirror those of an earlier age" (2001, 15–16).[17]

In a later paper, Howe (2006) investigates whether this same relationship could be found in the Netherlands, a country with high civic literacy that has not experienced a significant turnout decline among the young. While he finds a large knowledge gap between age groups, he notes that the decline in participation in the Netherlands across knowledge levels is considerably less steep than in Canada. The explanation, he hypothesizes, lies in the fact that the Dutch are more knowledgeable about their politics than Canadians are about theirs, especially for those with the least knowledge, as relatively few Dutch fall below a low threshold.

Howe links the idea of a political knowledge threshold to the wider concept of civic literacy—that is, the knowledge required to be effective citizens. This interpretation, that countries higher in civic literacy are likely to have smaller knowledge gaps, was tested in a comparative study (Grönlund and Milner 2006). We calculated the dispersion of political knowledge using the political knowledge questions in the national electoral surveys assembled by the CSES. Given the absence of common questions,[18] we were not surprised to find the overall means of correct answers to vary widely, from 31 percent correct in Israel to 64 percent in the United Kingdom. Hence, rather than using this score, our analysis was based on comparing variations from the national mean for each of three groups of respondents: those who had not finished secondary school; those who had finished secondary school but not college; and those who had finished college. This provided us with a comparative indicator of the education-based dispersion of political knowledge. When we compared the relatively low-civic-literacy English-speaking democracies (the United States, the United Kingdom, Canada, and New Zealand) with the high-civic-literacy Northern European democracies (Sweden, Norway, Germany, and the Netherlands), we found that the lowest educational groups in the Anglo-Saxon countries averages 13.3 percentage

POLITICAL KNOWLEDGE // 103

points below their countries' combined average score, compared to a gap of only 5.8 percentage points for the Northern European nations.

The countries with high civic literacy also score higher in the most important cross-national youth survey related to political knowledge, the National Geographic–Roper Geographic Literacy Survey, which assessed the knowledge of political geography of 3,250 young adults in 2002. This is the only international survey that allows us to place the political knowledge of young North Americans in a comparative context.[19] Besides questions asking the respondents to identify countries on a world map, there were also questions testing their knowledge of current events in international politics.[20] Out of fifty-six total questions asked across the ten countries surveyed, the average young American answered twenty-three questions correctly (just above the last-place Mexican youth), with young people in Canada (twenty-seven) and Great Britain (twenty-eight) faring almost as poorly. Sweden (forty) led, followed by Germany and Italy (thirty-eight each), France (thirty-four), and Japan (thirty-one).[21]

In part 2, we explore the institutions and policy choices underlying these differences. For now, we conclude that young people in North America tend to be less knowledgeable about politics than their counterparts in much of Europe, as well as being less knowledgeable than previous generations in their own countries. A brief exploration of where Finland, which was not included in the *National Geographic* survey, fits into this portrait is called for at this point, given our use of Finnish data in table 5.1. There is good reason to suggest that Finland fits roughly with Sweden and Germany, rather than with North America. A study by Nurmi (2007) put twenty political knowledge questions to a representative sample of 880 fifteen-year-old students, finding that, as elsewhere, politically knowledgeable young Finns were more likely to be male, have reading materials at home, spend less time watching television and videos, and discuss politics with parents who were more likely to be better educated. Table 5.2 provides the wording of the three, true/false questions most comparable to the questions posed to young North Americans, and breaks down the 880 respondents by the number of correct answers. The averages in table 5.2 compare very favorably to those of somewhat older (aged fifteen to twenty-five) North Americans, who were able to give an average of just over two correct answers in table 5.3 (below).

TABLE 5.2

Political knowledge of Finnish youth

QUESTIONS CORRECTLY ANSWERED	PERCENT OF RESPONDENTS
0	16.2
1	21.4
2	31.3
3	31.1

*The respondents were asked if the following statements were true or false:

The Coalition Party (Kokoomus) has ministers in the present Finnish government.

The present prime minister of Finland is a Social Democrat.

The Coalition Party in Finland is a left-wing party.

This suggests that while the economic problems that affected young Finns in particular, as well as Finland's unique political institutions that produce oversized coalition governments, have indeed bought down turnout rates, but so far have not had a similar effect on political attentiveness and knowledge. The latter are kept high, it appears, by Finland's very effective system of education (see part 3).

The Political Knowledge of Young North Americans

The *National Geographic* survey is still the best source of comparative data on the political knowledge of young people. But it has no questions like those in tables 5.1 and 5.2 about political life in the respondents' own countries. The contemporary challenge is to devise a battery of questions including ones that test knowledge of political actors and the institutional framework in which politics takes place, and that are suitable for use in cross-national research. Below we report on a first stab at this challenge. The analysis is based on two surveys conducted in 2006, comparing the political knowledge of young Americans and Canadians. Apart from the political knowledge questions per se, there were fifty-five questions designed to test possible sources or consequences of political knowledge.

The first of these, the Civic and Political Health Telephone Survey, was undertaken by the Center for Information and Research on Civic

Learning and Engagement (CIRCLE), and was conducted in May 2006 with a representative sample of 1,765 people[22] living in the continental United States, of whom 1,209 were aged fifteen to twenty-five.[23] The Canadian survey was conducted by me, using similar methodology,[24] in September 2006 with 877 respondents aged fifteen to twenty-five and 477 aged twenty-six and older. A third (451) of the interviews were conducted in French.

CIRCLE's earlier U.S. survey (Keeter, Zukin, Andolina, and Jenkins 2002) posed three political knowledge questions. For this second round, five questions were added (chosen from among those I had proposed). These questions were designed to be usable in Canada and to correspond as closely as possible to the five that had been slated for the second round of the European Social Survey in 2004. If on the resulting questionnaires the Americans answer every question right, they get a score of eight correct political knowledge answers; if the Canadians answer every question right, they get a score of ten. Anyone answering all the common questions right gets a score of seven (see the appendix). It is this combined score out of seven that serves as our main indicator of political knowledge. The figures in table 5.3 tell the basic story. We can compare the political knowledge scores of young people in Canada and the United States with each other and with those over twenty-five years in age in each country. Political knowledge is poor, especially among young people. Out of a possible score of seven, the means for correct answers are 2.12 for young Americans and 2.89 for those twenty-six or older. Canadian scores are a little better, at 2.57 and 2.93. While males are politically more knowledgeable than females in both age groups and both countries,[25] the difference is smaller among those under twenty-five. This is not, we should add, because young women are more knowledgeable than their elders, but because young men are significantly less knowledgeable than theirs.

A useful way to visualize these results is by the number of questions correctly answered. The difference lies not at the top but at the bottom, with 18.2 percent of young Americans able to give none of the seven answers compared to 11.3 percent of young Canadians. Adding those who could only answer one question, the proportion for the United States is 42.4 percent, while for Canada it is 31.7 percent. When we break the results down by question, the most glaring contrast is on international matters: 55 percent of young Americans are unable to name one permanent member country of the U.N. Security Council—in other words, they

TABLE 5.3

Average political knowledge (sum of seven answers)

COUNTRY	AGE	GENDER	MEAN	N
United States	15–25	Male	2.35	598
		Female	1.87	532
		All	2.12	1120
	26+	Male	3.34	292
		Female	2.50	343
		All	2.89	635
Canada	15–25	Male	2.91	424
		Female	2.26	453
		All	2.57	877
	26+	Male	3.45	211
		Female	2.46	236
		All	2.93	447

did not even know that the United States was a permanent member—compared to only 30 percent in Canada. But there is no shortage of political ignorance on domestic matters. Looking at tables 5.4A and 5.4B, we can see that 54.2 percent of young Americans are unable to identify citizens as the category of people eligible to vote (compared to 41.4 percent of young Canadians). Equally unsettling is a similar inability of young Americans to name even one cabinet secretary (55 percent could not do so)[26] and to identify the party that is more conservative (60 percent were unable to do so).[27] This latter figure is especially revealing, since no term is used more frequently and consistently to characterize the Republican Party. These numbers correspond to the 57 percent of Americans aged fifteen to twenty-five who could give two or fewer of the seven correct answers. In other words, somewhere between 55 and 60 percent of Americans between fifteen and twenty-five are effectively off the political map.[28]

These figures paint a stark portrait. Compared to 40 percent of fifteen-year-old Finns, over 55 percent of Americans born since 1991 were, in 2006, potential political dropouts, lacking a minimal understanding of the political world in which they lived. One answer to the question posed at the end of the last chapter—about whether the Ameri-

TABLE 5.4A

U.S. answers: Which party is more conservative?

AGE	ANSWER	PERCENT
15–25	Republicans	40.2
	Democrats	18.0
	Other or neither	21.1
	Don't know	21.1
26+	Republicans	53.4
	Democrats	16.4
	Other or neither	15.1
	Don't know	13.5

TABLE 5.4B

Which of the following best describes who is entitled to vote in federal elections?

COUNTRY	AGE	POSSIBLE ANSWER	PERCENT
United States	15–25	Residents	10.6
		Taxpayers	16.0
		Legal residents	19.5
		Citizens	45.8
Canada	15–25	Residents	11.4
		Taxpayers	8.1
		Legal residents	19.0
		Citizens	58.6

can rebound in youth political participation is likely to last—could be provided by a third round of the Civic and Political Health Telephone Survey, studying whether the mobilization of young people by the Obama campaign significantly reduced the political ignorance numbers.

Such a survey could be done rapidly, using the most sophisticated Internet polling techniques outlined in chapter 4. Although there is a risk when posing political knowledge questions that respondents will cheat and consult Google or Wikipedia, this can be reduced by setting time limits for answers. Moreover, such cheating may be less of a problem than imagined, at least for young people. This conclusion emerges from a recent experiment (Milner, Loewen, and Hicks 2007) whose findings are presented in chapter 6. In brief, the participants in the study were students aged eighteen or nineteen at a Montreal English-language junior college that serves a diverse population.[29] The study consisted of two surveys, one at the beginning and one at the end of an election campaign.[30]

Any fear of embarrassing uninformed respondents[31] proved to be unjustified. The concern arose when, to get enough respondents, we supplemented the face-to-face surveys with online surveys. We initially thought that some students answering online might look for answers on the Internet so as not to appear uninformed, but there were no discernible differences in the level of political knowledge between those who used the Internet and those who completed the questionnaire in person under supervision.

The scores were, as we expected, quite low: 20 percent to 25 percent had a grasp of both political issues and actors; 30 percent could identify the main actors, but were largely unaware of the issues; and 35 percent to 40 percent were effectively out of the loop. While we attempted to recruit ordinary students from general education courses with minimal admission requirements, we nevertheless could not avoid a certain self-selection bias—which, as in reported voting, means that however low our numbers, the numbers for the whole population represented are likely to be lower. In this case, the roughly 40 percent of the cohort who had left school before reaching junior college age—a group especially difficult to get to participate in surveys, or politics—was excluded. But even within the remaining 60 percent, the high level of attrition (despite repeated e-mails, supplemented by telephone calls) among those initially recruited who stated that they either did not expect to vote or were uncertain about voting reflects the fact that potential political dropouts tend not to find their way into surveys, no matter how they are conducted. There are more young people than we think who are disconnected from political life.

The Media and the Political Knowledge of Young North Americans

We can now turn to factors contributing to the level of political knowledge and differences among various groups, using the data from the

TABLE 5.5

Reported weekly media use

Over the past 7 days, on how many days did you:

Age	Country	READ NEWS ON THE INTERNET?	WATCH NATIONAL NEWS ON TELEVISION?	READ A NEWSPAPER?
15–25	United States	2.20	3.36	2.66
	Canada	2.09	3.75	3.09
26+	United States	2.15	4.67	3.78
	Canada	1.81	5.10	4.20

comparative study of the United States and Canada. Given what we have seen so far, the natural place to begin is with media use. Interestingly, as shown in table 5.5, young North Americans in 2006 reported using the Internet to read news on an average of roughly two days a week, less than the already low use of newspapers and television news programs. However, as reported in chapter 3, in the months leading up to the 2008 election, the Internet displaced newspapers in the United States as the leading news source after television, even rivaling television for young people.

The correlation coefficients set out in table 5.6 show that newspaper reading and, even more, reading news on the Internet significantly affect political knowledge, while the effect of watching TV news is also positive, but not as strong. (Significance is normally associated with a smaller than 5 percent possibility—Sig. < 0.05—that the relationship is due to chance; while a stronger measure sometimes used is that of a 1 percent possibility—Sig. < 0.01.) Overall, there is no avoiding the fact that the Internet must be part of any strategy to boost informed political participation, especially in the United States. The numbers for Canada in table 5.5 suggest that in that country, a strategy that emphasizes watching news on TV and reading the newspaper stands more of a chance of being effective. Examining the numbers more closely, we can see the real difference emerges when we break down the Canadian respondents by language. Keeping in mind that though the Canadian study, as is often the case, oversampled French-speaking Quebeckers,[32] we are still left

TABLE 5.6

Media use and political knowledge among Americans and Canadians
aged 15–25

OVER THE PAST 7 DAYS, ON HOW MANY DAYS DID YOU:			POLITICAL KNOWLEDGE (SUM OF 7 ANSWERS)
Read a newspaper?	r (Pearson correlation)		0.145*
	sig. (statistical significance)		0.000
	N (number of respondents)		1,993
Watch national news on television?	r		0.085*
	sig.		0.000
	N		1,999
Listen to the news on the radio?	r		0.026
	sig.		0.242
	N		1,988
Read news on the Internet?	r		0.269*
	sig.		0.000
	N		1,988

*Correlation is significant at the 0.01 level.

with small numbers[33] that give us a large margin of error, making conclusions tentative. Nevertheless, the basic findings are in line with other
efforts at comparing the two groups. Claes, Stolle, and Hooghe (2007)
also found higher levels of political knowledge among French-speaking/
high-school students in Quebec than among similar English-speaking/
Ontario students.[34]

Table 5.7 presents mean correct answers among the Canadian respondents, divided by age, gender, and language. Since the language dimension is limited to Canada, the table includes a column with the score
out of ten possible correct answers (as expected, the additional questions do not alter the overall relationships). While for those over twenty-
five, political knowledge is higher among English speakers, the opposite
is true for those aged fifteen to twenty-five. Not only are young Quebeckers more politically informed (4.10 average answers correct out of
10)[35] than their peers in the rest of Canada (3.55), but, unlike other Ca-

TABLE 5.7

Political knowledge in Canada

AGE	GENDER	REGION*	MEAN OF SUM OF 10 ANSWERS	NUMBER	MEAN OF SUM OF 7 ANSWERS
15–25	Male	ROC	3.91	285	
		Quebec	4.75	139	
	Female	ROC	3.22	303	
		Quebec	3.50	150	
	All	ROC	3.55	588	2.43
		Quebec	4.10	289	2.85
26+	Male	ROC	5.03	142	
		Quebec	4.65	69	
	Female	ROC	3.50	159	
		Quebec	3.19	77	
	All	ROC	4.22	301	3.00
		Quebec	3.88	146	2.78

*Respondents in Quebec were French-speaking; respondents in the rest of Canada (ROC) were English-speaking.

nadians and U.S. young people, the young Quebeckers are more politically informed than their elders (3.88).

This generational inversion is not surprising, given the late modernization of Quebec's educational system. In the International Adult Literacy Study—which, in the early 1990s, tested a sample of the population of twenty countries on their ability to comprehend written texts—the average score of French-speaking Canadians was well below that of English speakers (264.1, as opposed to 278.8). The gap dropped to five points when the test was repeated ten years later, with the bulk of the change due to the youngest group of respondents. Indeed, Francophones aged fifteen to twenty-five had not just reduced the gap but had actually surpassed their English-speaking counterparts, 292.7 to 290 (Bernèche and Perron 2005).[36]

The study finds a higher level of intention to vote among the young Quebeckers as well as, confirming the finding of Claes, Stolle, and Hooghe (2007), of greater attentiveness to politics, with 8 percent more Francophones than Anglophones responding "most of the time" when asked

TABLE 5.8

Media use by language spoken among Canadians aged 15–25

Over the past 7 days, on how many days did you:

		READ A NEWSPAPER?	WATCH THE NATIONAL NEWS ON TELEVISION?	LISTEN TO THE NEWS ON THE RADIO?	READ NEWS ON THE INTERNET?
ROC*	Mean	3.06	3.22	2.96	2.39
	N	587	587	586	581
Quebec*	Mean	3.17	4.82	2.86	1.49
	N	288	288	287	286

*Respondents in Quebec were French-speaking; respondents in the rest of Canada (ROC) were English-speaking.

the extent to which they follow political news. Keeping in mind the relatively low numbers and response rate in the Quebec sample, we shall suggest in chapter 9 that the difference is linked to the more politicized educational environment that young Quebeckers encounter.

For example, when we break down the responses to the question as to whether any of their classes require the students to keep up with politics or government through the media, we find a clear contrast between the responses of the Francophone and Anglophone students, with 66 percent of the former answering yes, compared to only 46 percent of the latter. This is reflected in the fact that young Canadians' reported higher levels of following the news via television is due, as we can see in table 5.8, to Francophones—who watch television news at more European than American levels.

Conclusion

In stressing attentiveness and political knowledge, I am challenging what is still the prevailing tendency among the political scientists and pollsters whose profession is to study political attitudes and choices. In many ways, we suffer from a professional deformation when it comes to informed political participation. There are a number of aspects to this. Most of the work concerns not whether people vote, but rather for whom they do, and why. And although such studies really deal only with the participants—whose number is declining—the language that journalists and the public use to discuss their findings ignores this distinction, describing an electoral outcome as if it reflects the choices of all the people. This is not surprising since, even if the journalists and pundits who cover elections are aware of the facts about electoral abstention, this reality is not at the forefront of their consciousness, given that the chances of their meeting a political dropout are low. This is true of political science professors as well. Despite whatever complaints we may have about them, students who take political science courses are the least likely to be political dropouts—and the minority who abstain from voting are likely to be among those who have replaced conventional with unconventional forms of participation.

Beyond this, political scientists, like journalists and other experts, are instinctive democrats. We naturally shy away from anything that would ostensibly put us in the camp of those who would keep the undeserving away from the ballot box, through poll tests and other such devices. As a result, we too readily and unskeptically accept the results of soft surveys that tell us that people are interested in politics, and we are less concerned about getting data from hard surveys, which test whether that interest is actually invested into effort to gain political information—i.e., to become informed citizens.

Consider how Blais (2000, 143) concludes his insightful analysis of possible explanations of voting and nonvoting. In a display of introspection that is rare among political scientists, Blais asks why he himself usually votes. His answer is that since he believes in democracy, it would be inconsistent to abstain. But, he adds, he would not vote if the parties or candidates were so indistinguishable that it made no difference who won. And on this note he ends his book, without considering the possibility that there might be differences between options that would make the outcome important to him, were he only aware of them. As an informed political scientist, he does not conceive of such a situation, yet that is precisely the situation for a large and apparently growing number of potential voters, especially young ones. For someone ignorant of relevant differences between political parties and candidates, they are all the same, and it makes no difference who wins.

So I end this part of my book with an exhortation to my colleagues: do not assume political knowledge, test it.

PART 2

INSTITUTIONS

6

Political Institutions

BOOSTING INFORMED POLITICAL PARTICIPATION

In this part of the book, we look at political institutions and their effect on informed youth political participation. So far, we have stressed the factors that contribute to a politically knowledgeable citizenry, and we have asked whether those factors can be counted on to produce politically knowledgeable citizens in the making. We have focused on universal trends, stressing developments in information and communications technology that recognize no national boundaries.

We have also noted another dimension to informed political participation, one associated with the notion of civic literacy. Whether a modern society is high or low in civic literacy is not a matter of individual capacity; rather, it is the degree to which that capacity is fostered by the institutional arrangements and policies particular to a society that accounts for differences in civic literacy. To simplify, the more intelligible the institutions, the more the otherwise similar citizen is capable of informed political participation. Institutions affect the supply, and hence the cost to the individual, of political knowledge, and of informed political participation.

In this chapter, we set out the wider framework of our approach to the relationship between institutions and informed political participation, applying that framework to different institutional arrangements, and asking if and how they affect the Internet generation. The bedrock of informed democratic participation is voting, and the institutions most directly concerned are those that set the rules of participation in elections—a subject we will turn to in chapter 7. This chapter will set the stage, focusing on wider governmental structures and the role of political parties. Chapter 7's assessment of the effects of alternate electoral systems leads into chapter 8's analysis of the effects of other electoral mechanisms relevant to the electoral participation of young citizens, such as eligibility to vote and timing of elections.

Political Institutions and Nonmaterial Redistribution

Political institutions form part of the institutional frameworks of functioning societies. Civic literacy, we noted in part 1, is high in societies with institutions that succeed in combining material and nonmaterial redistribution—reducing disparities not only in income and wealth, but also in intellectual resources. Bringing those at the bottom to higher levels of knowledge expands their economic opportunities, and also enhances their capacity to participate as citizens. Mahler and Skowronski note:

> In the economic sphere, the developed democracies . . . vary enormously on three critically important variables: the distribution of market income, the extent to which market income is redistributed by the state and the consequent distribution of post-government disposable income . . . Income inequality is negatively related to electoral turnout and turnout is positively related to the extent of government redistribution, even when other variables are taken into account . . . The mechanism by which turnout is associated with redistributive policies reflects a process whereby, as electoral participation declines, the actual electorate becomes less representative of the potential electorate with respect to income, which in turn has consequences for public sector redistributive policies. (2008, 2)

Particularly in the United States, there are enormous disparities across income levels in all forms of participation, especially voting. One study found a gap of 34 percentage points in reported voting in presidential elections between people with incomes above $75,000 and those under $15,000 (Jacobs et al. 2004). These disparities can be even greater in low-profile elections for state legislatures and local offices. With turnout for mayoral elections sometimes in the single digits, local politicians are particularly responsive to the concerns of high-income constituents (Macedo et al. 2005, 37–38).

The relationship between low civic literacy, low voter turnout among the less educated, and economic inequality in the advanced industrial democracies is explored at length in my earlier work (Milner 2002a), to which the interested reader is referred. An empirical confirmation of this relationship[1] emerges in the follow-up study introduced in chapter 5 (Grönlund and Milner 2006). Political knowledge, we found, tended to be more dependent on level of formal education in countries where income is more unequally distributed, and less tied to education in the

European welfare states. This relationship is illustrated in figure 6.1. The scores on the Gini index (.00 indicates perfect income equality among households, and 1.00 indicates that the top 10 percent earn all the income)[2] for the countries considered to be old democracies by the Comparative Study of Electoral Systems appear on the horizontal axis, while the vertical axis represents a measure (the F-value) of the variance due to education. The larger the F-value, the more education levels determine political knowledge levels in the country.

FIGURE 6.1

Average disproportionality scattered against the F-value of the effect of education on political knowledge at the country level.

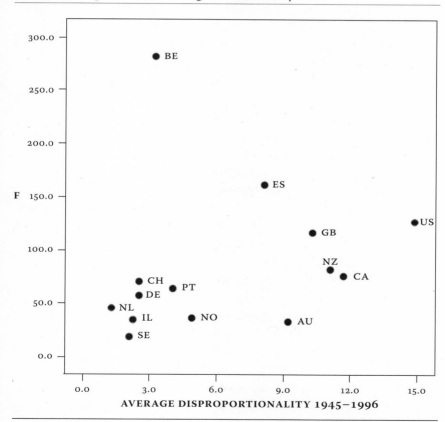

NOTE: County abbreviations follow the two-letter standard of the ISO. http://www.world atlas.com/aatlas/ctycodes.htm

In the case of income, the Gini score tells us how well income is distributed, as—though less elegantly—does our measure of educational dispersion in relation to political knowledge. As we can see in figure 6.1, the countries are scattered along a more or less linear pattern (with Belgium being the significant outlier).[3] We see a strong linear association: in countries where income is more equally distributed, political knowledge is not primarily dependent on formal education, whereas in countries where economic resources are less equally distributed, education tends to drive political knowledge.

Figure 6.1 illustrates how the relationship between material and non-material redistribution is manifested in political knowledge. The countries with the lowest income inequality (on the left of the figure) tend also to be closer to the bottom of the figure, which is where education least affects political knowledge. As I have shown in earlier work (Milner 2002a), the causal link is bidirectional. Not only do countries with more developed welfare states tend to make greater efforts to disseminate information to those citizens at the bottom, but in countries where those at the bottom are better informed, those citizens are more likely to participate politically—supporting parties that favor redistributive policies and that, as a result, are in a better position to enact them.[4]

Of course, there are many factors unrelated to political knowledge or participation impinging on the choice by parties in power to implement redistributive policies. Whatever its origins, greater socioeconomic equality gives those at the bottom a better chance of becoming politically informed. But there is a set of institutions not at all related to material redistribution that could have a similar effect. These are political institutions that enhance the intelligibility of politics and public affairs. Their effect is through what I have termed nonmaterial redistribution, reducing the cost of necessary knowledge—which is higher for those low in educational or economic resources. Civic literacy is boosted by the combination of policies and institutions that promote both material and nonmaterial redistribution.

Institutions and Informed Voting

In their analysis of turnout variations in elections for the European Parliament, Franklin and his colleagues conclude with a statement that is at the heart of the approach taken here: "Turnout seems above all to be affected by voters' awareness of the consequences of their decisions" (Franklin 1999, 220; see also van der Eijk, Franklin, and Marsh 1996). The more institutions are able to simplify the relationship between their actions and political outcomes—that is, the lower their cost of political knowledge—the more political systems will encourage citizens at the margin to vote. One general application of this principle takes the form of coherence versus fragmentation. Other things being equal, countries that divide power between executive and legislative branches, between two chambers in a legislature (see Arnold 2007; Gordon and Segura 1997), and between federal and regional governments are reducing the potential for citizens to be aware of the relationship between their actions and political outcomes. Presidential systems, federal systems, and bicameral legislatures, whatever their other benefits, render the link between one's choice as a voter and its institutional effect less visible and comprehensible. While they may not be appropriate in large, pluralistic countries for other reasons, unitary,[5] unicameral, parliamentary systems reduce the cost of gaining the knowledge necessary to cast an informed vote or otherwise participate meaningfully in politics.

There is another, temporal, dimension to the intelligibility of institutions. Those at the margins in political knowledge and attentiveness are at a distinct disadvantage if institutions affecting the outcomes of their choices are subject to frequent changes. This is especially the case with regard to party programs and leaders—which, as we shall see in chapter 7, are linked to the electoral systems in which they operate. Frequent changes like those experienced in the United Kingdom, the United States, and Canada lead to a failure to perceive differences among the parties, and, especially for younger generations, lead to abstention from voting (see, e.g., Vowles and Stevens 2008).

Institutional factors help clarify the differences alluded to earlier between Sweden and Finland. The two countries are similar in many ways; indeed, there are those who argue that, in socioeconomic terms, Finland is today's most successful practitioner of the Scandinavian model (Andersson 2009). And, as shown elsewhere in this volume, Finland, like Sweden, manifests the characteristics of a society high in civic literacy— yet its voter turnout is significantly lower than Sweden's. International IDEA figures show turnout in Finnish parliamentary elections to have been roughly 5 to 10 percentage points lower than in Sweden, with the difference doubling in the mid-1990s.

We noted in chapter 4 that this latter development is related to the higher proportion of political dropouts associated with significantly greater Finnish youth unemployment, and we suggested that there is an institutional dimension to this discrepancy. Every four years, Swedes vote at the same time for their national, regional, and local representatives. A national government is formed, most often dominated by the Social Democrats and supported by the Greens and the Left Party; sometimes, as in 2006, it produces a coalition of the other parties.

In Finland, citizens vote in separate elections (at intervals of two years) for the members of Parliament and local assemblies, and also separately, every six years, for a president who has real power. The winner, like Tarja Halonen, the current president, may very well be the candidate of the major party left out of the oversized "Rainbow Coalition" government, which is composed of almost all the remaining parties and dominated by the other two large parties. If we add to this the fact that Finland's unusual proportional electoral system gives individual candidates an incentive to compete against others from the same party, we can reasonably conclude that Finnish citizens at the margins of political knowledge are less aware than their Swedish peers of the consequences of their decisions. One indication of this is that, despite the waning of the president's power since 1970, turnout for presidential elections has exceeded that for parliamentary elections, which was not the case before the advent of rainbow coalitions.

Finnish voters, thus, like those in the United States, and unlike their Nordic cousins, elect a president with real powers separately from the members of the legislature. Overall, however, when it comes to institutions affecting electoral participation, unitary and unicameral Finland is closer to the other Nordic countries than to the United States. Hence, even with the recent U.S. rebound, and declines on the Finnish side, electoral turnout in Finland remains appreciably higher than in the United States. Finland is thus the exception that proves the Nordic rule: its Nordic cousins are countries whose political institutions are among the best at simplifying the relationship between citizens' actions and political outcomes. The best contrast in most, if not all, of the dimensions relevant to informed political participation is provided by the United States, to whose institutions we now turn.

American Institutions and Political Participation

Most directly related to the political knowledge side of informed political participation are rules favoring the dissemination of information
relevant to elections. In my earlier book,[6] I systematically compared
advanced democratic countries along these lines and found the United
States lagging badly behind the Nordic counties in ways I touch upon
below.

The Nordic countries are among the strictest when it comes to facilitating equal, limited party access to television during campaigns (see
Milner 2002a). The United States is at the opposite pole. There are no
legal restrictions on such access, since it is protected by the American
constitution, according to the Supreme Court's interpretation of freedom of speech in the First Amendment. Hence parties and candidates
need money to get TV time. This sets the United States apart even from
Canada, which, like most democratic countries, provides free television
and radio time to the parties during election campaigns. The need for
money is exacerbated in the United States by expensive primaries, which
are in effect elections for the party nominations. This gives leverage to
those individuals and interests with large amounts of money, and tends
to exclude those who do not—including young people, who generally do
not make political contributions.[7]

Building on the pathbreaking efforts of Howard Dean in 2004, the
Obama campaign proved successful at counteracting the role of big
money with an immensely successful Internet-based fundraising campaign among small donors. But the Obama campaign's success at fundraising is without precedent, and it pushed campaign spending to equally
unprecedented levels. Short of institutional changes that we have no
reason to expect, it is certainly premature to suggest that the influence
of big money in American politics is waning.[8]

The absence of legally enforceable campaign spending limits on parties and candidates, combined with the high cost of television advertising needed for name recognition, will continue to keep entry costs high
for candidates. This is exacerbated by an institutional context of frequent,
winner-take-all elections that lead to exaggeration and negative campaigning (see chapter 7). One well-known result is the powerful advantage of incumbents, exacerbated by the drawing of congressional district
boundaries in keeping with partisan considerations. With the effective

exclusion of parties and candidates unable to raise a great deal of money, competitiveness is sapped, and informed political participation inhibited. This effect is exacerbated by procedural idiosyncrasies in American electoral regulations discussed in chapter 8. Specifically, the registration procedure forces "prospective voters to navigate the obstacle-ridden path to the voting rolls," and rules for voter identification allow "many states [to] have onerous requirements that make it particularly hard for poor people and racial minorities to vote."[9]

These and other idiosyncratic practices discussed in chapter 8 have in common an important but seldom stressed feature that characterizes the institutions that administer elections in the United States. In other countries, electoral administration is nonpartisan and, at least for national elections, centralized. Hence, rules apply equally and throughout the country, and when reforms are proposed, the presumption is that, once adopted, they will be applied in the same way in every electoral district. The United States is exceptional in that no such single body exists. States administer elections and determine rules for registering to vote and conducting elections, not only to state offices, but to Congress and even the presidency. Rules affecting district boundaries, ballot forms, voter and candidate eligibility, counting methods, and so forth are often partisan in their intent and outcome, to the advantage of the party that dominates the state legislature.[10] The result is that, when it is in the interest of that party, the requirements make it hard for those lacking in educational and economic resources to inform themselves sufficiently to vote.

Moreover, because of the absence of nonpartisanship and the narrow jurisdiction of the state agencies, broad initiatives to enhance electoral participation in the United States are left to nonprofit groups and civic educators (Levine 2007, 41). A simple contrast can be drawn with the role and activities of Elections Canada, the public agency that administers Canadian federal elections. In completing its mandate to inform Canadians about all aspects of voting in federal elections—eligibility, dates, candidates, district boundaries, ballots, and polls—Elections Canada has responded to declining youth turnout with a series of efforts to boost youth electoral participation (see chapter 8). It is able to do so credibly and without political interference or backlash, despite the occasional partisan grumblings of politicians, because it is manifestly nonpartisan.

The same is true of such agencies in other countries. In Sweden, as we shall see, various state agencies act to foster political participation in a nonpartisan manner, a reflection of institutional arrangements under which political parties are represented on the boards of agencies proportional to their electoral support. In addition, under Sweden's unitary structure, agencies of the central government can create mechanisms for identifying problems wherever they occur, and set policy guidelines for local and regional councils and relevant voluntary organizations to follow in their implementation. Such coordination is far more difficult to attain in Canada, given its federal distribution of powers and lack of proportional representation.

Institutions, Parties, and Political Participation

In the above instances, institutions facilitate or inhibit citizens' being in a position to vote directly, through such mechanisms as eligibility rules, but also indirectly, by influencing the choices of political parties to present a candidate, spend money, etc. The key factor is the degree to which institutions facilitate differentiation in the programmatic commitments of parties (see Franklin 2004; Gordon and Segura 1997). The incentives built into electoral systems weigh heavily here, but so does the effort of the media to bring out such distinctions, as opposed to playing up individual personalities. The relative influence of the public service media is an important factor here, not only among its audience, but also in setting wider standards of professionalism that apply even to the commercial mass media (Althaus and Tewksbury 2000).

From the point of view of the individual, the crucial factor seems to be party identification. Institutional arrangements that make it easier for citizens low in political knowledge to identify with a particular political party foster higher turnout.[11] Soule sees the weakening link to u.s. political parties as a defining characteristic of the context in which the new generations arrived at political adulthood in the last decades of the twentieth century:

Party affiliations waned and many citizens registered as "Independents"...
Political parties gave way to candidate centered elections, which require individuals to possess higher levels of knowledge. Political campaigns tended to rely increasingly on professionals rather than volunteers... Only

14.1 percent of NES respondents reported that they were very much interested in political campaigns in 2000 . . . Only 3 percent worked for a political party or candidate, protested or demonstrated. (2001, 5)

While there is some disagreement in the literature about the effectiveness of party mobilizing efforts (see Rosenstone and Hansen 1993; Huckfeldt and Sprague 1991), research confirms that party identification is positively associated with political participation.[12] This is as expected because, in responding that they identify with a political party and naming it, those low in political knowledge are indicating the use of an effective shortcut for casting a minimally informed vote. Generally speaking, institutions that lead to each party's speaking with one voice tend to foster such identification, whereas lack of apparent consistency in a given party's program or concerns can inhibit it. Hence, party identification tends to be higher in the United States and the United Kingdom than in Canada, since in the former countries, the same parties contest both local and national elections. Conversely, as we shall see in chapter 7, party identification is lower in those three countries than in continental Europe due to their electoral systems, which give parties an incentive to try to be all things to all people.

The frequent use of referendums, for example, in Switzerland and California—where ballot initiatives are very frequent—effectively invites voters to bypass parties. When used appropriately for exceptional decisions, like EU membership for Sweden, or sovereignty for Quebec, referendums can be mobilizing instruments, providing parties with an opportunity to flex their political mobilization muscles. But when the frequency reaches a tipping point, a negative effect prevails. The same is true with the frequency of elections.

The coherence of a party's image is affected by a number of quite specific characteristics, such as the rules of eligibility for participating in the nomination of candidates. Public party financing is also likely to have a positive effect on party identification, giving parties the resources to recruit and mobilize supporters—though there may be a tipping point here, too, if the financing is so generous as to facilitate parties' hiring professionals rather than recruiting volunteers for mobilizing activities. We have already noted the benefits of public support for political party access to the media. And closer to our civic education orientation here are programs that subsidize the political education activities of parties.

For example, in Sweden, study circles commonly serve to familiarize supporters with, and consult them about, party programs and strategies in the period before an election, during which time such circles can account for up to half of those offered (see Milner 2002a, chapter 8).

Finally, as might be expected, a close race boosts not only turnout but knowledge, since more attention is paid to close races by the candidates, the media, and, thus, the voters. There is a clear institutional dimension to such closeness—or, put more broadly, competitiveness—in elections. Proportional electoral systems make elections more competitive, but the closeness of the race is also affected by factors noted in the discussion of American specificity—namely, the partisan drawing of district boundaries to favor incumbents, and the application of registration and voting rules to discourage certain minorities from voting.

Political Parties and Youth Participation

The effect of the institutions discussed up until this point affect young people in a manner similar to other citizens, except where money is concerned. But political parties in almost all democratic countries are currently facing extraordinary difficulties in recruiting young people. A recent paper (Goerres 2008; see also Mair and Biezan 2001) describes parties as "old school," finding only one partial exception—Denmark—in eighteen European countries to the trend of both declining and aging party membership between 1990 and 2000. The problem is often deeper than just attracting members: identification with a given party is inconceivable for many young people, who are culturally disconnected from the whole world of party politics.

The situation in Britain is a good example. The U.K. Electoral Commission notes that party politics seems to repel young voters, so that attempts by political parties and government agencies to engage them are almost invariably doomed to failure, and dismissed as crude electioneering. The result is that youth involvement in the political parties is left to small elites effectively cut off from the wider youth culture (Electoral Commission 2002).

A similar situation apparently prevails in Canada: Cross and Young (2004), who refer to the "graying" of political parties, estimate the average age of Canadian party members to be fifty-nine.[13] In a second study, they probe what proved to be an exceptional group, young party members.

These young people were clearly exceptional: "their upbringings . . . primed them to join parties, as their parents are likely to have belonged to political parties, . . . initiated regular discussions of politics . . . inculcated habits of news consumption [and] exerted a pull toward partisan activity that outweighed the broader societal push away from partisanship" (Young and Cross 2007, 2). Moreover, they themselves see that they are outside the dominant youth culture. When asked to compare participating in political parties and issue-oriented interest groups, the majority rated interest groups equal to or higher than parties.[14]

This is not surprising, since parties are perceived by young Canadians as ineffective vehicles for achieving change, and, unlike issue-oriented interest groups, as hierarchical and unwelcoming of young people, producing what Young and Cross term a culture clash. Canadian parties, like parties elsewhere, have limited resources, and they have made fewer efforts to recruit young people than older citizens. This pattern can be expected to continue, since it seems likely that, unless some way is found to overcome the culture clash (could there be a Canadian Obama?), efforts among the young are likely to prove less than fruitful (see Goodyear-Grant and Anderson 2008).

Some observers see in this not a decline in political participation but the replacement of party-related attitudes and activities by engaged citizenship, in the conceptualization of Dalton set out in chapter 1. There is good reason to be skeptical, however, of voluntary associations as substitutes for political parties. That is generally not what we are finding in Europe, or even in Canada—especially French Canada.[15] We take up this question in chapter 9.

Compulsory Voting

If we are not prepared to abandon party and election-related forms of participation, we have another alternative available to us, a kind of fast fix: compulsory voting.[16] Fining people who abstain from voting without a valid excuse is a sure-fire way of augmenting turnout, as we can see in the turnout rates in Australia and Belgium, the main democratic countries where compulsory voting is used today.[17] But we are interested in informed political participation: ultimately, the justification for compulsory voting rests not on whether it brings more citizens to the polls, but on the increase in their political attentiveness and knowledge.

POLITICAL INSTITUTIONS // 129

This is not to reject the value of increased turnout for its own sake. Given the turnout numbers presented in chapter 4, it is reasonable to argue that since we are about to face an electorate composed of generations for whom abstaining is more common than voting, drastic policy responses like compulsory voting are called for, especially since we know that it affects mainly those low in education and income (Lijphart 1997b).

Of interest here, however, is attaining a satisfactory level of informed political participation among emerging generations. What, if anything, do the data tells us about whether requiring non-voters to vote would result in their becoming more politically informed?[18] A recent work (Milner, Loewen, and Hicks 2007) took up this question on the premise that if evidence could be found that obliging people to vote would lead to a more politically knowledgeable and engaged electorate, it would convince skeptics that compulsory voting is a good thing, since a major criticism of compulsory voting is that it brings unmotivated and poorly informed citizens to the polls.

Previous research had been unable to confirm any relationship between being obliged to vote and efforts to make an informed choice. Ballinger (2007) found that Australian respondents, who under Australian law are obliged to vote (and most Australians do), are no better informed about their political institutions than British respondents are about theirs. Bilodeau and Blais (2005) found no evidence that citizens in Western European countries with compulsory voting discuss politics more than those in noncompulsory countries. And in examining the behavior of immigrants to compulsory-voting Australia and of immigrants from Australia to New Zealand (which does not have compulsory voting), the researchers could find no effects either way of compulsory voting on reported levels of political discussion, interest in politics, and elections. For their part, using Belgian survey data, Engelen and Hooghe (2007) found that respondents who said they would not vote if it were not compulsory were both less knowledgeable about and less engaged in politics (see also Czesnik 2007).

But such data are only suggestive. In the absence of a change in electoral law within a country allowing for a before-and-after quasi-experiment, there is no unambiguous empirical basis for testing this proposition, and even in such a case, the test would be complicated by the fact that many of those voting out of obligation will not have been attentive enough to realize that the obligation has been lifted.

The study under discussion (Milner, Loewen, and Hicks 2007) took an experimental approach. As chapter 5 briefly discussed, the experiment was conducted among students at a Montreal junior college[19] who were eligible to vote during the March 2007 Quebec provincial election.[20] The working hypothesis was that those who face a financial incentive not to abstain can be expected to learn more about politics, discuss politics more frequently, and follow the news more frequently than those who do not face a similar incentive. To test this, we recruited a group of students to participate in a study about "youth attitudes," consisting of two surveys administered approximately one month apart, at either end of the provincial election campaign. Those who completed both surveys were entitled to receive $25. However, to receive this money, a randomly selected subset of the students were also required to vote in the provincial election.[21] Accordingly, we were left with two groups, one of which faced a financial disincentive if they chose not to vote, and the other of which faced no such disincentive. By comparing differences between these two groups in political knowledge, media news consumption, and reported discussion about politics, we are able to draw inferences about the effects of incentives like compulsory voting on first-time voters. Taking away a financial incentive to vote in this way allowed us to adequately approximate losing money through a fine, while conforming to ethical limitations.

We recruited participants in over sixty classes most likely to contain students who would be at least eighteen on Election Day, targeting students in courses with minimal admission requirements. Interested students were asked to fill out a registration form that asked ten unrelated questions, one of which was if the student expected to vote in the upcoming Quebec election.[22]

Once the election was formally announced, 205 students who filled out the forms and who were eligible to vote were invited by e-mail or telephone to complete the questionnaire in a classroom in either of the college's two campuses, during the lunch break on a given date. The 205 students included 119 who indicated that they did not expect to vote or were unsure about voting, with the balance made up by drawing randomly from the rest of the applicants. Half were randomly assigned to two treatment rooms, and the other half to two control rooms. To our disappointment, only 55 of the 205 turned up as instructed. All were given instructions, a research consent form, and a questionnaire, the only difference being that the treatment group was informed of the future obligation to vote. The subjects were not told that the survey would be associated in any way with the election, only that there would be a second questionnaire in approximately one month's time.

To bring our sample back up to desired levels, we e-mailed or telephoned those who did not turn up after the first invitation, as well as another 255 of the remaining students who had filled out the forms. We offered each student the option of completing the attached survey by e-mail or completing it in a secretary's office on the college campus at a time of their convenience (within a five-day window).[23] Once again, assignment to treatment was randomly determined. After attrition at the end of the first round, we had 82 subjects in the control condition, and 101 in the treatment condition. Analysis of the completed surveys showed no significant differences between the control and treatment groups in political knowledge, political discussion, or media usage.

The second round of the survey was administered in the five days prior to the election, with the deadline coinciding with the close of polls on Election Day. The second questionnaire was completed by 143 students completed the second questionnaire (all but 6 completed it electronically).[24] Excluding those who failed to fill out consent forms, we had 55 subjects in the control group, and 66 in the treatment group at the end of the study.[25]

As already noted, the first observable result was the unexpectedly high attrition rate; the second was the low level of political knowledge even of those who did persist. The knowledge questions, preceded by questions about media usage, political discussion, and attitudes toward political involvement,[26] tested for a rudimentary knowledge about matters relevant to Quebec politics. They ranged from the positions of the parties on the issues (e.g., on raising college tuition), to relevant political facts (e.g., "name the party in power when the election was called"), to knowledge about the election (its date, and eligibility to vote). There were eleven political knowledge questions in the first survey, and twenty in the second.[27] The percentage correctly answered in the second survey served as our political knowledge measure.

Both political attentiveness and knowledge were low. Our subjects reported consuming news on the radio, television, and the Internet and in newspapers a mean of less than two days per week.[28] In the first survey, the subjects on average answered fewer than one in three knowledge questions correctly. In the second survey, the percentage of correctly answered questions rose to 43.1 percent, an unimpressive improvement since the majority of the questions had been asked in the first round.

In relation to our hypothesis, no significant difference in knowledge scores in the second round between groups under treatment and control conditions was found. Moreover, we found no evidence that the subjects had increased their general engagement with politics through discussion: both groups reported engaging in conversation with friends and family on average somewhere between "rarely" and "sometimes" by the end of the campaign. Only in media usage was there any difference (though it did not attain significance): subjects in the treatment condition reported consuming all forms of news 2.43 days out of 7, compared to an average of 2.05 days out of 7 for those in the control condition. Since the extra media attention did not seem to bestow any political knowledge benefits, we could not conclude that either it or financial disincentives from abstaining from voting made for more informed citizens.

Based on the lack of evidence that young people who were obliged to vote made efforts leading them to be better informed than they would otherwise be, we cannot support the imposition of compulsory voting solely as a means of boosting informed political participation. This does not preclude possible merit in the idea. Though we cannot say that those low in education and income brought to the polls by compulsory voting would be sufficiently informed to be able to make electoral choices that reflect their interests, and thus potentially change electoral outcomes in their favor,[29] their presence could be expected to induce parties to make a greater effort to address the expressed concerns of these groups (Milner, Loewen, and Hicks 2007). The problem is that such arguments will not convince those who feel that democracy is better served by keeping unmotivated and poorly informed citizens at home on Election Day, nor those who do not like the idea of being obligated to do what should be a matter of choice.[30] Unable to show that compulsory voting will make better citizens, we are thus forced to beat a strategic retreat from including it in the measures proposed to deal political dropouts.

Institutions of Deliberative Democracy

If compulsory voting is a way of bringing into the political process those lacking the requisite skills and knowledge, deliberative democracy can be seen as a means of getting those with these resources to invest them in political engagement. In chapter 1, a certain skepticism was expressed toward the claims of exponents of deliberative democracy that consultative forums, which invite involvement by interested citizens in certain decisions, could reduce the democratic deficit. There are, however, three other types of ongoing or recent activities in North America that deserve attention, since they appear to have the potential of surmounting the limitations of these forums: citizens' assemblies, deliberative polls, and focus groups. I discuss these as well as voting advice applications, now used in most European countries.

Citizens' Assemblies

Canada is known as a pioneer in this area, with citizens' assemblies established to consider electoral system reform in the provinces of British Columbia and Ontario. The selection process ensured that the assemblies' members were socioeconomically representative of ordinary citizens,[31] and the fact that the proposed reform was then submitted to a referendum added another layer of democracy to the process. The problem is that, especially in the case of Ontario, it is difficult to find evidence that these assemblies increased political knowledge beyond that of the several hundred participants.

Note that such an assembly has an important quality: it excludes elected politicians. This is important with electoral system reform, since it keeps at bay not only partisan interests, but also the vested interests of incumbents to get reelected. The advisable alternative, then, is not for such decisions to take place through normal political channels, but rather via an expert investigatory commission composed of members whose nonpartisanship is beyond question. Would replacing the assembly with such a commission have had any less effect on informed political participation?[32] Judging by the British Columbia experience, one could contend that a citizens' assembly can attract more media and public interest (see Milner 2005b), but this was not the case in Ontario. The crucial factor is the degree of effort by agencies set up to inform the population before the vote in the subsequent referendum. While British Columbia seems to have been more effective than Ontario at this, New Zealand (where a commission was used) did an exemplary job of informing its population prior to the referendums in 1992 and 1993, and the first mixed member proportional, or MMP (see below), election in 1996.

In Ontario, an attempt was made to extend the work to young people through a parallel student assembly, created to engage the province's high-school students in a discussion about electoral reform. One hundred and three young people were selected among applicants to participate in a four-day gathering to learn about electoral systems, and the values and outcomes associated with them. At the close of the conference, the participants chose an electoral system. The next stage was to take the discussion and materials to schools that had signed up to organize their own classroom assemblies on electoral reform. At the end, participating students cast votes for the preferred electoral system, and the combined results were sent to the citizens' assembly. According to the draft report on the student assembly,[33] 2,372 students took part, a rather low number compared to alternate methods of civic education outside the classroom, which will be discussed in chapter 10.

Deliberative Polls and Focus Groups

Because it requires bringing members spread out over a large territory together for many hours, as well as giving them access to experts and resources, the assembly process is highly cost-intensive, and thus limited to a small number of persons. Somewhat greater, though still relatively small, participation is possible in deliberative polls (see, e.g., Luskin, Fishkin, and Jowell 2002) and focus groups. Participants in the polls are surveyed at the beginning and again at the end of a weekend, during which they are given relevant information on the subject at hand. Such polls thus constitute a useful antidote to the universal tendency of pollsters to ignore the quality of opinions[34] in asking people's opinions and attitudes without first testing on what knowledge they are based.[35] Recent versions of these polls have been conducted online (Fishkin, Iyengar, and Luskin 2004), suggesting a potential beyond the small numbers attainable with groups that meet in person.

The deliberative focus group is similar, in that individuals are given information about a specific subject and asked their opinion afterward. The difference is that a focus group is structured in such a way as to encourage deliberation in an effort to arrive at a consensus. If that deliberation is face-to-face, the deliberative focus group suffers from same limitations as citizens' assemblies. But here, too, a potential online extension exists.

In November 2006, a deliberative experiment was held in Turku, Finland, on the question, "Should a sixth nuclear power plant be built in Finland?"[36] While the initial experiment was limited to a small group of individuals, the organizers developed an electronic version that has a potential of widening the process. They created a mechanism for real-time democratic interaction through an online forum using webcams and microphones, avoiding the costs and complications of travel and accommodation. While the method is still new, with the spread of on-line access and the relevant technology and skills, it could constitute a important breakthrough in reducing the costs and set-up time for ar-ranging genuine efforts to gauge informed opinion on important issues of the day—especially among young people, who are advanced in such technological access and skills.

Overall, though one can envisage using such methods to inform those who fail to vote or otherwise participate due to lack of knowledge, deliberative polling as a means of reaching potential political dropouts is still far off. It is clear, as the Finnish experimenters found in the responses to their surveys, that those willing to participate in the deliberative ac-tivities were already more informed and interested in politics than those refusing (let alone, we can be sure, those who did not even respond to the survey).

Voting Advice Applications

A similar self-selection process seems to take place with regard to a re-lated use of Internet technology to inform public opinion, called voting advice applications (VAAs). First developed in the Netherlands and Fin-land in the mid-1990s, VAAs have been adopted in most European coun-tries. They consist of a multiple-choice questionnaire, typically con-taining twenty to thirty-five statements on current political issues. Users give their opinions on each of these statements and are then shown how closely their views match those of the parties competing in the election. Statements used as bases of comparison cover the key policy areas, typically giving users a way of indicating the extent to which they agree or disagree with the statement presented. For example, a 2006 Belgian VAA asked if "the use of soft drugs should be legalized," with response options ranging from "completely agree" to "completely disagree" (Wag-ner and Ruusuvirta 2009).

In a number of countries, such as Germany and the Netherlands, the agencies responsible for civic education have developed standard VAAS. Media corporations have also developed popular VAAS, notably in Finland, Belgium, and Norway. Other VAA providers include teams of political scientists and civil society organizations. To construct a party or candidate position database, VAA providers usually ask parties or candidates to respond to a questionnaire, though some instead search party manifestoes, websites, and press releases as well as media reports. Congruence between users' and parties' positions is measured by calculating the distance between their respective preferences. VAAS usually allow users, and in some cases parties, to also weigh statements according to the importance they place on the issue. At the end, the users receive graphs showing how well their opinions match those of the parties or candidates.

Among the most effective is the Swiss VAA, smartvote (see Ladner, Nadig, and Fivaz 2009), first offered during the 2003 parliamentary election campaign, and since then in about twenty national, communal, and cantonal elections. In the four months leading up to that 2003 election, smartvote and its civic education versions were used about 940,000 times[37] (compared with about 2.3 million votes cast). Moreover, a version of smartvote was developed to meet the specific needs of students, young voters, and civic educators for the October 2007 election.[38] The website for young people and first time voters, my-vote.ch, also enabled users to identify their own political positions and which politicians or parties best reflected them, but it was shorter, with simpler wording. To spread the word, its designers collaborated with a textbook publisher, teachers' associations, and youth organizations, and provided a training course to give teachers an overview and explain how the site could be used for civic education.

One problem was reaching first-time voters who did not attend an educational institution offering lessons in civic education. The solution came in joining forces with *20 Minuten*,[39] Switzerland's most widely read free daily newspaper, and owner of the largest Swiss online community information platform targeted at those under thirty-five. Two and a half months before the election, the platform went online. Twice each week during this period, the German-language edition printed a complete page dedicated to the upcoming elections, similar to what was published on the Internet. The platform website provided the issue-matching system, as well as several pages of relevant facts and ideas. During the campaign period, fliers were distributed at chosen youth events, and advertisements were placed to promote the *20 Minuten* online platform and the MyVote website. The combined platform and website accounted for 8 percent of the total smartvote use.[40]

Among smartvote users polled, almost 40 percent (or 5 percent of all Swiss voters) reported that the use of smartvote had influenced their decision to vote. Against this must be set the fact that the typical smart-vote user is male, well-educated, and relatively high in income, hardly the profile of potential political dropouts, although both are relatively young (the average user was 37.5 years old). In Switzerland, turnout reached its nadir in 1991, but that was the first year when eighteen- and nineteen-year-olds were able to vote. Since then, according to data assembled by Lutz, there has been a gradual improvement, especially among young voters (Ladner, Nadig, and Fivaz 2009).

Are smartvote and MyVote in some part responsible for this? That is hard to prove, but even harder to deny. While at this point the VAA is not in itself a solution to the problem of low informed political participation, the designers of the VAAs—including the Bundeszentrale für politische Bildung, the federal agency responsible for civic education in Germany, which administers the German VAA, the Wahl-o-Mat—are investigating how they can be adapted to wider citizen-education uses. Can this kind of online service bring inadequately informed young citizens to a sufficient level of knowledge and thus, potentially, to the voting booth? We return to this question in chapter 10, when we set out a series of ways to bring the issues—and the political parties' stances on them—to the civic-education classroom.

There is some reason to be hopeful here. A recent survey (Ruusuvirta and Rosema 2009) shows that 75 percent of Dutch citizens aged eighteen to twenty-four used the Dutch VAA, Stemwijzer, in the 2006 election. Still, most countries do not give their citizens access to such online voting advisors. It is no coincidence that VAAs have not crossed the Atlantic. In nonproportional electoral systems, parties have strong incentives to be all things to all people, and the best way to do this is to be vague on many issues, so as to allow individual candidates to create an image that conforms to voters' expectations without publicly breaking with the party program. This would be impossible with VAAs, which force parties and candidates to explicitly set out their positions. That is another reason why North Americans should look to Europe for electoral system reform—the subject of chapter 7.

Conclusion

Countries that combine material and nonmaterial redistribution have higher rates of informed political participation, but institutions matter, too. The more institutions are able to simplify the relationship between voters' actions and political outcomes, and to foster party identification—both of which reduce the cost of political knowledge—the lower the proportion of political dropouts. Other things being equal, countries that disperse power complicate the relationship between acts and outcomes, and make it harder for citizens to see that relationship.

When it comes to bringing citizens at the margins into the mainstream of informed political participation, American institutions in particular perform poorly. In relation to elections, there are problems with the role of money, the incentives for partisanship in a decentralized electoral system, the use of active registration, and the frequency of elections and ballot measures.

Compulsory voting has not been shown to boost informed political participation, while deliberative polls, focus groups, and citizens' assembles have had minimal impact, given their limited reach. Yet they have an untapped, long-term potential via online applications that transcend their limitations, with implications for the very nature of our democratic institutions.

7

The Electoral System

I n part 2, we seek to identify institutional arrangements found in advanced democracies that manage to maintain relatively high levels
of informed political participation among young citizens, despite the
universal transformations described in part 1. In the previous chapter, we
set out the principle that such institutions foster citizens' awareness of
the consequences of their decisions by simplifying the relationship between their actions and outcomes. We pointed to the potential advantages
of unitary, unicameral, parliamentary systems in this regard, suggesting
that the principle applied especially when these are accompanied by
complementary party structures and, especially, electoral systems. The
effect on informed political participation of different electoral or voting
systems, the set of institutions through which ordinary citizens choose
who will make political decisions on their behalf, is the subject of this
chapter.

Alternate Voting Systems

When it comes to electoral institutions, a crucial quality associated with
fostering citizens' awareness is proportionality, which, as Franklin put
it, "enhances the predictable consequences of the voter's choice" (1999,
220). Fully developed, proportionality of party representation to its
popular support—in short, proportional representation, or PR—is a principle that extends beyond the mathematical formula for allocating seats
in the legislature. PR is applied to representation in local and regional
assemblies, even school boards and various councils in which parties
have a legitimate place, as well as to the regulations governing media
access and party financing. The underlying principle is to ensure that
all legitimate political positions among the population are given public
expression at an equitable level. Integrated into the political culture, PR

simplifies the relationship between actions and outcomes, driving down the cost of political knowledge. This chapter argues that—especially when combined with unitary, unicameral, and parliamentary institutions—PR promotes a politically knowledgeable population, and thus informed political participation. In this analysis, I follow the logic of Lijphart (1984, 1999), who places democratic countries on a continuum from what he terms consensual to majoritarian democracy, in which the proportionality of a country's electoral system is the most important distinguishing element. A second dimension of consensualism concerns the relationship between institutions at the local and regional levels and those at the center.[1] As conceived here, this dimension draws attention to the relationship between voting systems and political party organization— i.e., how political activities oriented toward macro-level national politics are integrated with those concerned with micro-level local matters.

It should perhaps be stated at the outset what is *not* being claimed. The argument here, as elsewhere in this volume, rests on the objective of informed political participation. As noted in the previous chapter, unitary or unicameral systems are not necessarily appropriate in all circumstances, as powerful second chambers and constitutionally entrenched regional governments (federalism) can play a necessary role in fostering integration in large countries geographically divided along sociocultural lines. Similarly, an electoral system based on single member districts may, in some cases better ensure the representation of minority groups. India comes to mind here. Given local circumstances, as well as prevailing values, proportional systems may not be appropriate.

It is because of this that we do not here enter the discussion about the relationship between alternate electoral systems and government efficiency. The absence of a single party majority—far more likely under PR than in the Anglo-American system of single member plurality, or SMP—leads some to claim that SMP produces governments that are more efficient (e.g., Barker 1994). This is a view contested by Lijphart (1999), among others, and clearly does not apply to SMP countries unable to produce single party majorities, such as Canada in the last decade, nor to the stable governments produced for generations under PR in Scandinavia.

The underlying objective of PR electoral systems is to attain proportionality between representation in the legislature and popular support, and thus not exclude parties with relatively weak, but nevertheless real, support. Hence, at its simplest, citizens participating in PR elections are more likely to be able to find, and place in office, representatives from parties that stand for policies and principles that they support.

PR-elected national legislatures are common is Europe, but only in New Zealand among the Anglo-American democracies. Britain, Canada, and Australia share a set of political institutions known as the Westminster model, though Australia uses a form of PR to elect the upper chamber of its legislature. The United States rejected other elements of the Westminster model, but it has fiercely maintained SMP—that is, the principle under which the members of the legislature gain their seats by virtue of having won the highest number of votes in a geographical district. While SMP is the term commonly used by students of comparative institutions, the system is often referred to by the phrase "first past the post"—whose origins lie in the British passion for horse racing— or the American expression "winner take all." Among the main Westminster countries, only Canada retains SMP for all its regional (provincial) as well as national elections. While there has been quite intense debate in recent years about replacing SMP in British Columbia, Quebec, Prince Edward Island, Ontario, and New Brunswick, little has come of it.[2] In the United States, alternatives to SMP have effectively been limited to the municipal level.[3]

While second ballot systems (used in France) or preferential ballots (used in Australia) have certain potential advantages, when it comes to the principle of enhancing the predictable consequences of the voters' choice, only PR systems qualify. Though several forms of PR meet this criterion,[4] the only practical form of PR that could be implemented under North American conditions, in my view, is mixed member proportional (MMP). This is because it is the only form of PR that allows voters to continue to have their own geographically based individual member of Parliament or Congress—something North Americans are exceedingly unlikely to give up, even in exchange for the claimed benefits of PR. Hence this chapter looks at the MMP form of PR in investigating PR's effects on informed political participation. The logic of MMP is straightforward but not evident at first glance, so the first task is to set out that logic.

The word "mixed" in MMP is somewhat misleading; sometimes the more apt word "compensatory" is used. Under MMP, each voter casts two votes: a party vote for the whole list, or slate, of a party, and a district vote for a constituency representative. The holders of constituency seats are decided by plurality—just as under the SMP system—and the party vote determines the total number of seats to which each party is entitled. The constituency seats it has won are subtracted from that total in order to establish the number of list seats it will have—occupied by representatives to be drawn from its lists, who will not represent a particular constituency. Constituency candidates can also have their names placed on the lists, so that if they do not win their constituency, they still have a chance to be elected; this is common in Germany, New Zealand, and Scotland.[5] The overall result is proportional, though the extent to which the outcome diverges from perfect proportionality is affected by several factors.

The first factor is the threshold used in almost every PR system to discourage the proliferation of small parties. In New Zealand, for example, to qualify for list seats, a party must either receive at least 5 percent of all party votes or win at least one constituency seat. North American voters would probably insist on such a threshold, as this limits the number of parties that win seats, typically to four to six parties.

The second factor is the percentage of overall seats available for list seats. In Germany, this is 50 percent; in New Zealand and Scotland, it is about 42 percent. In addition, New Zealand's outcomes are more proportional than Scotland's since the territory covered by the party lists is large (the entire country), while in Scotland, each list covers a regional district containing approximately one-eighth of the population. The result is an effective regional vote threshold that somewhat reduces overall proportionality.[6] North American voters would very likely insist on the Scottish model—so the lists would be based on relatively small regions with which the representatives can identify—as well has have the electoral law specify, as it does in Germany, that placement on the list is determined by party members (or their elected delegates), rather than by party officials. In addition, North Americans would probably want to add an element of openness to the lists: in Sweden, for example, a popular candidate low on the party's regional list is moved to the top if more than 8 percent of the party's supporters in the region indicate such a preference through what is known as the personal vote.

These aspects and other more technical ones—such as the actual mathematical method for allocating seats[7]—can be customized to suit local circumstances. All, however, are satisfactorily faithful to the basic principle of proportionality so as to fit the arguments presented in favor of PR systems.

Many reasons have been advanced for replacing SMP by PR. The starting point is fairer representation for parties and sectors of society in the legislative and governing process, putting an end to what can be highly distorted patterns of representation. To see the need for this, look at Canada at the beginning of the millennium, a textbook case of the kind of distortions that can occur under SMP. These include: one-party dominance,[8] decimation of parties,[9] regionalization of parties,[10] enfeeblement of the opposition,[11] victory for the loser,[12] and hyperpolarization.[13]

Because of strong regional identities exacerbated by the electoral system, SMP's most discernible effect in Canada is to regionalize party representation. But its effective exclusion of the Green Party from representation may be more salient when it comes to informed youth voting. The proportion of young people who express sympathy for the Greens in polls is not much different from that in Northern Europe, but the electoral system in Canada effectively excludes the Greens from winning seats in that country. This leads many of the Green supporters, if they bother to vote, to vote strategically for another party, while their European counterparts face no such dilemma since they can see their support finding its way into the legislature and even national policy.

Thus we can see a direct, if weak, relationship between PR and youth political participation, since PR makes it possible for that small proportion of knowledgeable young people who feel unrepresented by the parties that can win seats under SMP to have their votes for the Greens and other minor parties count toward representation. Moreover, PR can encourage the participation of women and members of visible minorities,[14] since it enhances the possibility of their being elected to the legislature. This is because of the simple fact that PR systems use lists from which, unlike winnable single member districts, it is hard to exclude women or identifiable minorities.

We should, therefore, not be surprised that there is a relationship between PR and voter turnout. One comprehensive assessment (Farrell 2001) based on turnout in thirty-nine democracies where voting was not compulsory in the last election before the year 2000 found turnout averaged 68.2 percent in nonproportional systems compared to 70.8 percent in proportional systems.[15] In an earlier work (Milner 2002a, chapter 5), I calculated the difference in turnout in municipal elections under PR and non-PR systems in three countries where both are or have been found (Switzerland, Norway, and Australia), finding higher turnout under PR in each case.[16]

PR and Informed Political Participation

So far, we have only explored the tip of the iceberg; the more powerful relationship between PR and informed political participation lies beneath the surface. An indication that political knowledge is an intervening variable in the relationship between electoral systems and turnout can be found in the results of the National Geographic–Roper Geographic Literacy Survey. In the eight mature democracies in the survey, young people in the three with SMP electoral systems (the United States, Canada, and the United Kingdom) scored lowest, while those in the two PR countries (Sweden and Germany) ranked at the top in geopolitical knowledge. In between were the countries with mixed systems—Italy and Japan, as well as France, with its second ballot system. How could these seemingly unrelated variables be connected?

Proportional systems bring more sectors of the community in under the umbrella of democratic institutions. This applies both to groups linked by ascribed characteristics such as gender, and to groups united by programmatic objectives, such as environmentalists. More choices mean the fewer potential voters excluded from identification with a party or candidate. In the United States, more voters turned out for elections in which prominent third-party candidates took part. For example, Ross Perot increased turnout in the 1992 presidential election: Lacy and Burden (2000) estimate that voting increased by 3 percent due to his candidacy. And in Minnesota's 1998 gubernatorial election, independent Jesse Ventura added 7 percentage points to the turnout rate, bringing younger and less educated voters to the polls. Overall, in their study of third-party candidates in the 1968, 1980, 1992, and 1996 presidential elections, Lacy and Burden find that between 24 percent and 34 percent of third-party candidate supporters would have stayed home on Election Day had their candidate not chosen to run.

The effect on turnout is obvious with regard to minor parties, but it applies also to mainstream parties whose supporters can, under SMP, find themselves living in districts in which their vote is certain to be wasted, since their party has no chance of winning the seat. However, this explanation is insufficient: even under PR, a single vote almost never changes the outcome. It is only when we incorporate the incentive that parties have under PR to mobilize all potential supporters, and not just those in winnable districts as is the case under SMP, that we begin to approach a full explanation. In the previous chapter, we saw this phenomenon in congressional districts in the United States, where there is far lower turnout in the many districts where one party is dominant. And here political knowledge enters, since fundamental to mobilization—especially when the electoral rules encourage this, as they tend to do in PR countries (see Bowler, Carter, and Farrell 2000)—is the task of informing insufficiently informed potential voters.

In the language of Gordon and Segura (1997), the electoral system—along with the party system and the legislative institutional structure—affects the availability, clarity, and usefulness of political information. Gordon and Segura find that, among other things, electoral disproportionality exerts a negative influence on political sophistication, that "measures of political sophistication . . . are really products of both capabilities and decisions."[17]

Of course political knowledge is not the only factor. Incentive effects built into different electoral systems are complex. Elklit, Svensson, and Togeby argue that the electoral system is a key part of the explanation for high Scandinavian, especially Danish, turnout. They see a sort of virtuous circle, combining Danish electoral institutions that foster the mobilization of weak groups, high competitiveness in national elections, and a high level of mobilization:

> Systems of proportional representation provide fairly good possibilities for new political interests to be represented in parliament, in particular in Denmark, where the . . . threshold is as low as two percent. This institutional framework has facilitated the mobilization of groups of citizens who felt that they were not well represented by the established parties, in particular with regard to issues like immigration, refugees, foreigners, and the European Union. The Progress Party and its successor, the Danish People's Party, have both been able to mobilize voters with few resources . . . Political mobilization . . . helps uphold the norm of civic duty. (2005, 12)

Denmark's remarkable level of voter turnout—even compared with its Nordic neighbors, which also have high civic literacy—is in good part due to the fact that young Danes vote at almost the same high level as previous generations, and that even citizens who express low interest in politics continue to vote. This is linked to the fact that the norm of civic duty is better passed along to new generations in Denmark.

Lacking citizens with a comparably strong sense of civic duty to vote, other countries have to rely on the incentives that their electoral systems place on political actors to mobilize support. But these are different under PR and SMP. A party contesting a PR election seeks to mobilize support everywhere, while one contesting an SMP election will concentrate resources on marginal districts, knowing that the choices of a relatively small number of voters can make the difference between monopolizing political power and having none whatsoever. With politics as a zero-sum game, distorting the opponent's position (through appeals to emotion, negative advertising, and the like), while keeping one's own policies vague so as to be able to shift with voter opinion, tends to pay off (Amy 1989). This is not the case with PR, where cooperation among parties is necessary and commonplace. All aspects of party strategy and the content of electoral programs are affected, often with a real, if hard to discern, effect on voter participation.

Consider, for example, the relationship between the incentives on party strategy built into SMP and the dramatic decline in democratic participation in Britain (18 percent fewer citizens voted in 2001 than in 1992). To defeat Thatcherism, Tony Blair pushed the Labour Party firmly to the center, creating what he called New Labour. Yet the powerful Conservative majority he overcame was in fact an artifact of the electoral system, highly vulnerable to defeat by a Labour–Liberal Democratic coalition, had the elections been fought under PR and not SMP. A "Lib-Lab" government would have enacted center-left policies similar to those of New Labour. But there is a profound difference between Blairite policies' emerging as a compromise program of government between parties of the center and left, and their coming from a party transformed almost beyond recognition. In the former case, normal under PR, a formal or informal coalition government implements a compromise program reflecting the expressed choices of a majority of voters, but constituent parties retain programs reflecting the evolving expectations of party supporters. The party need not, thus, renounce core principles when it enters the government, a renunciation that stokes cynicism toward politics and, in due course, discourages voters.

Even more important in the long term than the effect on attitudes, I contend, is a far less well known effect of the electoral system: how the interplay of built-in incentives influences the political knowledge of the citizens. Transforming Labour into New Labour alters the political map, changing the settings on the citizen's political compass. This is especially applicable in the context of an SMP environment, in which parties concentrate mobilization efforts, including information provision, on voters in marginal districts. For the citizen with limited knowledge, party transformation can mean no longer being able to make the basic distinctions that allow for meaningful choice.

In sum, voters are likely to be better informed under PR than under SMP, which, at the margins, can make the difference between having and lacking the minimal knowledge needed to cast a meaningful vote. This goes against conventional thinking, which assumes that voting under SMP is a simpler proposition, since it is typically a choice between, as the saying goes, keeping the bums in or kicking them out. But such conventional thinking views voters one-dimensionally. It ignores the reality of party identification, which develops over time. Parties that frequently change their programs and leaders in an effort to maximize short-term support are more likely to lose than gain long-term adherents. But SMP drives them to do just this. Unlike under PR, the volatility of their support is exaggerated: SMP blows up their strength when they do well, and shrivels it when they do poorly. This explains the frequent ideological shifts in the Westminster democracies to keep up with public opinion, compared to the more gradual evolution under PR in Europe.

Similar incentive effects can be seen in the vertical dimension of party strategy. The logic of SMP discourages parties from taking the risk of operating at levels other than the one at which they are best organized, which is a disincentive for a national party's investing in regions and municipalities where it is weak. Over time, this has the effect of gradually pushing national parties away from an effective presence in certain regions and localities. With parties less present at the base, vertical political links are weakened and vertical communication flows disrupted. Citizens find themselves with a political map on which side roads that connect the small communities to the main centers have been erased. The extreme case is Canada, where municipal political parties—in places where they exist at all—have no formal links to the parties operating at the federal and provincial levels. In the United States, in many regions, one of the two parties is effectively absent, while at the municipal level, where parties were traditionally present, over three-quarters of municipalities use nonpartisan elections to elect their public officials (Schaffner and Streb 2000, 2).

The opposite logic operates under PR. In the case of Norway, for example, once PR was adopted for the national legislature, its use spread to other levels and it became embedded in a system of vertically integrated relationships centered on the political parties. In Sweden, the introduction of PR led the Social Democrats to become active in municipal politics and then rural communes, which forced their bourgeois opponents to do likewise, a process completed with the municipal amalgamation reforms of 1974.[18]

The overall logic differentiating the two systems insofar as political knowledge is concerned is clear. Because PR systems are more conducive to the formation and durability of ideologically coherent parties that contest elections at more than one level, they provide potential voters with a political map that is relatively clearly drawn and stable across time and space. They make it easier for the potential voter to identify with a party, and to use that identification as a guide through the complexities of issues and actors over time and at various levels of political activity. In this way, PR fosters political participation, especially at the lower end of the education and income ladders, where information about issues and actors is at a premium.

Testing PR's Effect on Participation

The data are inadequate for directly testing this claim comparatively by using political knowledge as the dependent variable (with electoral systems as independent variable), or the independent variable (with turnout as dependent variable), since there is as yet no set of factual political knowledge questions used cross-nationally. Nevertheless, it is possible to derive insights from the responses to the political knowledge questions of the Comparative Study of Electoral Systems (CSES). In our 2006 article Grönlund and I examine the dispersion of political knowledge among educational categories by comparing the variation from the mean of the political knowledge score by the group with the lowest education. In a section of the article dealing with the effects of institutions, we report that average dispersion was lower in countries using PR, thus bol-

FIGURE 7.1

Gini indexes scattered against the F-value of the effect of education on political knowledge at the country level

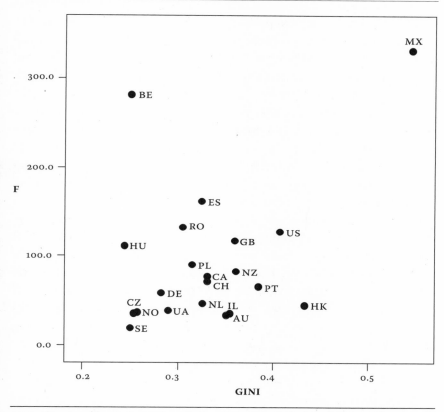

NOTE: Country abbreviations follow the two-letter standard of the ISO. http://www.world atlas.com/aatlas/ctycodes.htm

stering the contention that PR reduces the cost of the political knowledge needed to make an informed vote for those for whom the cost is highest—that is, those lacking in educational resources.

To get a clearer picture of this relationship, given the variety of electoral systems, we applied a classification using a sophisticated indicator linking the number of parties to the proportionality of the electoral system (the Gallagher Index). As we can see in Figure 7.1, for the CSES democracies (with Belgium again as the outlier), as predicted, as the number of parties decreases, education plays a greater role in political knowledge—in other words, that under more proportional electoral systems, political knowledge is more accessible to people with less education.

We found also that party identification, as anticipated in the discussion in chapter 6, increased political knowledge significantly—but more in majoritarian than in proportional systems. The logic underlying this relationship appears to be as follows. The subset of political knowledge questions asking respondents to distinguish among parties (e.g., "Which party favors policy x?") are more likely to be answered correctly by someone with a low level of education who identifies with a particular party than by someone who does not identify with a party. Moreover, the proportion of those who identify with a party is higher under PR, with its more stable political map. This means that party identification is more salient for distinguishing the politically knowledgeable among the poorly educated under majoritarian systems.

If we can apply to young people the logic that PR elections, and other institutions that favor stable party identification, reduce the costs of political knowledge for those for whom it is at a premium—and there is every reason to believe that we can—then we can better understand the even stronger relationship between proportional electoral systems and youth turnout. In examining differences in turnout level for voters aged eighteen to twenty-nine in fifteen Western European countries in the late 1990s, International IDEA (1999, 30) estimated that in countries using PR systems, the average youth turnout rate was almost 12 percentage points higher than in non-PR countries. International IDEA's interpretation stressed the electoral system's facilitating access to parliamentary representation for small parties. We have noted that this is the case for a minority of informed young people whose views are poorly represented under majoritarian systems. But there is also an effect on a larger group, those at the margins of political knowledge, which reduced the number of potential political dropouts.

Using U.S. turnout data, Donovan and Tolbert (2007, 2008) find that variation in turnout across states reflects campaign mobilization effects. They suggest that these effects are most pronounced among people with lower interest in politics, and especially among young people, because those with higher levels of interest are likely to participate in most elections regardless of how much interest is generated by competition for the contested position. Exposure to electoral competition is associated with greater political interest and knowledge, which, in turn, is associated with greater participation; the absence of electoral competition thus depresses interest among the most vulnerable to abstaining and reduces participation.

Since PR fosters electoral competition, it is reasonable to expect it to foster political interest, knowledge, and, thus, participation—in other words, to boost informed turnout. But we need to be wary of such predictions. The shift identified by certain observers cited in part 1 toward a culture that measures the value of an activity based only on its meaningfulness to the individual carrying it out will dampen political participation under any set of institutions. In New Zealand, which adopted the MMP system in 1996, turnout increased by about 3 percentage points in 1996, but the decline that marked the 1980s resumed in 1999. In Scotland, the 58.8 turnout in PR elections for the new assembly in 1999 declined to 49 percent in the elections in 2003 and 2007. In the London mayoral election, the percentage of registered voters turning out in 2000, 34.7 percent, was identical to that in the previous borough elections (Electoral Commission 2002, 23).

Since turnout was generally already in decline, it is certainly possible that the adoption of PR may have kept it from accelerating in some or all of these cases. Moreover, we need keep in mind that proportionality is far from fully institutionally rooted in these countries. Scotland, which operates in the context of Westminster's dominating SMP environment, has only recently introduced semiproportional STV in local elections. In New Zealand, PR has only entered local elections in fits and starts,[19] and the country has not yet adopted fixed election dates, an important complementary institutional arrangement to PR elections (see chapter 8). Hence we are far from attaining the political knowledge effects from a simplification of the political map that a full-fledged PR institutional environment would bring.

In sum, while there is no mystery to the higher overall levels of voter turnout under PR, there is no guarantee that adoption of MMP in a country with low turnout will raise it. In our study of Switzerland, the only country without compulsory elections that uses a variety of electoral systems in local elections, Andreas Ladner and I found that though PR municipalities had higher turnouts to begin with, they were no better at withstanding the turnout decline experienced at all levels in Swiss elections in the 1990s (Ladner and Milner 1999).

PR and Turnout: The Case of Canada

What effects, if any, could we expect the adoption of PR to have on informed youth political participation in Canada or one of its provinces? It would bring to the polls knowledgeable young people who feel their views to be unrepresented by the parties that can win seats under SMP. This is the group that the International IDEA data pointed to, and it is this group's voting that helps explain the turnout spike in New Zealand's first MMP election in 1996 (Karp and Banducci 1998).[20] But the group contains few potential political dropouts. Rather, given their educational and political knowledge levels, a good number can be expected to vote as their political views moderate with age.

If the outcome of the April 2009 referendum had resulted in British Columbia's changing its electoral system, we might have seen some future improvement in turnout, due to the province's relatively large number of Green supporters whose votes would have counted. But, for Canada as a whole, their numbers appear not to be large enough to perceptibly boost overall turnout levels, given that young Canadians tend to be mainstream in their political attitudes (O'Neill 2001).[21]

But timing is also a factor. Had MMP been instituted in the 1990s, it seems fair to suggest that, given the importance of habits developed during youth, the additional competitiveness could have had a small but not insignificant long-term effect, by developing the habit of voting among a greater proportion of young people. Similarly, were Canada to adopt MMP now—during a period of recurrent, short-lived minority governments—the inter-party cooperation thus fostered could reduce the cynicism toward politics in the political culture into which young citizens are socialized, and therefore could indirectly foster the habit of voting among a discernible number of young people.

Much would depend on whether the provinces and other jurisdictions followed suit. Much would also depend on whether complementary measures were adopted. Electoral reform need not take place in a vacuum: the small dent that adopting PR should make in the democratic deficit could be enlarged if other reforms were introduced along with it. Given Canada's size, composition, and Constitution, federalism—and, very likely, bicameralism—will be a fixture. But, as we shall see in the chapters to follow, there are institutional reforms complementary to the potential positive effects of PR, such as voting dates, voting age, and the dissemination of information during election campaigns, that lie well within the reach of Canada and its provinces.

I do not raise the possibility of similar reforms for the United States, given the impossibility of changing that country's electoral system. This is clear from the fact that Barack Obama, who put change on the American political agenda, did not include political institutions as a dimension of the change required. Even he cannot raise the political capital needed to change the electoral system. But there is potential in the grass-roots networks kindled by his presidential campaign that could be mobilized toward more specific changes, such as making redistricting nonpartisan and thereby reducing the number of uncompetitive districts. Another possible target is the winner-take-all "unit rule" method that forty-eight states use to allocate their electoral votes. This has led to a two-tiered system, in which a shrinking number of battleground states are spotlit in the campaign, with voters in the remaining states left on the sidelines[22]— the consequences of which are especially acute among young adults, who are a third more likely to vote in the battleground states.[23]

Conclusion

If democratic countries were to adopt a PR system appropriate to local circumstances, there would be a positive effect on the turnout of the young and not so young, but we should not exaggerate its overall impact. For one thing, there are not that many countries where such a transformation can take place, since most advanced democratic countries already use a form of PR, while the United States is incapable of even considering such a change. Of the relatively few countries that still use SMP, Australia has resolved the turnout—though not informed turnout— problem through compulsory voting. This leaves, among the countries under consideration here, only the United Kingdom and Canada.

We have investigated the possibility of Canada's going from SMP to PR as a sort of test case, concluding that if it were to happen, it could have a real, though small, positive effect on turnout. While efforts at change at the provincial level have fizzled, continuous minority government in Ottawa has unexpectedly revived discussion of federal electoral system reform. If change is to come, however, Canada's federal system ensures that the process will be a slow one, characterized by different systems' operating in different provinces and in the federal Parliament.

But this could prove to be a constructive development, making Canada, heretofore the textbook case of the problems with SMP, a kind of laboratory of the effects of alternate electoral systems.

Something like this has been taking place in the United Kingdom in recent years, with different variations of PR implemented in Scotland, Wales, Northern Ireland, and London. Moreover, given the widely expressed active dislike of the major party candidates by many young Britons (Electoral Commission 2002), bringing PR to Westminster, should the Liberal Democrats be in a position to force it upon a Labour minority, stands a better chance of resulting in a perceptible increase in youth turnout. Despite the attitudes of the major parties, this should not be ruled out. The election of a minority government—a real possibility at the time of this writing—could force electoral reform onto the agenda. Nevertheless, as proved to be the case in Quebec, any impetus for change is likely to be short-lived if it is left to politicians, who naturally see merit in the voting system that put them in office.

Beyond this, we need to be wary of expecting that any institutional reform, electoral or otherwise, will shelter us from the effects of the powerful technological and cultural forces shaping emerging generations. But this does not mean we should do nothing. Political institutions are man-made and can be remade. Changing them for the better should be on the platform of every party and candidate claiming to want to boost informed political participation by young people. Such reforms will not resolve the problem, but—combined with the implementation of specific programs and measures like those set out in the next chapters— they can still have a significant effect.

8

Who Should Vote, and When?

In this chapter we continue to examine election rules, focusing on those directly affecting first-time potential voters. Measures along the lines discussed in this chapter would complement the reforms intended to promote higher general levels of informed political participation that are outlined in the last two chapters. Indeed, these reforms can also indirectly affect youth turnout. In particular, the initiatives proposed to augment the level of electoral competitiveness have been found to push local American party organizations toward making an effort to mobilize young citizens.[1]

We begin with one very simple way to increase the number of young people who vote: reduce the voting age to, say, sixteen. Were that done throughout the democratic world, millions more young persons would participate in the democratic process. This rather simple argument voiced by youth advocates has so far fallen on deaf ears. Very few jurisdictions have moved in this direction, citing, if challenged, the perceived scarcity of political knowledge and skills among young people. Critics quite legitimately ask, if young people do not vote at eighteen, why should we expect them to vote at sixteen?

Nevertheless, there is some support for just such a move among experts in the field.[2] The most powerful case for reducing the voting age is made by Mark Franklin, the prominent specialist in electoral participation, who asserts that there is indeed good reason to believe that some people who do not vote at eighteen might have voted at sixteen. Franklin is anything but an idealist when it comes to youth voting: indeed, he would prefer what he knows to be politically impossible—namely, raising the voting age back to twenty-one—since, as his work convincingly demonstrates, the voting age reduction implemented in the mature democracies starting in the 1960s (typically reducing it from twenty-one to eighteen) triggered a long-term decline in turnout.[3]

In this chapter, we begin with a discussion of Franklin's arguments in favor of lowering the voting age, proceeding to place voting age reduction in the context of other institutional reforms—in particular, a system of fixed election dates. We conclude by setting out some of the more specific measures taken to boost electoral participation among young people and other vulnerable groups, focusing on Scandinavia and Canada.

Lowering the Voting Age

Franklin's argument, first encountered in chapter 4, can be summarized briefly. Lowering the voting age left a statistically identifiable footprint in the electorate. Each election added to the population of potential voters a group of citizens less likely to turn out than would have been the case if the voting age had remained at twenty-one, a process apparently reflected in the declining turnout in every country that had lowered the voting age. The reasons for this, Franklin argues, are clear. The ages eighteen to twenty-one are inappropriate for a first experience with voting, because the period immediately after leaving high school is fraught with the problems of early adulthood. Building on the analysis of Plutzer (2002), Franklin maintains that the costs of learning to vote are higher if one's first election falls in a period during which one is only starting to establish the social networks that will frame future choices, including political ones. Those aged eighteen to twenty are typically in a period of transition, in the process of withdrawing from their home and school environments without fully settling into another, and are preoccupied with things other than public affairs and hence more likely to develop the habit of nonvoting. It is the habits young people develop during their first opportunities to vote that are at the bottom of the long-term trend. Since, to an important degree, voting is habitual, turnout decline will accelerate as newly eligible cohorts of potential voters, set in their nonvoting ways, replace older cohorts with developed voting habits.

Given the impossibility of restoring the voting age of twenty-one, and given a choice between reducing it to sixteen and leaving it at eighteen, Franklin opts for the former because people aged sixteen would be engaged by the political process at a less unsettled time in their lives. This would get more young people to the polls and instill in them the habit of voting. There are several reasons: first, because parents are better able to set an example for sixteen-year-olds than for eighteen-year-olds; and second, because sixteen-year-olds are better integrated into the networks of the community than their older siblings. This second contention corresponds to Franklin's (2005) findings that, based on U.S. turnout data since 1972, length of residence in the neighborhood has a significant positive effect (second only to that of education in overall importance), especially on young adults. Young adults who had lived in the neighborhood all their lives were 21 percent more likely to vote than those who had recently moved there (compared to 7 percent more likely for the electorate as a whole).[4] According to Franklin, long-time residents have had the opportunity "to become enmeshed in social structures that expose them to expressive engagement on the part of acquaintances and friends . . . Length of residence is a precondition that makes it easier for friends and acquaintances to shepherd young adults into the habit of voting" (Franklin 2005, 23–24).

While this conclusion is intriguing, it is far from proven.[5] Moreover, Franklin's argument runs up against what we learned about changes in the role of family and peer groups in the new informational environment in chapters 2 and 3. And, given its less than positive depiction of young citizens, it is not the kind of argument likely to be taken up by youth advocacy groups. One can find more typical arguments presented before the Electoral Commission of the United Kingdom, which was charged with investigating and reporting on reducing the voting age. The commission's report drew on the work of several independent bodies established to make recommendations on ways to encourage youth participation in England, Scotland, and Wales, as well as the Commission on Local Governance in England, all of which looked favorably upon a reduction in either or both of the minimum ages for voting and candidacy (Electoral Commission 2004, 8). The issue was placed on the political agenda by the "Votes at 16 Coalition" campaign, in which the British Youth Council played a leading role. However, after considering the issue in depth, the commission declined to recommend lowering the voting age.

The commission first considered the arguments of the coalition's spokespersons that other important rights and responsibilities accrue at sixteen in the United Kingdom, especially the right to marry and join the armed forces, as well as the liability to pay income tax. It noted that these are in effect "split rights," which a sixteen- or seventeen-year-old may exercise only with the consent of a parent or guardian, and added that a new army recruit, unlike a new voter, must first go through basic training. (This is an analogy applicable to the argument introduced below, in which lowering the voting age is linked to compulsory civic education.) In the end, the commission could not find a basis for disagreeing with public opinion, which its own surveys and investigations had found to favor retaining the current minimum age:

> The Commission has looked for clear evidence on which to base any change in the current voting age, and to date has found insufficient justification for such change . . . Even among young people themselves, our experience has been that there has been no significant or even consistent majority of young people calling for the right to vote and indeed many felt that they were not ready for the responsibility any earlier than 18 . . . On the basis of the evidence currently available, there does not seem to exist a sufficiently strong argument that change now would affect the level of political engagement between young people and the political process . . . Although the Commission has met large numbers of mature and politically literate 16 and 17 year-olds in the course of this review . . . these have been almost by definition self-selecting representatives of this age group. (Electoral Commission 2004, 61–62).

The commission's report is a useful source of comparative information relevant to the issue. In a large majority of countries, the minimum age is eighteen, with a few still retaining the age of twenty-one. Among the small number that allowed people younger than eighteen to vote, only one—Brazil, where the voting age is sixteen—qualified as significant in size and solidly democratic. The others are Iran (age fifteen), Cuba and the Isle of Man (sixteen), and Nicaragua and Indonesia (seventeen). The report singled out developments at the municipal level, focusing on six German states where the voting age had been lowered (see also Aarts and van Hees 2003). The first change came in 1995, when the minimum age for municipal elections in Lower Saxony was reduced from eighteen to sixteen. Five other states, including Hesse, followed suit (though Hesse later reverted to age eighteen).

The commission assembled survey data for the municipal elections in the Lower Saxony cities of Hanover and Braunschweig in 1997. Some were promising. In Hanover, turnout among those aged sixteen and seventeen was 56.5 percent, compared to 49.1 percent among those eighteen to twenty-four, and the overall turnout of 57 percent. In Braunschweig, with the same overall turnout, turnout among those sixteen and seventeen was 50.4 percent, compared to 44.5 among those eighteen to twenty-four. Somewhat similar results emerged from another set of figures from municipal elections in 1999 in the former East German state of Saxony-Anhalt. Across all the main cities, the turnout rate for those sixteen to eighteen was around 33 percent, similar to that for those eighteen to twenty-one, but better than the 24 percent for those twenty-one to twenty-five—though below the 38 percent turnout overall (Electoral Commission 2004,15–16). Though these results did not convince the Commission, they would seem to confirm Franklin's expectation. But there is also the possibility that it was a matter of novelty, and that the turnout of those aged sixteen to eighteen would fall in subsequent elections, a theory that it would be useful to test.

The most interesting test will come in Austria, given recent developments in that country. Following up on actions taken by the Austrian states of Carinthia, Burgenland, and Styria, the Austrian Parliament passed a law in 2007 making Austria the first European Union member to allow sixteen-year-olds to vote in national elections. The measure was backed by four of the five parties—only the rightist Freedom Party opposed the measure—and was part of a larger reform package that also introduced absentee ballots.[6] With about 200,000 sixteen- and seventeen-year-olds, out of an electorate of 6.3 million, eligible to vote for the first time, the first test came in an election that took place on 26 September 2008, in which the country's two far-right parties made large gains, collectively winning 29 percent of votes. It is suspected, though I have seen no evidence of this, that the two developments are related. If true, that would not help the case for reducing the voting age.

Austrian turnout data over the next several elections should help us assess Franklin's contention that reducing the voting age to sixteen will boost turnout. For now the question remains open. Moreover, even if it does marginally boost turnout, that would not be enough to persuade those who fear it would open the door to uninformed and thus unready electors. We suggested in chapter 6 that compulsory voting cannot be counted on to augment informed youth voting; the same, we would expect, would be true of lowering the voting age. Given changes in the role of the family and of neighborhood-based networks, I have less confidence than Franklin does in the political-socialization capacity of these institutions.

Like the Electoral Commission, I am skeptical of the net benefit of simply reducing the voting age. Unlike the commission, however, I would not rule it out. Britain has introduced compulsory civic education, and voting at sixteen potentially allows for greater integration between what goes on the classroom and the choices the students will be in a position to make as citizens. Indeed, since many young people in the United Kingdom drop out of school at sixteen, the course can be given at an age when they are still at school and nearly eligible to vote. Nevertheless, we need to move carefully here. It is no coincidence that many initiatives have taken place at the municipal level. In the discussion of civic education in chapter 10, I argue that something similar needs to be done in North America, combining, in a given province or state, the experimental lowering of the voting age and a complementary compulsory program of civic education at age fifteen and sixteen.

In the United States, with its distinct set of institutional arrangements, young people face the additional difficulty of registering to vote. Franklin's argument is acutely salient for the United States due to the fact that getting registered to vote is easier at sixteen and seventeen, when one is closer to home. One way to deal with the situation without formally lowering the voting age has been proposed by FairVote:[7] allowing citizens to register at sixteen, and (as is now done in several states) to vote in primaries at age seventeen if they will be eighteen at the time of the next election (a date known in advance, due to fixed voting days). Even those opposed to lowering the voting age, unless their opposition is based on partisan considerations, should favor such a measure, since it would enhance the proportion of young persons actually able to vote when they reach the eligible age.

Election Dates in Parliamentary Regimes

Active voter registration, like a number of other distinctive aspects of election-related institutional arrangements in the United States, has been seen to be detrimental to informed youth political participation. This is not the case for the u.s. system of fixed election dates: for all federal, most state, and many municipal, offices, Election Day is always the first Tuesday after the first Monday of November, in every even-numbered year.[8] Were election dates unfixed, as they are in Canada, turnout would likely be even lower. The comparison to Canada might be unfair, since fixed election dates are more readily compatible with a presidential system like that of the United States, in which—unlike in a parliamentary system—there is no need for the executive to maintain the confidence of the legislature to stay in office.

But proposing fixed election dates in parliamentary systems like Canada is to push against an unlocked door in many places, including several Canadian provinces. Chapter 6 argued that parliamentary systems, which are found in most mature democracies, are more conducive to participation than presidential ones, since by fusing rather than fragmenting power, they better meet the criterion of fostering citizens' awareness of the consequences of their decisions. We here address the possible advantages for parliamentary systems of the adoption of fixed election dates. And our primary focus is on Canada and other Westminster countries, for the usual reasons—but also because surprisingly, as we shall see in table 8.1, many of the other parliamentary countries use a version of fixed election dates.

In recent years, Canada has been moving slowly but steadily toward fixed election dates, though there has been insufficient discussion of the phenomenon and its implications. Soon after taking power in 2006, the new minority Conservative government changed the law with regard to voting dates, as it had promised it would during the election campaign. In this, it was following the examples of British Columbia, Ontario, Newfoundland, and New Brunswick. The law fixing election dates, which came into force in May 2007, established that federal elections will take place on the third Monday in October, four years after the previous general election. Unfortunately, in the minority government context, neither the governing nor the opposition parties respected the spirit of fixed elections; and an escape clause in the law[9] was invoked by the government to force an early election in October 2008, two years before Parliament was scheduled to expire. Given that the election produced another minority government, the situation remains in flux—to say the least.

Turnout, which had risen in 2006 from 2004, dropped sharply in 2008—in part because, as the polls showed, citizens were not persuaded that an early election was justified. Hence there is good reason to expect that turnout would have been better had the election taken place on the set date. But before looking at the relationship between fixed election dates and informed political participation, we need to address the question of whether, given the Canadian experience, fixed election dates are in fact compatible with parliamentary government, a question raised when parliamentary elections do not deliver single party majorities.

This question cannot be answered without returning to the discussion of electoral systems. SMP usually produces majority governments, which are readily compatible with fixed election dates—as has so far been the case in the above-mentioned Canadian provinces. But when no party wins a majority, Canadian politicians and media tend to treat the minority governments that emerge as short-lived aberrations, undermining Parliament's capacity to serve out its full fixed term. This is not the case under PR, since PR elections are not expected to produce majority governments. Political actors thus act accordingly to form coalitions or garner sufficient support for minority governments to provide, as a rule, reasonable assurance of longevity.

The effort by the Canadian opposition parties to form a coalition at the end of 2008 suggests that Canadian political actors may be beginning to accept the real possibility of quasi-permanent minority government in Ottawa, and thus coming to think beyond the short term in developing positions about the formation and longevity of governments—and even, possibly, ready to look again at the idea of moving toward an electoral system based on proportional representation. Only then would Canada have real, rather than merely legislated, fixed election dates; only then would it be in a position to take advantage of the potential benefits of fixed election dates presented below.

The standard argument for fixing election dates is fairness: to remove from the party in power an unfair advantage of calling an election when it serves its partisan interests to do so. This is also the reason why parties in power tend to try to avoid introducing fixed dates. Conversely, once fixed dates appear on the agenda for public discussion, it is difficult for parties in power not to take action without appearing to be acting out of partisan interest. Of course, with political parties held in less than high esteem, fair treatment of political parties is not an argument that can readily mobilize public opinion these days. But it is a different story when it comes to enhancing public participation, and that is the story we have to tell.

The first question to be posed is whether, as many assume, parliamentary institutions are incompatible with fixed election dates. In reality, in

TABLE 8.1

Election dates in parliamentary and mixed systems

UNFIXED TERM	FIXED TERM	FLEXIBLE FIXED TERM
Australia	Chile	Austria
Canada	Cyprus	Belgium
Denmark	Estonia	Czech Republic
Iceland	Finland	Greece
India	Germany	Hungary
Ireland	Korea	Israel
Japan	Latvia	Italy
Malta	Lithuania	Spain
New Zealand	Luxembourg	
United Kingdom	Netherlands	
	Norway	
	Portugal	
	Slovakia	
	Slovenia	
	Sweden	
	Switzerland	

addition to four Canadian provinces, three Australian states, and the newly created assemblies of Scotland and Wales, a fair number of countries combine fixed election dates with parliamentary systems of government. Table 8.1 illustrates the situation in thirty-four comparable democracies. Overall, while American-style, rigidly fixed election dates are rare in parliamentary and mixed systems, only a minority of countries with these systems allow the head of government to effectively set the legislature's election date. Of course, as we can see in the list of countries in the second column in the table fixed election dates are a natural fit with proportional systems of elections.

In the classification set out in table 8.1, only ten democracies are unfixed—that is, set no legal constraints beyond the maximum term length on the head of government in choosing the election date. Even so, their experience varies, since the head of government's capacity to exercise discretion is not simply a matter of laws and regulations; historical and institutional factors come into play, in some cases resulting in elections that regularly take place in quite a predictable cycle.[10]

Classifying the remaining countries is more complex. A definition of a fixed system as one where, as in the United States, there is nothing the executive or legislature can do to alter the date of the next legislative election would exclude any parliamentary system that permits premature elections—that is, only Norway would be left.[11] The other countries' rules allow for early elections but place obstacles upon opposition parties' ability to force such an election. For example, a vote of no confidence supported by a majority of members voting may be required, or, as in Sweden and Germany, legislators may be required to make an extraordinary effort to vote confidence in an alternative government before any premature election can be called. All of these countries set a known, fixed term for their legislatures that is, as a rule, respected. And if a premature election does occur, the law sets out clear rules for the date of the subsequent regular election, for instance leaving it unchanged or moving it to a similar day in a later year.[12] Whether the law specifies a single day or sets a range of weeks within which it must take place constitutes a second dimension of the level of fixedness.[13] To incorporate these variations, I divide the countries that are not in the unfixed column into "fixed term" and "flexible" columns[14] in table 8.1. Even if we exclude the mixed (parliamentary-presidential) systems like Finland in the group, the fixed date category still has the most cases, and it is more the rule than the exception in parliamentary regimes.

Why Fixed Election Dates?

Until recently, like most political scientists interested in political institutions, I had given little thought to the rules concerning election dates. In the 1990s, an invitation to join a group of foreign observers of German federal elections, trips necessarily organized well in advance of the election date, made me conscious not only of the fact that Germany had fixed election dates, but also of the advantages this afforded. And Germany's parliamentary system was known and respected for its innovative democratic reforms and high level of informed political participation. It was a natural next step to reflect upon the possible relationship between the rules concerning voting dates and electoral participation, especially among young people. In presenting the main arguments advanced in the debate over fixed election dates,[15] I start from the general and move rapidly toward those specifically salient to informed youth voting.

The most frequently cited advantage of the fixed system lies in its relative transparency, inhibiting the ability of parties in power to use the calling of an election as a means of furthering their chances of reelection. With election dates known in advance, efforts of governments to buy voters with their own tax money become visible; in unfixed systems, it is often only retrospectively—after the election has been called—that such efforts become apparent. A second, related set of arguments concerns the administrative benefits of being able to plan ahead.[16]

The most frequently heard argument against fixed election dates is related to campaign spending. If the u.s. case is indicative, then fixed election dates promise longer and more expensive campaigns. But need the United States be the model in this regard? Overspending can be countered by a combination of tight financial controls limiting the period of campaign spending, and an appropriate choice of election date. Sweden's choice of the third Sunday in September corresponds and contributes to expectations built into the political culture. Campaigning begins in mid-August, at the end of the vacation period, which marks the beginning of the political season. For parties to begin earlier can be counterproductive, given limited resources. And we should not neglect the fact that if the agencies charged with administering elections know the date well in advance, they can reduce their costs.[17]

An October election date, as Canada's law specifies, is a good choice for countries in the Northern Hemisphere, because their legislatures are not in session in the summer. It means avoiding the spectacle of a dysfunctional parliamentary session in the weeks before an election campaign is about to begin, a session in which strategies are geared toward improving the party's electoral prospects rather than the country's welfare. Such spectacles contribute to the growing cynicism about politics and, indirectly, it is fair to presume, to declining political interest and participation.

There are a number of ways in which fixed voting dates can impact upon informed electoral participation. Related to the above is the absence—or at least the reduction—of media speculation over the date of the next election and the various strategic considerations involved in its selection, which should leave more room for public discussion of the actual issues and priorities and thus, on balance, create a more informed electorate. In addition, diminishing the ability of governing parties to manipulate the timing of elections for political or partisan purposes should strengthen public confidence in the political process and help reduce the prevailing cynicism about politics.

Timing also affects individuals, allowing for interested citizens to plan their participation well in advance. Hence, fixed elections should make it easier to attract candidates needing to reconcile possible political careers with other obligations. This applies especially to women, who often have more family responsibilities than men, and to those not employed in professions, such as law, that readily lend themselves to political involvement. A longer period of notice should also make it easier to recruit more and better campaign volunteers to mobilize and inform electors. The ability of the United States to attain high levels of mobilization of this kind is pertinent here.

Better candidates and more and better informed volunteers should indirectly boost informed turnout. A more direct effect of election dates selected to optimize participation and known in advance is that they can make it easier for certain classes of citizens to make themselves available to vote. This applies particularly to potential voters with seasonal constraints. In the case of students, fixed election dates could be chosen to avoid, for example, times when college students are moving between home and school, or taking final examinations.

High turnout can be achieved without fixed election dates, as Denmark clearly illustrates. Nevertheless, for countries with habitually low youth turnout, like Canada and Britain, fixed election dates can and should be part of a systematic effort to address the problem.

In addition, fixed election dates complement concrete measures designed to actively boost informed political participation. The planning and staging of any and all public events—such as seminars, adult education activities, and public information campaigns—to raise awareness, interest, and involvement in public affairs can only be made easier by knowing the date of the next election well ahead of time.

Among these concrete measures is a set that applies specifically to young people. In the last part of this chapter, we will briefly survey various initiatives outside schools that different countries have taken to encourage young people to participate in elections; many such initiatives would be facilitated by knowing when the next election will take place. In addition, as with lowering the voting age, there is a link to what goes on at school. Fixed election dates can be effectively integrated into the content and activities of civic education courses, the subject of the final part of this book. A major thrust of our approach is to bring spokespersons into the classroom both virtually, through Internet-based information provided by the political parties, and physically to present their positions on relevant local, regional, national, and international issues. It goes without saying that an upcoming election with the date set in advance provides an excellent opportunity for arranging these activities. In planning the civics courses targeted at young people about to become citizens and voters, educators who know the exact date of the next election (and the associated deadlines for nominating candidates, adopting campaign platforms, etc.) will find it easier to identify and schedule visits from knowledgeable resource persons.

A case in point that will be considered in chapter 10 is simulated, or mock, elections. The simulation carried out during the 2004 Canadian election serves as a good example of the potential drawbacks of unfixed election dates. The prime minister put off calling the election until May, resulting in a 28 June election date. This was too late to allow for a simultaneous mock vote, so each participating school chose its own day for students to cast their votes. Overall numbers were clearly kept down by the election date's lateness and uncertainty. In contrast, the fact that the date was fixed in advance for the May 2005 and 2009 elections in British Columbia resulted in a much higher participation rate. The over 450 schools that participated in the latter provincial mock election equaled almost half the number that took part in the 2004 federal mock election.[18]

Other Measures

A less constructive aspect of the fixed election date in the United States is that it must be a Tuesday. Though of less direct consequence for the young, change here could make a difference. While we do not know if adopting weekend voting, as many other countries have done, would boost the U.S. turnout, we can reasonably expect that a regulation requiring employers to give employees sufficient time off to vote, as is the case in Canada and a number of other countries, would have at least a marginal positive effect, especially on low-income citizens of all ages, who have a lower turnout rate.

There are a number of other policies and programs unrelated to civic education that attempt to enhance political participation. These are typically targeted at a particular segment of the population, including but not limited to young people. A wide range of such policies and specific measures has emerged in recent years in the countries under consideration. A useful early list of suggestions along these lines was provided by International IDEA (1999), and many of them have been taken up and developed in different places.[19] These include various efforts to register young citizens, election simulations, and specially targeted artistic and cultural events. One recommendation was to make first-time voting a rite of passage, for example by sending congratulatory birthday cards to new voters, explaining how and when to register for elections, or by adding an element of public spectacle through a proposed National Youth Voter Registration Day.

Even those measures that do not specifically target young people tend to affect the new generation as much as, if not more than, other generations. In the United States, as noted in chapter 6, it is up to voters to register,[20] while in most Western democracies, registration is passive: the eligible citizen is automatically placed on the voters' list. Hence many organized efforts take place on and off American college campuses to register young citizens—work that is largely superfluous in other countries, though some special effort is still typically needed in countries with passive registration, such as Canada, to get those turning eighteen onto the roll of voters right away.

Fitzgerald (2003) shows that young people are substantially more likely to vote if they can register on Election Day (something that has been possible in Canadian federal elections since 2001), and that being able to vote early in advance polls and to register at state motor-vehicle agencies also has a positive, although smaller and not statistically significant, effect on youth voting. Moreover, young people are significantly more likely to be contacted by a political party in states with Election Day registration and, to a lesser extent, those with advance voting and mailed ballots. Given the complications related to rules for the registration of college students away from home (Niemi 2008), and the strength the Obama campaign showed among young people in 2008,[21] it is hard to imagine local Republican officials, given the opportunity, removing barriers to encourage them to vote. Citing a study at the Massachusetts Institute of Technology, a *New York Times* editorial noted:

Administrative barriers, such as error-filled voting lists or wrongful purges of voter rolls prevented as many as three million registered voters from casting ballots. Another two million to four million registered voters were discouraged from even trying to vote because of difficulty obtaining an absentee ballot, voter ID issues and other problems . . . Another nine million eligible voters tried to register but failed to because of a variety of hurdles, including missed deadlines or changes in residence.[22]

Benefits could also be derived in many states from improvement in the provision of special voting facilities for the handicapped, translated ballots for members of linguistic minorities, and placing the polling places in convenient locations, such as nursing homes. As noted in chapter 6, the inconsistency in these services and provisions in the United States is related to the absence of a single body to administer elections, set district boundaries, and determine rules for registration to vote and election for national office. The absence of such a body allows states to reduce turnout by measures designed to discourage voting by citizens in categories likely to oppose the party in power in the state.[23]

We cannot here do justice to the various proposals advanced to address the situation (see, e.g., Council of Baltic Sea States 2006; Ellis, Pammett, Gratschew, and Thiessen 2007; European Parliaments Research Initiative 2009; Wisse 2006; Youniss and Levine 2009). In keeping with the approach taken elsewhere in this book, we set out examples of recent initiatives in Scandinavia—in particular, Sweden—and Canada.

With turnout having fallen below 80 percent for the first time, Sweden initiated a program called Time for Democracy early in 2000. Mechanisms were instituted, mainly via the Swedish Associations of Local Authorities and Regional Councils, for supporting projects aimed at boosting democratic participation, especially among those groups in the population where it was low. Two targets were priorities: ethnically diverse urban communities, and young people.[24] Projects focused on strengthening local democracy; developing conditions for youth involvement and participation; democratic initiatives based on information technology; innovations in citizen education; and new forums for dialogue between politicians and citizens. Money was also allocated to voluntary organizations promoting political participation, and for the staging of seminars and other events on the theme. The program funded the publication and distribution of the voters' magazine *Röster* ("Votes"), which, according to those responsible for its distribution, was used quite widely by teachers of social studies and civic education.

Extra resources were made available to political parties to provide information to underrepresented groups—including young people, immigrants,[25] people with low incomes and education, senior citizens, and people with disabilities—and to recruit them to run for office, especially at the local level, with funds to give them with the needed training. "Ambassadors" were appointed and trained to act as information officers among immigrant groups. Some consideration was given to opening the vote to sixteen-year-olds—an initiative taken in at least one municipality, Eskiltuna, in the greater Stockholm region. The program also established citizens' initiatives, through which residents (including adolescents and noncitizens) could bring issues to the municipal assembly.[26]

The latest phase of the program, called Participating Sweden, was launched in February 2006. Its main thrust was to evaluate and build upon existing programs and experiences. New funding was focused on five municipalities to further develop and test different methods of fostering the involvement of the low participation groups, not only during but between elections. In addition, twelve communities (all with low turnout in the most recent election) were given grants to work with local nongovernmental organizations (NGOs) to raise awareness about upcoming elections and Sweden's political institutions.

Parallel to this, Sweden began another program, Democracy in the New Century, in 2004. This program provided for the creation of a new, single-purpose agency to run elections, which makes information about the voting process available on its website in a number of foreign languages. Related changes included simplifying the processes of voting at polling stations, and of postal voting for voters residing abroad as well as those in Sweden. In the next part of the book, we will return to Scandinavian initiatives related to civic education, including mock elections (known in Sweden as *skolval*) and youth parliaments, an area in which all the Nordic countries, especially Norway, saw quite interesting developments. Initiatives similar to those in Sweden took place in Norway and Finland, and a smaller number of them occurred in Denmark, where the focus has been on enhancing citizen influence through a 2007 structural reform of municipalities. One interesting recent Danish initiative has been to post draft parliamentary bills online in user-friendly format, for citizen input.

Like Sweden, Finland and Norway have targeted groups with particularly low levels of participation. Finland's stress has been on improving bureaucratic responsiveness through the use of electronic feedback systems in, for example, the Ministry of Justice. The Ministry of the Interior has been mandated to strengthen local democracy, to develop mechanisms to counter the trend toward declining citizen involvement through what is called a Municipal Democracy Audit. One interesting aspect touches on citizenship education, in the form of exchange visits by teachers and local officials or elected politicians, so that each side can learn from the other through hands-on experience.

Comparing these countries with Canada is complicated because of Canada's federal system, which inhibits the coordination of central, regional, and local initiatives (see Milner 2009b). This rules out, for example, following the Scandinavian approach, which stresses involvement in local politics. Nordic decentralized unitary institutions facilitate the local carrying out of activities in accordance with guidelines set centrally. To have any kind of full overview of comparable developments in Canada, we need to look separately at institutions at the federal, provincial, and local levels. Hence, in closing this chapter on parallel developments in Canada, we limit ourselves to briefly setting out measures to address the decline in youth voting that have been undertaken by, or in coordination with, Elections Canada, the independent body that administers federal elections.

In response to the strikingly low turnout in 2000, Elections Canada made reaching young people a priority,[27] beginning with efforts to get those turning eighteen onto the voters' rolls. The main initiatives include mock elections, special events, contests, and games (such as crossword puzzles containing democratic words such as "vote," "assembly" and "elections," and an online trivia quiz in which players answer questions about Parliament and elections). One contest asked students to create public service announcements telling their peers why democracy is important, and why it is important to vote. Another contest, in partnership with four student associations,[28] involved the production of posters for display on campuses across Canada during the 2004 election.

Elections Canada supported the running and publicizing of mock federal elections in the schools (discussed in chapter 10). It also contributed to a youth voter education kit as part of Youth Vote 2004 and 2006, an education and media initiative launched by the Dominion Institute.

Along with the latter and other public and private donors, Elections Canada supported a series of surveys, carried out by Innovative Research, on issues related to youth political participation, as well as facilitating sixty-three debates including all the candidates and held at high schools and colleges. Elections Canada also funded musical events organized by Rush the Vote,[29] at which performers in Ottawa, Toronto, and Edmonton encouraged voting and democratic involvement, and worked with the Historica Foundation to develop a new YouthLinks education module on citizenship and voting, entitled "Voices."[30]

Access to and information about these and other such efforts are on Elections Canada's website (http://www.elections.ca/home.asp), which provides relevant information to young people and their teachers in an accessible format. It provides links to basic information about elections, members of Parliament, and candidates, and to learning resources in the following categories: general—reports and publications, as well as facts and figures about elections; resources for students— information on organizing elections in schools; and resources for teachers—information on how to make learning about elections enjoyable, broken down by the targeted age group. The final section of the website, titled "Get Involved," has links to basic information about voting and the electoral system, and about how to become a candidate and start a political career. The site also provides links to various youth-related and other organizations and lists relevant events and games. The interested reader might want to consult the Elections Canada website before turning to the following chapters, on civic education.

EDUCATING TOMORROW'S CITIZENS

9

Civic Education outside the Classroom

It is time to focus on the institution whose mission is to impart knowledge. Chapter 2 pointed out that recent developments have placed a mounting burden of political socialization on the public school. But its exploration of the school as agent of socialization stopped at the school door. In this final part of the book, we go inside, into those aspects of education that influence informed political participation. In chapter 10 we enter the civics class, exploring how it can carry out its civic education mission, giving substance to guidelines drawn earlier in the book for fostering habits of attentiveness to public affairs that match the world of information and communication of the emerging generations, with potential political dropouts as prime targets. In this chapter, we set the stage for that discussion by placing the civic education classroom in the wider educational and community context.

In my earlier work on civic literacy (Milner 2002a), a full chapter dealt with education. The emphasis was on adult or lifelong education, on the premise that when it comes to civic literacy, what is learned as an adult is more important than what is acquired in one's youth. Correspondingly, when the chapter did address the education of young people, it stressed the development of a literacy habit during the period of compulsory schooling. Data assembled in the chapter pointed to the correlation between countries' scores (especially for students at the lower percentiles) on tests of citizens' knowledge, such as the Trends in International Mathematics and Science Study (TIMSS) tests of sixteen-year-old students in mathematics and science, and the level of functional literacy among adults. It was clear that school systems of the countries high in civic literacy were better at encouraging a larger proportion of students to read newspapers and books, use libraries and maps, write letters, etc., habits they retained into adulthood. Moreover, the acquisition of such habits seemed to be distinct from the content of civics courses, the long-term effects of which were unclear. Given the uncertainty about whether information acquired in these courses was retained into adulthood, civic education, though encouraged, was not given top priority among the recommended policy measures.

There is still obvious truth in these observations. We do not know enough about the long-term effects of civic education, but we can be certain of the benefits of inculcating habits of literacy throughout the curriculum.[1] Nevertheless, the urgency of the situation with regard to political dropouts obliges us in this last part of the current book to return to the school and the place of civic education in it.

The fact that better-educated citizens are more likely to be informed and participate politically is confirmed in a wide range of research literature. This suggests that one effective approach to boosting informed political participation would be to raise the level and length of schooling. The problem is that while the average number of years of education has increased, political knowledge apparently has declined. Clearly, the causal relationship at the individual level is a complex one. Does more schooling make better citizens, or is it just selection bias—that is, the more resource-rich and motivated students stay in school?

Some studies are encouraging. Milligan, Moretti, and Oreopoulos (2003) show that extra years of schooling mandated by compulsory schooling laws increase the likelihood of becoming politically involved and thus have a strong effect on voter turnout. Another study that investigated the relationship suggests that something more than selection bias is at work, finding the potential for educational attainment, in the form of the degree of availability of two-year colleges in given geographical regions, to correlate positively with differences in civic-related attitudes and reported behavior in those regions (Dee 2004).

But what is taking place in these colleges that promotes informed political participation? Controlling for characteristics associated with self-selection, Nie and Hillygus (2001) show that college students majoring in the social sciences and humanities are more likely to vote and discuss politics, as well as to participate in community service and politics upon leaving college, a finding extended to longer-term political engagement by Hillygus (2005). She concludes that a curriculum that develops language and civic skills contributes to democratic participation more than any other aspect of education.

There is thus good reason to believe that the school, in both fostering habits of literacy and teaching civic skills, contributes to informed political participation. However, since postsecondary social science and humanities education for all is not attainable, or indeed desirable, we are brought back to where we left off in chapter 8, the age group targeted by a reduction in the voting age, whose members are in the latter years of compulsory schooling. If our prime targets are the potential political dropouts, we cannot rely on fostering civic skills in college. The challenge is to apply the lessons learned from education at higher levels to developing and putting into place a system targeted at young people nearing the end of their compulsory secondary education.

This chapter begins by summarizing the contributions of recent, cross-national research touching upon civic education. We then focus on what might be termed the external dimension: the activities outside of school that various jurisdictions have tied to the provision of civic education. This sets the stage for our exploration in the next chapter of different approaches to teaching civics in the school.

Some Recent Findings

A good place to start our search for a comprehensive comparative study of civic education is an Australian report (Civics Expert Group 1994). In setting out its research program, which was quite innovative for the time, the Australian Commission on Civics and Citizenship commissioned a survey of international best practices in civics education to guide its deliberations. The survey results proved disappointingly meager. Ultimately, the report could do no better than describe what it saw as the three alternate approaches to civic education, approaches it associated respectively with the United States, Britain, and France, noting that recognized instruments for comparing the three on the basis of their results simply did not exist.

Writing in 2000 about what was known at that time about the provision and effects of civic education for young people, I drew attention to the then-ongoing twenty-eight-country comprehensive Civic Education Study of the International Association for the Evaluation of Educational Achievement (IEA). I expressed the hope that once the study was completed, it would significantly add to our knowledge of the effects of courses intended to raise the level of political knowledge of adolescents.

The completed first phase of the IEA study had assembled case studies from twenty countries, based on research into what the country experts agreed that a fourteen-year-old civic education student should know. In addition, researchers from several of the participating countries carried out qualitative case studies, in the hope that the resulting observations could be used to develop an information-gathering instrument to assess students' civic knowledge, civic attitudes, and levels of civic engagement in the study's second phase. In their report, the researchers emphasized the precarious position of civics in the schools, as well as the absence of adequate training for teachers of civic education (see Torney-Purta et al, 1999).

The results of the second phase of the IEA study (see Torney-Purta, Lehmann, Oswald, and Schulz 2001) emerged in a series of publications in the first few years of this century. The sample was large, composed of 90,000 fourteen-year-old students in twenty-eight countries, and 50,000 seventeen- to nineteen-year-olds in sixteen countries). The study sought to understand how young people learn about civic responsibilities, and how they become involved in political communities, both in and beyond the school. A great deal of useful information was provided, identifying differences among students, teachers, and schools over such matters as learning explicitly about voting and elections, openness of classroom climate, and the role and participation of the student council. The study's usefulness was diminished, however, by the failure of its efforts to produce an appropriate dependent variable, an indicator of outcomes to which differences in these matters could be linked.

The dependent variables used consisted of questions that surveyed the students' future intentions to be an informed voter (discussed in chapter 4), their expectations of community participation, and—most important, at least for this observer—a test of what was termed civic knowledge, which promised rich data about the political knowledge of young people in a large number of countries. There were thirty-eight questions in IEA's civic knowledge questionnaire—the specific contents of which the IEA jealously guarded. At least some of the questions, observers like myself assumed, would allow for a cross-national comparison of youth political knowledge. Unfortunately, this turned out not to be the case. The first indication of this problem was in the report's ranking of countries by average civic knowledge score, rankings that failed to correspond to the findings of other political knowledge studies, such as those reported in chapter 5. It soon became apparent why this was the case.

Presumably to gain approval of the national representatives, questions were eliminated that might appear to place a given country at a disadvantage—i.e., the factual questions. What remained in the end were items measuring the students' familiarity with democratic concepts, and skills in interpreting political communication. Rather than testing factual knowledge, the questionnaire tested vocabulary, logic, and appreciation of democratic principles.[2]

This left as the dependent variable the extent to which the students responded positively to the questions that surveyed their intentions to be attentive voters and expectations of community participation. We have, however, already noted the limitations of using a fourteen-year-old's expressed intentions as a predictor of future behavior, rather than as an indicator of the social desirability of a given attitude. Since socially desirable aspirations are culturally based, using rates of intention to vote for cross-national comparisons is problematic.

Thus, in the end, despite the large samples and number of countries involved, the study proved more valuable for comparing individuals than countries on the relationship between what went on in the schools and student attitudes toward political participation. The key finding in this regard is that intended informed political participation correlates most significantly with the degree to which students believe that they and the groups they join can make a difference in what happens at school. This relationship is stronger than simple membership in a governance organization like student council, or taking a civic education course, though these do contribute (Torney-Purta and Barber 2004).

For our purposes, then, the IEA study's main contribution is to direct us toward further investigating, and comparing, what happens in the school, both in the classroom and beyond it, but to do so in a manner that allows us to link school activities not only to students' attitudes toward future citizen responsibilities, but also to their factual political knowledge.

This challenge was taken up in a small way in the author's comparative study of young Canadians and Americans (Milner 2007, described in chapter 5), which used factual political knowledge as the dependent variable, and which also posed two questions that correspond to those of the IEA about what happens in the school. One asked whether the

TABLE 9.1

Relationship between civic education in class and political knowledge in
Americans and Canadians aged 15–25

		POLITICAL KNOWLEDGE (SUM OF 7 ANSWERS)
Do any of your classes require you to keep up with politics or government, either by reading the newspaper, watching the news or using the Internet?	r (Pearson correlation)	0.092*
	sig. (statistical significance)	0.002
	N (number of respondents)	1,184
In classes that deal with history, government, social studies, or related subjects, how often do teachers encourage students to discuss political and social topics with people of different opinions?	r	0.162*
	sig.	0.000
	N	1,232

*Correlation is significant at the 0.01 level.

students' classes required them to keep up with politics or government,
whether by reading the newspaper, watching television, or using the Internet. Table 9.1 shows a positive relationship between such a reported
requirement and political knowledge among young North Americans,
and an even stronger one when the question becomes one not of requirements but of reported classroom behavior by teachers,[3] a finding
corresponding to that in the literature discussed in the latter part of this
chapter.

This latter finding is not unexpected. Campbell (2006) argues, based
on his findings, that the degree to which political and social issues are
discussed has a greater impact on civic proficiency than the mere fre-

quency of social studies classes.[4] As noted earlier, Andolina, Keeter, Zukin, and Jenkins (2002) find that students who participate in open discussions in class and who learn to communicate their opinions through letter writing and debate are much more politically active than those who do not have these experiences. And a North Carolina study finds that "young people who reported having to stay current on political events showed higher levels of political knowledge . . . and interest in voting" (Henzey 2003: 32).

A Natural Experiment about Civic Education

In the students' responses to the first question in table 9.1, about whether any of their classes require them to keep up with politics or government through the media, there is a clear contrast between the responses of the Francophone and Anglophone Canadian students, with 66 percent of the former, but only 46 percent of the latter, answering yes. This reflects the greater politicization of the Quebec school environment (noted in chapter 5), but it is nonetheless surprising in light of the fact that, unlike Ontario, Quebec has no compulsory civic education course. Indeed, Ontario's civic education requirement, the only one of its kind in Canada, makes Ontario a suitable candidate for a comparative case study for an investigation of the effects of compulsory civic education.

While a comprehensive study of this kind has yet to be carried out, a set of data from Elections Canada made available to me casts light on the relationship between this requirement and electoral participation in the form of a natural experiment, using turnout data for recent Canadian federal elections. As noted in chapter 4, for the 2004 and 2006 elections, Elections Canada created a very large sample of eligible voters so as to be able to estimate turnout by age group. Based on the results of the study, it reported that while overall turnout increased by 4.4 percentage points in 2006, the estimated increase for those aged eighteen to twenty-four was 6.8 percentage points, from 37.0 percent in 2004 to 43.8 percent in 2006.

While in Canada, as opposed to the United Kingdom, the law does not permit recording who in fact votes, the methodology used by Elections Canada permitted a close estimate. It used a sample of people previously registered who voted at the polls on Election Day[5] plus almost three million people who either registered at the polls and voted on Election Day,

TABLE 9.2

Youth turnout in the 2006 Canadian general election

	AGE GROUP	CANADA	ONTARIO	ROC*
Born between January 1, 1985, and January 23, 1988	18–20.1	40.8 (±2.6)	41.8 (±4.3)	40.2 (±3.4)
Born between January 1, 1981, and December 31, 1984	20.1–25.1	42.5 (±4.2)	46.8 (±8.9)	40.0 (±4.2)

*ROC = rest of Canada, outside Ontario.

voted at advance polls, or voted by special ballot—i.e., away from their polling place.

One already noted anomaly was the major shift that had occurred among those under twenty-five who had been eligible to vote in the previous election: their turnout rate jumped a hefty 9.9 percentage points. It was suggested that this number was too high, possibly reflecting the overrepresentation of university students in the sample. Nevertheless, such overrepresentation, being consistent across the country, should not affect our experiment, which contrasts youth turnout in Ontario, where more than one-third of Canadians reside, with that in the rest of the country.

The experiment tests the possible effects of civic education on youth turnout. In recent years, most provincial education systems have seen changes in the approach to civic education, with more emphasis on volunteerism and community values. But only Ontario, the province with one of the lowest levels of reported federal election youth turnout (Milan 2005), instituted a required civics course for all high-school students. Ontario took this initiative in 1999, as part of an updated high-school curriculum. The fifty-five-hour course, "Profile for Civics," is given over six weeks in the tenth grade.[6]

Thus, among the eighteen- to twenty-four year-olds eligible to vote in both 2004 and 2006, there were young Ontarians who had taken this course, and others who had not, identifiable by their birth dates. Moreover, since no other province instituted compulsory courses during that

TABLE 9.3

Youth turnout in the 2004 Canadian general election

	AGE GROUP	CANADA	ONTARIO	ROC*
Born between January 1, 1985, and June 28, 1986	18–19.5	37.5 (±3.4)	38.2 (±7.9)	37.1 (±2.5.)
Born between January 1, 1983, and December 31, 1984	19.5–21.5	36.1 (±3.1)	38.8 (±6.8)	34.5 (±2.9)

*ROC = rest of Canada, outside Ontario.

time, the level of turnout in 2004 and 2006 of Ontario young people who had been required to take the course and those who were too old to have done so can be compared with the same age groups in the other provinces, the latter serving as a control group for this natural experiment. The results of the experiment for each election are presented in tables 9.2 and 9.3. The cutoff ages for the 2004 and 2006 elections provide two categories (for Canada as a whole, Ontario, and the rest of the country): young people who would normally have reached tenth grade before the compulsory civics course was introduced in Ontario (the bottom rows of the tables), and those who reached tenth grade earlier (the top rows; the upper cutoff age for this category was chosen to give a roughly equal sample of the two groups). The numbers are thus greater in 2006, since more students who had taken the course were now at voting age.

If there is a positive relationship between civic education and voting, it is not found in the tables. Indeed, the numbers point in the opposite direction. In 2004, the subgroup of Ontarians at an age to have taken the course turned out at the same level (38.2 percent) as those older who did not (38.8), while there was an improvement for the corresponding age groups in the rest of Canada, from 34.5 percent to 37.1 percent. Such a small difference may be dismissed as merely statistical, except that it grew significantly in 2006: those young Ontarians of an age to have taken the course had a much lower turnout (41.8 percent) than those who were not (46.8), while this time there was no difference between the corresponding age groups in the rest of Canada (40.2 and 40.0 percent). Given the confidence limits (in parentheses) for the data,[7] it is still possible that the difference is only in the samples and not among the overall population. It does suggest, however, that if there is a relationship, it is a perverse one.[8]

Is it possible that developments were taking place in this period in Ontario during this period that may account for this result? We have noted that the elections in those years were far more competitive than those in 2000 and before. Since Ontario is the major battleground in Canadian competitive elections, it is possible that this effect was more salient than elsewhere in the country. In 2006, the older Ontario group would have been eligible to vote in two competitive elections, whereas most of the younger group would have been eligible for only one. Therefore, Franklin's theory would suggest that this might have something to do with the unexpected higher turnout among the older group in Ontario.

Nevertheless, we are left with the plain fact of the failure of compulsory civic education to boost turnout, the low level of which had prompted its introduction. Part of the explanation must lie in the course itself, and the context in which it was introduced. One element of the context was a complementary new curricular requirement. Along with the civic education course, the 1999 Ontario regulations required that students complete forty hours of community service before graduation from high school.[9] While such activity is encouraged in other provinces, I am not aware of its being compulsory outside Ontario, though it is common in American states (see below).

Henderson, Brown, Pancer, and Ellis-Hale (2007) surveyed Ontario college students about taking part in volunteering, community service, and other forms of civic and political engagement. Using a quasi-experimental design, they surveyed 1,768 first-year Ontario college students who had completed high school in 2003. Because the government, at the same time, had shortened the high-school curriculum from five to four years, the 2003 high-school graduating class contained two cohorts, only one of which was required to complete a mandated community service requirement (as well as take the civics course). The authors were thus able to compare two groups of students who had very similar backgrounds, but who differed in whether or not they had been required to perform the community service to obtain their high-school diploma. To the authors' surprise, they found "no differences in current attitudes and reported civic engagement that might plausibly be attributed to participation in the mandatory service program" (849). They were surprised further to find that the civics course, which was compulsory for the same cohort, had an apparently negative effect on reported interest in politics and consumption of political media content. The authors' only explanation was that the age groups are "on opposite sides of a critical political responsibility cusp (18 years) in our society," given the average age difference of a year and a half between the two sample groups—an explanation partially confirmed by the fact that when the authors controlled for age, the effect on political media consumption "fades to statistical nonsignificance" (857).

However, unless this age effect is more salient in Ontario than elsewhere in Canada, the puzzle remains unresolved. Henderson, Brown, Pancer, and Ellis-Hale (2007) found greater political interest among subjects who described themselves as having engaged in service than those who did not, a relationship quite opposite to that when the engagement resulted from being required to perform service in high school, leading the authors to suggest, based on the literature (see below), that the explanation may lie in the mandatory nature of the so-called volunteering program.

To understand the possible effect of the mandatory nature of the requirements, especially of the civics course, we need to distinguish perception from reality. Something that is mandatory but, to your knowledge, that has always been so, is very different from something imposed on you and not your peers. This is exactly what distinguished the two groups in the experiment on the effects of the community service requirement—and with regard to the civics course requirement. Ontario teenagers entering tenth grade in 2000 found themselves unexpectedly saddled with two obligations that their older peers and siblings had managed to avoid, a civics course and forty hours of volunteering.[10]

As the civics course has become a normal component of the curriculum, one assumes that students are less negative about it, and so are the schools, which appear to have been generally less than happy about the new requirements when they were introduced. The provincial government imposed the new curriculum (which was revised only a few years later) with little fanfare or support. It is fair to say that, overall, there was little concerted effort on the part of education administrators and teachers at the various levels to successfully implement the new program.

One reflection of the low priority of the course for many school boards (notably the large ones of Toronto and Ottawa) was their refusal to even allow the civics teachers to be interviewed for a research study (Lewis 2009). Though thus unrepresentative, the results of the interviews in areas where the school board permitted them do shed some light on these findings.[11] The teachers generally complained that the course was too short and expressed dissatisfaction with the curriculum and text-books. They consistently noted that the students came to the course unacquainted with current events and lacking any desire to participate politically. Thus the students, naturally enough, found "The Canadian Context"—the largest unit in the curriculum—boring. This impression was confirmed by Goodyear-Grant and Anderson (2008), who asked a self-selected—and hence more likely to be positive about civic education—group of Ontario high-school students if they enjoyed learning about politics in school. A clear majority responded negatively.

Moreover, Lewis (2009) finds clear inconsistency in the content of the courses, even within the same schools—especially in the importance given to institutions. Such flexibility can be constructive, but only in the hands of trained and experienced teachers. Anecdotal evidence suggests that this was seldom the case: school principals tended to treat civics as a dumping ground for teachers who were inexperienced or even un-trained in social studies or history. Thus, not only did the students feel unfairly burdened by a new requirement, but the school environment reinforced the sense that the new course was unwelcome.

In sum, there is good reason not to be surprised by the results; rather, it would be surprising if the course had boosted political participation. If it is understandable, given the depoliticized environment of young Ontarians, why the government should have taken this sort of action, it is also understandable why it may have backfired. Now, a decade after the course's introduction, given that its initial negative effects are no longer a factor, there is an opportunity to rethink the content and ap-proach, as well as the selection and training of the instructors, subjects approached in comparative perspective in chapter 10.

One focus of that analysis will be on Sweden and Norway, which have emphasized improving civic education in recent years. A study of the effects of Swedish reforms suggests that they may have encountered problems analogous to those in Ontario. In Sweden, civics courses de-signed to teach students about politics and develop their civic compe-tence are compulsory in the final years of secondary school and in upper secondary school. Past research with upper secondary students found that the civics courses have a positive effect on political knowledge.[12] All students had been required to study civics for a minimum of 90 hours (out of 2,150 hours of teaching time), with the students in theoretical (precollege) social science programs required to study it for 300 hours. This changed with a reform implemented in the latter 1990s. One aspect of the government's push toward equalization in education—the slogan was to create a "school for everyone"—was to reduce the disparity in civic education by raising the minimum number of hours required.

Persson and Oscarsson took advantage of this change to conduct a "before and after" experiment, testing if implementation of the reform reduced the differences in reported political participation, political knowledge, political attentiveness, and trust between students in vocational and theoretical programs. Indeed, their findings show that, on a number of indicators, the gaps between citizens who were in vocational and theoretical programs are decreasing—which, the authors note, "could at first glance seem to support the absolute education effects model" (2008, 17). However, the decrease turns out to be mainly a consequence of lower scores among students from theoretical programs after the reform, which is hardly what the reform's designers had in mind.

For Persson and Oscarsson, these results clash with conventional wisdom that more civic education leads to improvement in the various dimensions of democratic citizenship. This would be true if young people arrived at secondary school with a static level of political interest and civic competence. But there is no reason to assume that the general decline in political knowledge spared Sweden. So neither we nor the authors should be surprised by the decline in the scores of the precollege students. Indeed, it is reasonable to surmise that the vocational students' scores would also have declined, had there been no increase in their number of hours of civic education.

If, as the study reveals, Sweden—just like Canada, though much higher in civic literacy—is facing a decline in the political knowledge of emerging generations, the lesson is not that civic education should be abandoned. Quite the opposite: it becomes more urgent to get civic education right.

Civics in the Community

As we noted, in addition to introducing a compulsory civic education course, Ontario also added the requirement of forty hours of so-called volunteer community service. Here the inspiration was clearly from south of the border, where the activity is often called "service learning." According to the Education Commission of the States, service learning "involves learning and intellectual skills, performing needed service and producing real results that command respect. Service-learning provides students with the skills and virtues that enable them to participate fully in a civil society and contribute to the sustainability of our democracy."[13] As already indicated, even when they do not require it, U.S. high schools and colleges frequently impose powerful institutional incentives for such service. According to the commission, twenty-four laws related to service learning were adopted by U.S. states between 2000 and 2008.[14]

In approaching this topic, we need to emphasize the methodological caveat raised at the outset concerning surveys about such activities and interests. Studies showing a causal relationship between reported community service and positive attitudes toward political participation and civic engagement should invite skepticism, given that students are motivated to answer both types of question positively for the same reason. As argued in chapter 1, we consequently need to be wary of extending the meaning of political participation to include community service.

This is not meant as an objection to sending students out into the community, as there are certainly benefits to be had, for example, in greater acceptance of diversity, or in breaking down class and racial barriers.[15] Indeed, much of the ample literature about cases of youth civic engagement in the community is concerned with this "human rights" or "intercultural" dimension.[16] Our concern here is with the claims associating service learning with civic engagement, and thus, implicitly at least, to informed political participation. The question that needs to be posed, but often is not, is an empirical one: does student participation in community service activities, especially when such activities are compulsory, lead to greater political knowledge and higher levels of participation in elections and in other forms of political participation? The question cannot be posed, however, if the definition of political participation is expanded to incorporate such experiences and positive attitudes toward them.

In studies testing the relationship between community service and informed political participation using methodologies that eschew self-fulfilling prophesies, the findings—like those of Henderson, Brown, Pancer, and Ellis-Hale (2007)—leave one skeptical. A brief review of this literature suggests that, as in the case of civics teaching, context matters.

TABLE 9.4

Relationship between volunteering and political knowledge in
Americans and Canadians aged 15–25

Have you ever spent time participating in any community service or volunteer activity,
or haven't you had time to do so?

COUNTRY		POLITICAL KNOWLEDGE (SUM OF 7 ANSWERS)
United States	r (Pearson correlation)	0.205**
	sig. (statistical significance)	0.000
	N (number of respondents)	1,129
Canada	r	0.074*
	sig.	0.031
	N	853

*Correlation is significant at the 0.01 level.

**Correlation is significant at the 0.05 level.

Consider the comparative study of the United States and Canada cited earlier (Milner 2007): like other such studies in the United States, the American version of the questionnaire (see Lopez et al. 2006) posed a large number of questions about involvement in voluntary associations of various kinds. The most general question is shown in table 9.4, which demonstrates that the effect of positive responses to these questions on youth political knowledge is significant, especially for u.s. students (see Milner 2007).[17]

This is not to suggest that young Americans are made into better citizens via such activities, while Canadians are not, but rather that context matters. It is those u.s. students who are most likely to be politically knowledgeable that are most affected by the incentives to engage in such activities, and thus respond in surveys that they have done so

With regard to the effects of the activities themselves, opinion is divided among u.s. observers as to whether community service is complementary to informed political participation. One study finds that service experiences failed to change "the students' assessments of the value of elections [and] definitions of what civic responsibility is and should be" (Hunter and Brisbin 2000, 625).

Those who see a problem lay the blame on an approach that downplays politics in both community service and civic education. According to Westheimer and Kahne (2004), too many civic education programs in the United States embrace a model of citizenship that fosters a commitment to service as a substitute for participation in democratic deliberation and decision-making. As Westheimer writes in a later article:

> My colleague Joseph Kahne and I spent the better part of a decade studying programs that aimed to develop good citizenship skills among youth and young adults. In study after study, we come to similar conclusions: the kinds of goals and practices commonly represented in curricula that hope to foster democratic citizenship usually have more to do with voluntarism, charity, and obedience than with democracy. In other words "good citizenship" to many educators means listening to authority figures, dressing neatly, being nice to neighbors, and helping out at a soup kitchen—not grappling with the kinds of social policy decisions that every citizen in a democratic society needs to learn how to do. (2006, 5–6)[18]

Similarly, a study of college students[19] finds that they "received much more encouragement and opportunities to get involved in service, but hardly any into politics . . . While there are ample and readily accessible opportunities for community service . . . they do not know how to find out who their assemblyman was, or how to get involved in a campaign, or even how to register to vote . . . Schools feared being charged with being partisan" (Beem 2005, 10). And, clearly, fears of being labeled partisan were not unfounded. The Corporation for National Service, a major funder of service learning, explained its refusal to allow participants in the youth service program Americorps to attend the "Stand for Children" rally in Washington, D.C., by asserting that "National Service has to be non-partisan . . . it should be about bringing communities together by getting things done.[20] Strikes, demonstrations and *political activities* [my emphasis] can have the opposite effect . . . [they] divide and polarize."[21]

Conversely, it appears that more-positive outcomes tend to result when the political dimension is explicitly included. Stroupe and Sabato (2004) compare the results of civics classes that used the National Youth Leadership Initiative[22] curriculum, which explicitly links service learning to knowledge of partisan politics, with a control group of similar classes that did not use the curriculum. The study found that the initiative's programs have substantial, positive effects on students' levels of political knowledge and, to a lesser degree, on their likelihood of future political participation.

While the above provides only a taste of the literature, it makes the point: where community service has a political dimension, it has a greater potential of contributing to informed political participation. In sum, the key distinction is not between volunteering and classroom political discussion, but between an environment surrounding the civic education class that welcomes, and one that discourages, partisan political discussion and involvement.

With this in mind, we return to the findings from the U.S.-Canada comparative study that differentiate the Francophone and Anglophone Canadians. In chapter 5, we noted that the average political knowledge score of the 289 young French-speakers, all from Quebec, was higher than that of the English speakers in the rest of Canada and the average U.S. score, suggesting that this has something to do with the Francophones' being in an educational environment that encourages them to follow news in the media. In this chapter, we drew a link between requirements that students keep up with politics or government through the media and political knowledge. While the effect on political knowledge is similar for the Francophone and Anglophone Canadian students, as noted in chapter 5, more of the former (66 percent) reported such a requirement than the latter (46 percent).

The other side of the coin emerges in table 9.5, where we break down by language the effect of participating in community service or a volunteer activity on political knowledge set out in table 9.4. We can see that, unlike for their counterparts in the rest of Canada, for the young Francophones, there is no statistically meaningful relationship between political knowledge and participating in community service or a volunteer activity. The coefficient for young English-speaking Canadians is also just below statistical significance, due to the lower numbers than in table 9.4. The difference between the two groups emerges most clearly when we include those twenty-six and older—for whom, as we can see, even in spite of the low numbers, such service has a strong effect on the political knowledge of Anglophones but virtually none on that of Francophones. The combination of these factors explains the difference in responses to the question surveying political attentiveness among the young Canadians: when asked the extent to which they follow what is going on in politics, 8 percent more of the Quebeckers respond "most of the time."[23]

The numbers in figure 9.1 correspond to the findings (noted in chapter 6) of a study suggesting that young Quebeckers are more likely than

TABLE 9.5

Relationship between volunteering and political knowledge among
Anglophone and Francophone Canadians

Have you ever spent time participating in any community service or volunteer activity,
or haven't you had time to do so?

LANGUAGE	AGE		POLITICAL KNOWLEDGE (SUM OF 7 ANSWERS)
English	15–25	r	0.079
		sig.	0.058
		N	586
	26+	r	0.21*
		sig.	0.000
		N	300
French	15–25	r	0.087
		sig.	0.158
		N	267
	26+	r	0.040
		sig.	0.651
		N	133

* Correlation is significant at the 0.01 level.

other young Canadians to engage in political rather than civic activities.
Altogether, these and other studies suggest that young Quebeckers find
themselves in an educational and media environment more conducive
to attentiveness to traditional political processes—such as elections, political parties, and government policies—than the environment of their
peers in English-speaking North America, which places greater stress
on civic engagement via voluntary, nonpartisan activities and organizations unconnected to government policies.[24] In this, it would appear
that Quebec is closer to Europe, where, generally speaking, there is less
emphasis on community volunteering than in the United States, and
where partisan politics is less in contradiction with civic engagement.
A compilation based on the International IDEA civic education database
(see chapter 10), using data from civic education experts mainly from
Europe, shows that while 82 percent of participants rated classroom instruction as important in their countries, only 28 percent accorded equal
importance to out-of-class, community-based activities.

We are thus reminded that context matters, whether in the content of a civics course or in participation in community service. From the point of view of informed political participation, a civic education program that places great emphasis on service learning, even if appropriate in the context of U.S. institutional arrangements, may not be effective elsewhere. Canada may very well be an example of such a poor fit:

> Models of citizenship are surprisingly devoid of government and politics. The role of discussion and debate, of political parties, of protest and demonstration, and of political ideologies do not appear to form a central component of citizenship ... They do little to reinforce the difficulty of attempting to reach decisions within the reality of competing interests, values and demands. Citizenship ought to include simple elements such as joining a party, attending debates, contacting officials and reading the newspaper. But it ought also to include running for office ... Citizenship ought to include an understanding that while politics might be "messy," its avoidance is impossible. (O'Neill 2009, 18).

Applying what we have learned in this chapter to Ontario's decision to emulate U.S. practices, a trend that other Canadian provinces appear to be following,[25] we arrive, tentatively, at a guideline for the discussion to follow. We should not eschew civics courses, as Quebec has done. Despite a context more conducive to political discussion, Quebec too has seen a significant drop in turnout in recent provincial as well as federal elections.[26] Nor should we limit civic education to the classroom. Instead, our guideline tells us that in designing an external complement to in-class civic education, we need to find ways to give expression to and incorporate the political dimension.

How to do this is the subject of the next chapter, in which we try to identify what seems to be effective cross-nationally, beginning with activities in the school but looking outside the classroom as well. We then turn to civics courses per se. We bring to bear our concern with making the environment of young people rich in political information, targeting those lacking access to such information on their own. And without excluding the role of voluntary, civil-society organizations, our approach emphasizes complementarity with national and local government programs in education, media support, political party financing, information dissemination, and the like.

10

The Challenge of Civic Education in the Internet Age

have argued from the start that we face a serious challenge in the phenomenon of political dropouts, and that any effective response to that challenge must address the upcoming generations' political knowledge and attentiveness. As a result, civic education lies at the core of any solution. As the Ontario experience dramatically illustrates, however, that does not mean that merely requiring students to take a civic education course or to perform community service will have the desired effect. Moreover, the literature does not allow us to identify a clear path to effective civic education or, indeed, to systematically evaluate what is available. Nevertheless, while some remain skeptical (e.g., McDevitt and Chaffee 2000), most studies—including some mentioned below—suggest that civic education can increase political knowledge and close knowledge gaps between advantaged and disadvantaged groups.[1] On the other hand while there is a connection between learning about politics in school and expressing the intention to vote as an adult, there is a dearth of evidence that this intention is actually carried out (see, e.g., J. Phillips 2004).

If merely boosting turnout were our objective, we would ignore civic education in favor of compulsory voting. But our ultimate objective is informed political participation. As indicated at the outset, enhancing political attentiveness is crucial in itself, whether or not it translates into higher turnout. Moreover, even if we cannot yet empirically demonstrate this convincingly, we have good reason to expect that it will indeed have that effect.

The challenge is thus to optimize the potential of civic education to boost informed political participation. The starting point of such an approach is never to lose sight of the needs of those who can most benefit from it: young people from backgrounds weak in the resources conducive to informed political participation. The courses should be given when they are still at school, as close as possible to voting age, the emphasis should be less on increasing political knowledge per se than on fostering the long-term habit of attentiveness to public affairs. A key dimension lies in integrating the course content with the communications networks that link members of the Internet generation, so as to break down the barriers between the political world and the world of the young adult.

Meeting this challenge requires more than a verbal commitment on the part of the relevant authorities. Generally speaking, there has been some progress. Civic education no longer tends to be associated with the old conformist, good-citizen approach. We have seen a reversal in the decline in courses related to civic education, which renders some-what inaccurate this description from the beginning of the decade of "social studies [as] a low status area of the school curriculum [in which] politics . . . receives attention for only a small part of the few school hours reserved for the subject [by] teachers [who often] . . . have limited political knowledge" (Dekker and Portengen 2000, 467).

There are signs of such attitudes giving way to a renewed interest in civic education, prompted by the growing deficit in youth political par-ticipation. While government agencies have taken the lead elsewhere, in the United States it was the private sector—for example, the Center for Civic Education (see below)—that has been at the forefront of efforts to promote civic education. But these efforts can be less than welcome in the schools. In trying to prepare young people for a rapidly changing world, especially in light of the economic tsunami that hit at the end of 2008, schools must juggle a set of mounting expectations. Hence, while the demand for civic education in the schools has been growing, we cannot say the same for the schools' capacity to supply it. To paraphrase a recent comprehensive report on citizenship education in England, political literacy is an area of particular weakness due to teachers' lack of confidence in the subject matter, and the fact that it is perceived as being dry and difficult to teach (Kerr et al. 2007).

This incapacity is exacerbated by the uncertainty over what is ef-fective. There is a general consensus that the conforming, good-citizen approach is outdated, but not about what should replace it (see, e.g., Borhaug 2009). In chapter 9 we looked at civic education in the form of service learning, expressing some misgivings about this strategy. This is not to advocate a return to the classroom-based, good-citizen approach; it is, rather, to insist that the relationship between classroom and community be one of integrating with, not escaping from, political life. In the next section of this chapter, we shall explore what this might entail.

Civics outside the Classroom

There is some evidence that different kinds of activities outside the civics classroom—both in and beyond the school, but complementary to what goes on in the classroom—have a real potential to help develop habits of informed political participation. In this section, I briefly describe some of the more promising of such activities, with an eye to creating an educational environment conducive to developing habits of paying attention to politics—especially among those lacking the resources to do so on their own.

In so doing, I pay little attention to organized activities not related to the goals of civic education, such as social clubs and sports teams. While a link can be drawn between such activities and civic engagement, it has largely been confined to the United States, emerging out of the social capital and political socialization literatures cited in chapters 1 and 2. As noted with regard to voluntary activities outside of school, incentives like résumé padding are a key factor here. Students who want to get into a good college are encouraged to join clubs and teams, and thus report having done so on surveys. This concern with producing a record of involvement that will further their careers applies to some extent also to membership on student councils and participation in other activities related to school governance. I do not deny that a democratic climate in a school can enhance the work in its civic education classes, as well as being a desirable objective in its own right. Moreover, as noted in the discussion of the IEA study in chapter 9, there is some cross-national connection between participation in such activities and intended political participation. However, membership on the student council or its equivalent unfortunately tends to be restricted to the minority of students who bring to school the skills and motivation to participate.[2] An apparent illustration of the effects of extracurricular activities can be found in our comparative North American survey. Tables 10.1 and 10.2 show the responses of those in the sample who were still in school to two questions about such activities, and links the responses to the students' level of political knowledge. As we see in table 10.1, the number of groups in which the students say they participate is significantly related

TABLE 10.1

Relationship between participating in school groups and political knowledge in Americans and Canadians aged 15–25

Are you currently participating in any organized groups or clubs in high school, such as sports teams, band, or chorus?

COUNTRY		POLITICAL KNOWLEDGE (SUM OF 7 ANSWERS)
United States	r (Pearson correlation)	0.169*
	sig. (statistical significance)	0.001
	N (number of respondents)	393
Canada	r	0.081
	sig.	0.234
	N	216

*Correlation is significant at the 0.01 level.

TABLE 10.2.

Relationship between type of school group and political knowledge in Americans and Canadians aged 15–25

Do these groups include student government or organizations concerned with social or political issues?

COUNTRY		POLITICAL KNOWLEDGE (SUM OF 7 ANSWERS)
United States	r (Pearson correlation)	0.249*
	sig. (statistical significance)	0.000
	N (number of respondants)	235
Canada	r	0.088
	sig.	0.312
	N	135

*Correlation is significant at the 0.01 level.

to political knowledge only in the United States. And, as we see in table 10.2, this is also the case when we look just at those involved in student government or groups dealing with social or political issues.

Without going so far as to conclude that in the United States, more-knowledgeable students from resource-rich home backgrounds are most likely to report involvement in groups in general, and in those concerned with student government or social or political issues in particular, I do contend that context matters. The ambivalence expressed in chapter 9 with regard to the effects of participation in community service upon informed political participation also applies to involvement in school groups. Hence, without excluding extracurricular involvement in the community or school, we stress the development of a habit of attentiveness to the political world. This need not be passive: later in this chapter, we provide examples using role playing to connect the civics class with the political world outside. The goal is to transcend the perceived dichotomy between political life and real life, the notion that politics is somewhere out there, separate from what goes on in here. As we shall see, the use of simulations[3] combined with innovative applications and uses of media, both new and old, is a key element in developing the skills and habits of attentiveness to political life.

Mock Elections

Simulations probably are the most frequently used method of breaking down the barrier between the world of public affairs and that of real life. We know that simulations can be effective in promoting informed political participation. Even as simple an activity as watching a presidential debate with others in school was found to significantly and positively enhance students' self-reported confidence that they could cast a knowledgeable vote in the election (Syvertsen, Flanagan, and Stout 2007). A good example of a more elaborate simulation along these lines was a collaborative effort by 75 Pace University students and 650 students from twenty-five high schools before the 2004 U.S. presidential election. The college students were in a course on presidential politics, in which much class time was spent preparing for visits to the high schools from October to December 2003. The high-school students played the role of delegates to presidential conventions in January 2004, building and proposing planks in the national party platforms, and nominating presidential candidates.[4]

The high-school students were divided into fifty Democratic and Republican delegations, representing each U.S. state; each school provided two delegations. The Pace students worked with each delegation to draft a state party platform on the eight issues the delegates debated at the conventions, compiling a reference work that was given to every delegate and placed on the project's website. Breaking the students down into state party delegations and asking them to understand issues from the perspective of the state parties (rather than their own) helped them understand how a state articulates its interests through the nominating process (see Malone and Gregory 2005).

Another innovative program on a smaller scale took place in Florida in a class of nineteen young women from troubled backgrounds, who were fifteen to eighteen years old at the time of the 2000 presidential election. The program included lectures in class, meetings with representatives of local organizations, and visits to local Democratic and Republican headquarters, city hall, and a homeless shelter. Zeiser (2001) notes: "The mock presidential election was one of the big successes of the project. The students even shared what they learned with the whole school, by making informational campaign posters and hanging them in the hallway outside their classroom . . .The increase in civic knowledge gained was dramatic. The average post-test score was 76 percent, a statistically significant increase over the average pretest score of 56 percent" (289).

While there are many such specific initiatives, the simulations with the widest impact are mock elections. A comprehensive program of mock elections was initiated in North America in 1988 by Kids Voting USA, a nonprofit, nonpartisan voter-education program. Currently, the program operates in schools in about forty states. Teachers help students gather information about the candidates and issues in local, state, and national elections. On Election Day, the students cast their ballots in special booths, the younger ones going to the polls with their parents. Studies suggest that the program enhances political knowledge among young people (e.g., Meirick and Wackman 2004; Nie, Junn, and Stehlik-Barry 1996; Simon and Merrill 1998),[5] though it does not appear to affect the class bias in electoral participation (Eagles and Davidson 2001). In 2008, the Youth Leadership Initiative of the University of Virginia's Center for Politics[6] staged an online mock election, in which more than a million U.S. students of different ages participated over a ten-day period just before Election Day.

The first large-scale simulation in Canada was conducted to coincide with the October 2003 provincial election in Ontario: students in the ninth through twelfth grades in about three-quarters of the province's public high schools cast ballots identical to those used by real voters.[7] In all, the ballots of over 43 percent of Ontario high-school students were collected and tabulated.[8] This was followed by the Canada-wide Student Vote 2004, conducted in 1,168 schools with 265,000 participants—in which, as noted in chapter 8, participation was inhibited by the late setting of the election date.[9] Since then, a provincial mock election took place during the 2005 British Columbia provincial election. The fact that the voting date was fixed in advance, as advocated in chapter 8, clearly facilitated participation in Student Vote BC, which took place in a very high proportion of the province's schools.[10] In the subsequent 2006 federal election, participation rose to just over 2,500 schools, with 468,000 students participating; in the 2008 federal election, the numbers were 3,000 schools and 500,000 participants.[11]

High-school students in Scandinavia also take part in mock elections at the time of national elections. The Swedish Skolval (school vote) is similar to the Canadian Student Vote. In Sweden, students form election committees to represent the various parties and invite candidates to the schools to debate the issues.[12] Ballots identical to the official ones are counted in the same fashion as the national vote. The results of the student vote are reported in the newspapers, and also on television as part of the live coverage of the actual election results. Only 34.3 percent of Swedish high-school students participated in the first Skolval, held during the 2002 election, but in 2006, turnout jumped to a very impressive 86.66 percent. In a study observing sixteen Norwegian upper secondary civic education classes, Borhaug (2008) found that all the observed teachers spent some time on the mock election debate in a subsequent class and invited the students to react to it.

The Norwegian Skolevalg has been running mock elections since 1989 for all parliamentary and local elections, including the referendum on EU membership in 1994. It also carries out a survey of students, with a similar survey conducted among a representative sample of the Norwegian population. Both take place in the ten days before the election.[13] Approximately 70 percent of all high-school students participate in the mock election, and 30 percent in the election survey.[14] The project is financed by government agencies, and the Norwegian Social Science Data Services is responsible for the surveys. Overall results are reported online, while the school results are also distributed to the schools, so students can compare their choices with those of their peers.

Mock Parliaments

The Scandinavian countries are prominent among those that have developed youth parliaments. One was organized by the Finnish Parliament in March 2006 as part of its centennial celebrations. These are quite elaborate initiatives, as we can see in the case of Denmark in 2004. The process began in August, with an invitation to groups composed of eight or nine high-school students (and their teacher) to prepare a draft bill and submit it to Parliament. The Danish Parliament selected sixty of these bills, and the groups that had drafted them each chose three delegates. After further discussion and elaboration of the draft bills, largely on the Internet, each of the twelve committees of the Danish Parliament was sent five bills. Meetings of a Youth Parliament attended by the 180 delegates took place in the Danish Parliament, attended by the members of the twelve committees, with the general public able to follow the event on the Internet. Each committee framed a question, which was then posed orally to a cabinet minister during question period. The final session, held in April 2005, was chaired by the speaker of the Danish Parliament.

The most innovative aspect of this particular mock parliament was the committees' participation, integrated with the use of the Internet. Still, direct participation was limited to a relatively small number of young people. Even more promising is a new parliamentary simulation, also based on the work of committees, that has recently been developed in Denmark, Norway, and Sweden: interactive centers.

The centers are a response to dissatisfaction with existing efforts to bring students into contact with legislative institutions. As in other countries, these efforts traditionally took the form of student tours of parliamentary buildings, combined with lectures about the institution. With indications of young people's growing lack of interest in passive traditional forms of political participation, and the need to foster active youth political involvement, such visits were seen to resemble visits to a museum, and were deemed inadequate.

The solution was not to stop the visits, but to make them active. The Parliaments of Sweden, Norway, and Denmark created and funded interactive centers, called Democracy Workshops or Mini-Parliaments, which offer students in their last two years of compulsory school (these students are typically aged fifteen and sixteen) the opportunity to experience the parliamentary committee decision-making process through role-playing. In the case of Sweden, with a population of nine million, some 12,000 students visited the interactive center between its opening in fall 2006 and early April 2008.

The centers, located next to the parliaments, are designed to simulate the parliamentary process. Clearly, they could fruitfully be imitated in other mature democracies facing even larger democratic deficits. Each center's space is divided up to provide places for party caucus meetings, areas set up to resemble committee rooms, and a larger area for plenary meetings. In Oslo, there is also a room for press conferences, in which students have to defend their positions in response to questions from real journalists.[15] Otherwise the process is similar in all three countries (the details here are derived from an observation of the Swedish Democracy Workshop in Stockholm). After preparation in their civics classes prior to the visit, students in groups of fifteen to thirty-five meet trained facilitators who also work as parliamentary press or information officers, and who guide the students through a simulated half day of a key aspect of the work of a member of Parliament. Each student is given a card with the first name of an individual MP and his or her party, and placed on a committee responsible for dealing with one or two issues. During my visit in spring 2008, one committee was considering whether the punishment for graffiti should be made harsher, and another whether boxing should be outlawed. Both matters had come up in Parliament.[16]

First, the students get a chance to express their own opinions; they are then asked to express those of the legislator whose persona they have taken. (The card gives information about the legislator's party affiliation, age, gender, professional background, and so on. The five parties are fictitious, but their positions and names are based on those of existing parties. The party groups vary in size to reflect the actual composition of legislature.) The exercise begins when students in each committee go to their parties' caucus rooms (specially designed booths) and, basing their judgments on their assigned roles, work out a position on the legislative issue under consideration. Students are guided in their deliberations by instructions they receive on a computer screen in the booth, and they also have access to relevant newspaper articles and excerpts from TV and radio coverage. An added twist interrupts their deliberations with telephone calls and computer screen messages from interested persons —lobbyists, constituents, party activists, etc.—thus exposing them to efforts to influence the positions of MPs (along with, in the Norwegian center, public opinion as expressed by the journalists).

Debate over the bills is carried out alternatively in party groups and in committee meetings where all parties are represented. This means that the students not only have to arrive at a common party position, but also must work with representatives of other parties to form alliances or compromises in order to win majority support in the committee—keeping in mind that the proposals need to be adopted in a plenary of all the students present. When the bills come to the plenary floor, in a mock session of Parliament overseen by the facilitator acting as the speaker, there are speeches for and against each measure, and a vote is taken. In some of the scenarios, the prime minister—the spokesperson for the governing coalition—asks for a vote of confidence, and the members must reevaluate their views and take a stand on whether they want to support the government or bring it down. Finally, the students are asked to vote again, this time based on their own views on the issue, and to reflect on whether and how their positions changed during the simulation.

According to evaluations by student participants, these interactive, role-playing scenarios have helped them understand how laws are made and appreciate that MPs are subject to conflicting influences and the constraints of parties and interested persons. The use of a committee and caucus structure gives the students hands-on experience in making alliances and arriving at compromises, teaching them that a vote in Parliament constitutes the culmination of a long, but nevertheless comprehensible, legislative process. It also responds to a call by Chareka and Sears (2006) to tackle the widespread perception of politicians as ineffective, by emphasizing areas where individual politicians can make significant contributions.

One reason for dwelling on this case is that, in many ways—for example, the size of the group, and the time and preparation involved—it is applicable to what I propose below needs to be done in the civics classroom. First, however, a few other examples merit mention. The Finnish project called Hear the Citizen focuses on the executive rather than the legislature, inviting students to familiarize themselves with a selected government agency. Working in groups, they prepare background papers, proposals, and commentaries relevant to the mandate of the agency and receive feedback. As the process continues, relevant information and the content of discussions are placed on a website financed by the Ministry of Education, and a handbook of lessons learned is prepared. The final stage has each group presenting and defending its report before the concerned civil servants.

Activities such as these can readily be integrated into civics courses. We know this to be the case of the Scandinavian parliamentary committee simulations, in which participation is organized by civics teachers, and preparation for the visit takes place in class. In the case of Sweden's Democracy Workshop, one remaining drawback is that its capacity, while large, still limits access to a minority of the targeted students—unlike the Skolval, with its 88 percent reach. With funding limited, the great majority of Swedish participants live within easy access of central Stockholm. This is not the case with Oslo's Minitinget, which, given Norway's smaller population, is able—by extending hours to allow three classes access each day, and paying the travel costs for students from outside the Oslo area—to offer its service to a majority of students during their first year of upper secondary school, when civic education is compulsory.

But even where only a minority can participate, unlike in mock parliaments and the like, the students involved constitute a cross section of the country's students overall—including the potential political dropouts—rather than the self-selected leaders of the future.

Another type of activity that ought to be mentioned here is more commonly found in the United States, as it is closer to the service-learning model. A good example is Project Citizen, a curricular module that seeks to promote competent and responsible participation in local and state government. The students first identify, research, and evaluate alternative solutions to a given problem. They are then expected to develop a public policy solution, along with a political action plan to get local or state authorities to adopt and implement their proposed policy. The work is presented at a public hearing before a panel of civic-minded community members. First developed in 1995, Project Citizen had been used by approximately 32,200 teachers and almost two million students as of September 2008. Project Citizen has been translated into more than forty languages and is used in more than forty-five countries. The Center for Civic Education conducted an assessment of it in 2004-5, surveying 522 alumni and comparing them to an equivalent group from the 2004 National Election Study of Americans their age. Ninety-two percent of Project Citizen's alumni reported voting in

November 2004, in contrast with 78 percent of those from the NES study (Walling 2007).[17]

Bringing the Political World into the Classroom

The above examples link the students to the political world by taking them out of the classroom.[18] Something similar can be accomplished via complementary initiatives that can be brought into the classroom via the Internet. A starting point here is to be found in applications to the civic education classroom of the voting advice applications (VAAs) discussed in chapter 6, especially the efforts of smartvote in Switzerland.[19]

This raises the wider question of bringing not only politics but politicians into the classroom, and not only virtually. In countries like Sweden, an important place is given to the positions taken by the different parties on relevant local, regional, and national issues. It is quite common to invite their spokespersons into the classroom (see below)—an activity that runs contrary to the typical North American insistence on keeping politics out of the classroom. Based on what goes on in the civics classroom, this fear of politics seems misplaced: politicians present clearly identifiable partisan views and are kept out, while teachers present their often partisan views (see Niemi and Niemi 2005) in the guise of objectivity.

It should be added that this is not merely a matter of personal choice: as set out in part 2, the institutional context matters. Fixed election dates facilitate planning civic education courses, especially lining up visits by political actors. While the United States, like Sweden, has fixed election dates, it does not have an electoral system suited to this approach. In the United States, one party is very likely to dominate politics in a given school's region, making it very difficult to avoid accusations of partisanship when inviting representatives of the different positions on controversial issues at a weight corresponding to the level of support for those positions in the population. This, of course, is exactly the context that a proportional electoral system establishes, allowing for the invitation of locally elected spokespersons of minor as well as major political parties.

A similar logic applies to the VAAs, and it is no coincidence that we have seen them develop in the context of proportional electoral institutions in Europe. Young voters are a particular target of the German

Wahl-o-Mat, since, as noted in chapter 6, it is supported by the federal agency responsible for civic education. The Wahl-o-Mat seems to have become especially popular during the campaign leading up to the September 2009 federal election, having been frequently mentioned in the media and used by over 15 percent of eligible voters. In the last two weeks before the election, at public question-and-answer assemblies in a score of upper-secondary schools concentrated in two provinces (Saarland and Rhineland-Palatinate), candidates filled out the Wahl-o-Mat questionnaires on big screens.

We can be sure that informal uses of the Wahl-o-Mat took place in civic education courses throughout Germany in this period, just as other VAAs are used—for example, in the civic education classes I visited in Norway in the week before the September 2009 election in that country.

We now turn to the civics courses themselves. Without getting too specific as to content, we envisage courses primarily targeted at students on the threshold of adulthood, a time that research suggests is optimal for the acquisition of political knowledge (Niemi and Junn 1998; Westholm, Lindquist, and Niemi 1990). From the International IDEA Civic Education Database (Milner, Nguyen, and Boylston 2008), we learn that in the just over forty countries[20] for which data exist, courses related to civic education are targeted only slightly more at students in the secondary or upper secondary level (aged fifteen to eighteen) than at those in the intermediate level (aged twelve to fourteen). A number of countries concentrate resources on the younger group because many students leave school at age fifteen. In countries where the great majority of young people are still in school at sixteen and seventeen, the literature suggests, limited resources should go primarily toward students of that age, rather than those in early adolescence, a stage of life not especially conducive to the kind of learning provided in civics courses.[21]

From the Civic Education Database, we also learn that almost all countries offer some form of civic education, which is compulsory in three-quarters of them, and authorities tend at least to say that it is important. Yet in just under two-thirds of the countries, civic education teachers do not have specific training related to the subject. Important exceptions in this regard are the Scandinavian countries, where there is a subfield for civics teachers in the teacher training program for undergraduates—as well as annual, university-based conferences for practicing teachers—in which social science professors are involved. It goes almost without saying that the kind of civic education innovations outlined below will require teachers trained not only in the content that such programs provide, but also in the skills needed to design and carry out simulations of various kinds.

As far as the United States (which is not included in the International IDEA database) is concerned, there have been important developments in civic education in response to a perceived decline in youth political participation. Around 1990, the declining interest in civic education gave way to increased concern, as most states developed or refined standards in high-school civics or government courses. The goal was to ensure that students acquired at least a minimal understanding of how government works, of basic democratic values, and of fundamental historical documents and events. To coordinate these efforts, the Education Commission of the States created the National Center for Learning and Citizenship, which provides an overview of what is being done.[22] It reveals, for example, that unlike in the core academic disciplines, most states have yet to establish statewide assessments of their civics standards. A 2006 analysis conducted by the National Center for Learning and Citizenship (see Lopez and Kirby 2007) found that all fifty states and the District of Columbia require that high schools teach civics or the equivalent, a substantial increase since 2003. But there has been no parallel improvement in accountability measures: only twenty-on states had measures such as examinations for civics courses or social studies, a proportion slightly lower than that for the countries in the International IDEA database.

It would be foolhardy, and indeed wrongheaded, to spell out what should be the content of the civic education curriculum—foolhardy because there is no one-size-fits-all formula to apply, and wrongheaded because the goal lies less in the content learned, than in the habits of attentiveness to political information acquired. Instead, we can identify certain general guidelines based on our limited knowledge of what is currently being done, and our understanding of the challenges imposed by ongoing changes, particularly in the communications world of young people.

There is a broad contemporary consensus on the first point—namely, that civic education must be a component of (though not limited to) the schooling of young people near the end of their years of compulsory schooling. There is also general agreement, as Delli Carpini and Keeter put it, that civics should be "taught in a realistic manner, introducing students to the conflictual, often unsettling nature of politics" (1996, 279).[23] But there is some disagreement over whether civic education should take the form of a stand-alone course or set of courses, or be incorporated into a wider social-studies curriculum. Practice differs sharply. According to the International IDEA database, civic education is a specific, stand-alone course in just over half (56 percent) of the countries included in the database. In the decentralized educational systems in North America, only a minority of states and provinces have a compulsory civics course. That is why the Education Commission of the States always refers to courses in civics, citizenship education, or social studies. (In Sweden, the course title includes both social studies and civics, with a specified political science component, along with economics, sociology, and human geography.)

The Education Commission of the States seeks to contribute to the process of harmonizing state efforts, especially through encouraging the creation and spread of course modules in multiple jurisdictions. The most important of these is We the People: The Citizen and the Constitution, the flagship program of the Center for Civic Education, containing materials designed to provide either a complete curriculum or modules that can be integrated into existing courses. More than twenty-eight million U.S. students have participated in the program since its inception twenty years ago. Other institutions that have been involved in this process include The New York Times and the Dirksen Congressional Center.[24]

The arguments favoring a stand-alone course are presented in a report investigating the application of a compulsory citizenship education course in English schools (Kerr et al. 2007). It concluded that citizenship education is best delivered as a discrete element of the curriculum because that approach increases the status and visibility of the subject, encourages the use of specialist teachers, increases the chance that the national-curriculum content will be used, and encourages the development of assessment plans and practices. In contrast, citizenship education delivered throughout the curriculum, the authors argue, can be uneven and inconsistent, especially because larger numbers of nonspecialist staff are involved, by default. According to the study, student feedback reveals that dedicated civics classes are more likely to provide opportunities for active and interactive teaching and learning approaches based around discussion, debate, group work, and the use of information and communications technology.

Whiteley (2008), also using data from a survey of British students, comes to a somewhat different conclusion: if citizenship is taught in dedicated classes, it weakens voting intentions compared to being spread widely among different subjects, such as history, geography, or politics. Still, he concludes, what matters in the end is less where it is taught, than that it cover a wide variety of topics.

The findings of a Canadian study (Goodyear-Grant and Anderson 2008) tend to support Kerr rather than Whiteley. Overall, it appears desirable to offer civic education in a particular set of courses, rather than spreading it out over different ones, not because of any intrinsic superiority of the former as a means of disseminating the content, but rather because of its form. Specific goals related to civic education can more readily be assigned, with outcomes monitored and necessary adjustments made, when the targets are clearer. Of course, there is a downside to this, which emerges in a comparison of what we have learned about Quebec and Ontario. If you place all your eggs in the single, small basket of a compulsory civics course and do not get it right, the result can be inferior to what happens when history and other classes encourage students to keep up with political issues and discuss them in class.

In planning the courses, one must also take into account not only the capacities of the teachers, but also what the students bring into the classroom in the form of assumptions and expectations. Based on a set of in-depth interviews with young Canadians, Chareka and Sears (2006) argue that citizenship education must start from, rather than ignore, young people's beliefs that political parties are all the same, and elections are useless exercises. The authors stress trying to break through young people's cynicism about voting by identifying concrete examples of how a vote can be an effective expression of their voice. The problem, the authors note, is that given student attitudes, the response still tends to downplay voting and elections altogether.

One manifestation of this can be found in the International IDEA database. The survey asked specialists about the importance given to five components of the content of civics courses, the results of which are set out in table 10.3. The questions allowed for six responses, ranging from no importance to high importance. As we can see, voting and voting procedures placed last in importance.

TABLE 10.3

The importance of types of civic education content

TYPE OF CONTENT	COUNTRY RESPONDENTS THAT RANKED THIS AS IMPORTANT (PERCENT)
Democratic values, good citizenship, and civic values	76
Community involvement	72
History and constitutional principles	69
Politics and international affairs	66
Voting and voting procedures	52

SOURCE: Milner, Nguyen, and Boylston (2008) using data from the International IDEA Civic Education Database.

Given the attitudes of young people, the reluctance to emphasize on voting, elections, and parties is understandable. Nevertheless, rather than simply resigning themselves to these attitudes, civics educators need to find ways, as suggested by Chareka and Sears (2006), to counter the underlying assumptions. A promising path, we suggest, lies in simulations in which young people experience the political activity rather than just learning about it.

A Modest Civic Education Proposal

We now outline a simulation project intended to do just this. The proposed simulation addresses a crucial dimension of the entire question: incorporating up-to-date channels of communication, electronic and otherwise.[25] Teaching skills and information relevant to political participation by the Internet generation entails cultivating media skills that fit the reading, listening, and viewing habits of that generation. Observers agree that schools—in and beyond the civic education classroom—must instill skills of literacy in the digital-age media, giving the students the capacity not only to obtain knowledge but to organize and use it as effective citizens (see Kirlin 2007). Again, it goes without saying that programs for learning such skills must be integrated into the training of civics teachers.

Comparing data from the 1998 and 2006 surveys conducted by the National Assessment of Educational Progress (NAEP) of the U.S.

Department of Education, Lopez and Kirby (2007) find that in only one area has there been a significant drop at both the eighth grade (23 percent to 18 percent) and twelfth grade (32 percent to 27 percent) levels—namely, on the question of whether "there have been visits from people in your community to learn more about important events and ideas." While the question is awkwardly phrased, the low and declining response it receives is worrisome, since a key to informed youth participation lies in appropriate arrangements for visits from the outside political world to the school. The very notion of keeping politics out of the classroom is wrongheaded in a mature democracy, a relic from the period when democracy was fragile, subject to threat from the top. In such circumstances, keeping the powers that be out of the classroom can be crucial. But in most Western countries today, the threat to democracy comes from the bottom, from abstention by the emerging majority. Hence the opposite principle needs to be applied: get politics, and politicians, into the classroom. The question is not if, but how.[26]

The kind of visits I have in mind are central to the concept of civic education. The idea is inspired especially by my familiarity with civic education in Scandinavia. For example, in Norway, "students study political parties and their programs, visit them, make projects where they present party platforms in class, they role play where they are representatives of political parties at upper secondary schools" (Borhaug 2009, 6.) Moreover, the courses are structured in such a way that the teachers can offer the section dealing with elections and parties to coincide with election campaigns. This is complemented by the textbooks, which stress forms of political participation, from membership in the parties or interest groups to street marches and demonstrations.[27]

In the Vasterbotten region of northern Sweden, where I have been a visiting professor for more than a decade, three colleagues and I recently surveyed the civics teachers in upper-level secondary schools (whose students are sixteen to eighteen) and high schools (whose students are fourteen to sixteen). A preliminary overview of the survey's results indicates a high response rate, especially from the former group.[28] One question asked what level of importance (1 is lowest. 6 is highest) was accorded in their civics courses to each of the following: field trips, group work or projects, simulations, case reenactments, participation in community or voluntary service, and guest speakers. By my preliminary calculations, of the sixty-seven responses, the average score for guest speakers was 3.2. In addition, roughly 25 percent of the teachers added comments about their choices to their responses. Visits from and to city councils were popular, as well as simulations like Minister for a Day. Because of a lack of resources for organized class trips, a number of teachers encouraged students individually to attend and tape or film sessions of political bodies and report on them to the class. The most frequent observation was the importance of adequate preparation before, and full discussion after, these different events.

I here set out a specific model based on these and other observations. It makes certain modest demands in the forms of scheduling and availability of resources that should not be beyond the capacity of most schools. The timing entails planning well ahead, in an effort to take advantage of upcoming elections, referendums, key votes in representative institutions, and so on in making arrangements to have elected spokespersons from different parties present their positions to the students. This can be done virtually if physical visits are not possible, but physical presence is preferable, because for most young people their only contact with politicians is through the media. As a result, many potential young voters are turned off by what they perceive to be the inauthenticity of politicians—an inauthenticity amplified, if not caused, by having to communicate via ratings-driven media that thrive on conflict. Giving young people direct access to political figures in the flesh rather than on the screen exposes them to another, potentially more authentic, side of those seeking their votes.

Planning such visits, as already noted, is facilitated by complementary institutional frameworks, especially fixed election dates and proportional systems of elections. The latter give small parties with distinct, principle-based positions that carry some measure of popular support —such as the Greens, Libertarians, or Christian Democrats—a better chance of having democratically elected, and therefore legitimate, spokespersons to represent them in the classroom. Such representativeness can also make the entire political system more legitimate in the eyes of the young people.[29]

The most important innovation in this proposal lies not in the role of the providers of the information, but in that of the recipients, the students. The proposed visit takes the form of a press conference (the model here is the press conference scenario incorporated into the Norwegian parliamentary committee simulation), at which the students play journalists attending the politician's presentation, on which they will be reporting in the medium of their choice: newspaper, radio, television, blog, Facebook, etc. Before they take on the role of journalist at the press conference, the students—usually in groups—prepare questions based on research into the issues, and the positions on them of the politicians and parties. In a later class, the journalist's report is presented to the other students and, where appropriate, beyond, via the chosen medium. The goal of such an activity, like the committee simulation, is to encourage an appreciation of the roles of politician and political journalist, and thus develop and improve habits of attentiveness to the news media, and to develop the skills needed for picking up meaningful signals about the political world in their chosen informational environment.

In keeping with the objective of targeting young people for whom the requisite home support and social connectedness is weak or nonexistent —i.e., the potential political dropouts—role-playing exercises need to be designed to minimize the advantage of students from resource-rich backgrounds. This is a strength of the parliamentary committee simulation described above, which provides all the information needed to play the role, placing no expectations on the students to bring with them any particular knowledge or skills. The same is potentially true of a well-prepared press conference simulation, in which those from resource-poor backgrounds are clearly at less of a disadvantage than they are in a more traditional civics-class exercise, which asks them to present their own views and back them up.

Simulations such as these can readily be integrated into the course materials. As noted, there is no one-size-fits-all formula, and I see little use here in reproducing texts setting out guidelines that have been offered in different contexts and that can readily be found on the Internet. With the range of course material available online, it is largely a matter of learning from—and adapting and refining to fit specific circumstances— the material most suited to delivering knowledge and skills relevant to democratic participation, as well as inducing the habits of attentiveness to relevant sources for acquiring and making use of that information. Web-based material has the added advantage that it can be incorporated into modules of civic education courses irrespective of location.[30] Much can be accomplished by learning from countries and regions that have maintained high levels of youth informed political participation. And, clearly, there is the need to train, or retrain, those who will be providing this education in an appropriate setting, one that optimally combines the complementary competencies of political scientists and professors of education.

Giving the course when potential dropouts are still in school, but when casting a vote is on their horizon, makes it possible to present attaining its objectives as something practical. A good analogy can be drawn to driver's education. When young people reach a certain age, it becomes practical—indeed, natural—for them to learn the rules of the road and their local geography; the same should apply to the age of citizenship and learning the rules about voting and political decision making, and the political maps situating the alternative political routes.

This brings us back to a measure discussed in part 2. In countries with elevated high-school dropout rates, concentrating on those nearing the voting age—sixteen- and seventeen-year-olds—means missing many of the prime targets. The main effort here, of course, should be at keeping students in school. But in many places, we are a long way from that. Reaching potential dropouts when they are still in school would entail lowering the voting age to sixteen. As we noted, interesting efforts in this direction have taken place, especially in Germany and Austria. But these are countries with relatively high levels of informed political participation by young people. Extending such efforts to North America could have more acute consequences, negative as well as positive. Opponents of lowering the voting age are right to raise doubts about the value of allowing millions more ignorant voters to help decide the country's future.

At the core is involving those soon to reach voting age in a civic education program focused on developing habits of attentiveness to public affairs. A key dimension of such a course is to bring the issues, and the political parties' stance on them, into the classroom. This entails integrating election-related activities and simulations, wherever possible, along with public-affairs media (old and new), and making a real effort to break down the wall between political life and real life that serves to justify political abstention. One example of how this could be accomplished has been set out in these pages. It was chosen because it is applicable in classrooms in any stable democratic country. There are, of course, other examples: simulations of municipal councils come to mind. One can readily conceive of such a simulation structured along the lines of, and using similar technology to, the Democracy Workshops that would reflect the composition, and recreate the decision-making process, of the local council. Ideally, a dedicated space could be established for this purpose in the local city hall.

In suggesting specific measures such as these, we must be tentative. A useful way to proceed would be through pilot projects. Following the German example, American states and Canadian provinces could serve as venues, instituting and funding such courses as pilot projects in a number of school districts. A second step, a pilot project for a province or state where such a course has been made compulsory for all students in the years just before they turn sixteen, would be to reduce the voting age to sixteen for a given period—say, two (preferably fixed-date) elections. This would constitute an excellent test of the overall effects of the application of the combined measures.

If such courses are well designed, taught by appropriately trained teachers operating in a welcoming administrative environment in the schools, and effectively integrating activities inside and outside the classroom, then lowering the voting age could make a difference. But there are no guarantees. If we wish to justify inaction, we could easily do so. We could interpret youth abstention as an expression of the good judgment of young people on the failings of political elites. Or, conversely—but with the same results—we could decide that democracy is best served when the ignorant abstain from participating. But, if these pages have taught us something, it is that given the forces at work, and the changes taking place around us, these are just rationalizations. Doing nothing is no answer. It is very true that we cannot know in advance if our interventions will succeed. Therefore—this is no small point—more and more-coordinated research is essential. But it is not enough.

Conclusion

In the 1970s, the Swedish Social Democratic Party youth wing claimed over 80,000 members; in 2008, it had a paltry 2,000.[1] That is an extraordinary drop. Although the party is still by far the largest in Sweden and still gets its fair share of the youth vote, it is no longer the vehicle for youthful idealism that it was in the days of Olaf Palme.[2]

Things have obviously changed. As in every comparable country, party membership, especially among the established parties, is down. Parties are not the agents of mobilization of the young and the not-so-young that they once were. But, as recounted in chapter 4, in contrast to most countries, Sweden has seen its turnout rate stabilized at over 80 percent, and the age gap in turnout has increased only marginally. Further, if we use as a criterion the theme on which we began many pages ago—the capacity to get climate-change policies onto the agenda of political parties, interest groups, and governments—environmentalists have clearly succeeded in Sweden, with the country having exceeded its Kyoto targets years ahead of the deadline and without expanding nuclear power.

The success story is one of a synthesis of conventional[3] and unconventional political involvement and mobilization, combined with the sophisticated application of the latest in communications technology. One manifestation of this success lies in the congestion fees that have significantly reduced the number of cars in Stockholm;[4] another is Swedish participation in Earth Day.[5]

Widening our focus, we see two parallel developments shaping the patterns of youth political participation in Sweden. One story is about fundamental transformations in forms of political participation. Indeed, it could not be otherwise: this is a country highly exposed to the economic and cultural realities of globalization, and at the forefront of broadband accessibility and associated technological developments described in chapter 3. But the parallel story that needs telling is of the relative dearth of negative aspects of this phenomenon, in the low number of political dropouts evident from the turnout numbers and political knowledge rankings cited in chapters 4 and 5.

The Swedish story is, of course, not the only one. The experience of several other countries in and beyond Scandinavia has much to teach us. Indeed, as noted, Denmark is the sterling performer in electoral participation.[6] But Sweden is especially instructive because, as we saw in chapter 8, it has made a concerted effort to face the challenges of declining youth political participation.

In the background to the story lies the durability of the Swedish or Scandinavian model of the welfare state. Since the welfare state's heyday in the 1950s and 1960s, Sweden has, by and large, successfully adapted it to the new globalized environment, without fundamentally undermining outcomes in health, income distribution, employment, and so forth. (see, e.g., Kautto et al. 2001; Brooks and Hwong 2006). Also at the macro level are policies associated with nonmaterial redistribution, about which I have written elsewhere. Specific measures include newspaper subsidies, public broadcasting initiatives, and a range of programs via schools, lifelong-learning associations, libraries, and other networks concerned with disseminating knowledge, and targeting adults at the margins of literacy and numeracy.

These programs are carried out within a framework of complementary institutions, including, in particular, those at the political level discussed in part 2. These arrangements consist of decentralized, unitary, unicameral parliamentary structures with relatively few elections and referendums; and elections that take place on the same fixed dates under proportional representation systems, with the same parties contesting all three levels (local, regional, and national), and with the state providing ample public support to assure diffusion of necessary information. This is a combination that conforms to, and operates upon, the principle of simplifying the relationship between citizens' actions and political outcomes. The result is a kind of virtuous circle connecting the policies of nonmaterial and material redistribution with institutions conducive to their continued effectiveness.

But while maintaining their basic structure, Sweden's political institutions have not been immutable. They have responded to the challenges manifested in the democratic deficit by developing and implementing micro-level measures that foster informed political participation on the part of a generation that has grown up in a world where the only constant is rapid technological change.

Initiatives described in previous chapters include a set of government-sponsored programs involving local authorities and public agencies, often acting in cooperation with civil-society organizations. Parliamentary initiatives were singled out, such as the Democracy Workshops that simulate the work of parliamentary committees. These initiatives, like their equivalents in Denmark and Norway, are designed and operated so that they can be closely integrated into the civic education curriculum.

In this manner, civic education reproduces at the micro level the virtuous circle of relationships at the macro level. This is not to imply that Scandinavian civic educators have all the answers to the challenges facing contemporary civic education. If they have better answers than their counterparts in most comparable countries, it is because the set of institutions in which they work place them in a position to address the challenges and adapt to the new realities. Despite the pressures on the schools due to the effects of globalization, compulsory civics or civics-related courses are solidly entrenched at the secondary (students aged fourteen and fifteen) and upper secondary (students aged sixteen to eighteen) levels. In addition, Scandinavian civics teachers are trained in specialized education programs at the university level; and the universities have a good deal of autonomy in designing these programs and making use of available academic resources, especially in the social sciences. Further, as stressed in part 2, civics teachers are, generally, encouraged to connect to the real world of politics through simulations and visits, and by bringing politics and politicians virtually and physically into the classroom.

One last factor bears mentioning in this regard: the success of Scandinavian schools at teaching English, so that by the age of fourteen, every student can understand an English-language text, website, or television program. This means easy access to materials in the dominant language of electronic communication, not only for the elite, but even for potential political dropouts. Immediate exposure for young people to international trends is accompanied by access by Scandinavian policymakers and educators to the best of what is available. Given the will to reduce the number of political dropouts, and the presence of conducive institutions largely lacking in the English-speaking countries, the Scandinavians are in a comparatively good position to find and implement the means to do so. How they choose to respond to the challenge will continue to bear watching.

Where does that leave the rest of us in terms of declining youth turnout? As far as other EU members are concerned, no generalization is possible. Some of the leading countries in Western Europe, like the United Kingdom and Spain, may be in trouble; others, such as Germany and the Netherlands, seem to be doing better. As noted at the end of part 1, Finland will be an interesting test. If the Finns cannot take better advantage of their high civic literacy and sophisticated communications technology to overcome the political dropout problem, this bodes poorly for the newer democracies to Finland's south.

Which brings us to North America. When this book was originally conceived, nearly ten years ago, the American outlook was rather bleak:

> Young adults often lack the ability to become involved in public life. Most important in this regard is lack of information—from general knowledge about how government works to specific knowledge about how to register and vote . . . Never having experienced a period in which their own participation has effected meaningful change on an issue that mattered to them, and raised in an environment that regularly tells them such action is unlikely to succeed, it is hardly surprising that they are disinclined to participate in public life. (Delli Carpini 2000, 343)

Underlying the problem is the approach signaled in chapter 9, which Delli Carpini characterizes as engagement having "become *defined* as the one-on-one experience of working in a soup kitchen, cleaning trash from a local river, or tutoring a child once a week . . . Missing is an awareness of the connection between the individual, isolated 'problems' these actions are intended to address and the larger world of public policy; a sense that these problems might be addressed more systematically and (at times) more effectively through other forms of civic engagement (from joining a community group to voting); the belief that politics *matters*."[7]

To what extent has this picture in the United States shifted over the last decade? Undeniably, the widespread and profound consequences of the failure of the unregulated financial markets make it much harder at the end of this decade to deny that government policy and, therefore, politics matters. In addition, mobilization first against the Iraq war and then behind the nomination and election of Barack Obama has meant that the new generation cannot be depicted as having "never experienced a period in which their participation effected meaningful change." If the Internet is to be an instrument of political mobilization rather than demobilization, a matter we left undecided in chapter 3, the Obama movement's accomplishments in this regard will weigh heavily.

As I write—despite the sophistication and depth of the movement's online network, the more or less intact charisma of Obama, and the competence and dedication of his advisors—cracks are starting to appear, a reflection of the toxic mix of years of financial mismanagement and relatively dysfunctional political institutions. Short-term economic prospects are at best uncertain, and when recovery does come, the political cost of raising the money from American taxpayers to pay for the stimulus and bank, auto, and homeowners' rescue programs will be exacerbated by the fragmentation and diffusion of responsibility inherent in American institutions. The 2012 election should be a crucial test; though it is quite possible that the die will be cast in the pretest, the 2010 midterm congressional elections.

Looking ahead, we need also to look back. We need to remember that as the Obama movement was getting off the ground, 55 percent to 60 percent of Americans aged fifteen to twenty-five were, for all intents and purposes, off the political map. Even if that number declined significantly in 2008, and we do not know if it did, it could easily rise again by 2012. The efforts of the many organizations working to boost civic engagement in the United States will continue to make a contribution, but progress will be inhibited by the immobility of American institutions.

Among Obama's impressive commitments to fundamental change— in areas such as health care, the environment, and education—there was nothing about underlying political institutions, no commitment to act even on a practical and urgent reform like nonpartisan congressional redistricting. A good argument can be made that without institutional changes of this kind, the most effective electronic mobilization strategy around even the most charismatic leader will not be able to prolong increased levels of informed political participation and thus reduce the number of political dropouts among upcoming generations. In sum, without diminishing in any way the accomplishments of the current administration and the movement behind it, we cannot assume any sort of breakthrough on the political dropout front.

Which brings us, finally, to Canada. In summarizing the approach here proposed, I have taken Canada as an example: Canadian conditions are not unlike those of most industrial democracies, though closer to U.S. than Northern European patterns. In my earlier book (2002a), at the beginning of this decade, I wrote that the prospects of Canada's choosing the European path of fostering civic literacy through nonmaterial redistribution were not great, but that the potential was there. The more recent data cited in this book, including the low youth turnout rates and political knowledge scores, as well as the apparent ineffectiveness of civic education in Canada's Ontario heartland, suggest that the prospects have diminished. Thus I am more apprehensive about what we can do, but nevertheless convinced that action must be taken in the form of measures outlined here. Whatever doubts we have about their effectiveness, we can be sure that without them, the situation will be worse.

In placing our approach within the Canadian context, we start from a set of institutional arrangements that are not especially conducive to high levels of informed political participation. Canada has a parliamentary system of government with a second chamber, albeit a weak one. It has a federal system, with powerful provinces jealous of their powers. It lacks a proportional electoral system, which results in weak coordination between national and provincial party politics, and, effectively, no coordination at all between these and politics at the municipal level. Moreover, the electoral system inhibits inter-party cooperation, something very much needed in the current period of chronic minority governments. While this is increasingly apparent to observers, the failure of electoral reform in the provinces that considered it, plus the vested interests of politicians in the voting system that allowed them to get elected, continues to keep the issue off the political agenda. Nevertheless, some progress has been made on fixed election dates, and—by U.S., if not European, standards—on state funding and tight regulations that moderate the power of money in politics.

Institutional change, then, if not on the agenda is still on the table, with one key exception. Given Canada's size, geography, and composition, a form of federalism is inescapable. But there must be far greater coordination and cooperation. This is especially true in our area of concern. When it comes to civic education, Canadian federalism presents a structural problem, since education in Canada is under provincial jurisdiction. If the primary goal of civic education is to develop the habits of attentiveness to political life, it is only in Quebec where the prime focus of such attentiveness—the province—is also the level of political decision making that designs and implements education policy. In most of the remaining provinces, especially Ontario, federal politics is the primary focus of whatever attention is paid. It is thus crucial that public bodies at the two levels involved in civic education and stimulating electoral and other forms of political participation cooperate closely.

It is time to recapitulate briefly the key elements in our approach. They can be summarized in the following five guidelines. The first follows directly from our understanding of the state of events in Canada; the remaining principles are more generally applicable.

1. *The national and regional electoral and educational authorities must make a coordinated effort* to foster informed political participation by youth, and to support related work by civil-society groups.[8]

2. *Compulsory civic education courses*, targeting especially those young people from backgrounds placing them at risk of becoming political dropouts, should be offered as late as possible in compulsory schooling. In terms of content, the object is to create a climate that is rich in political information and attuned to the communication networks of the Internet generation. Seeking above all to foster attentiveness to public affairs and break down the wall between political life and real life, the courses should make optimal use of simulation processes and techniques, and online applications such as deliberative polls and voting advice applications (VAAs).

3. *A complementary framework of political institutions* should be developed over time, consisting of:

   a. Appropriately timed, fixed election dates.

   b. Elections using a regionally based, mixed member proportional system of elections with district boundaries, eligibility rules, etc. tailored to the realities of the setting.

   c. Political parties that operate at the national, provincial, and municipal levels.

4. *Setting the voting age at sixteen* (as pilot projects) should be considered in jurisdictions with high dropout rates.

5. *A serious, coordinated academic research effort* should be made, combining the evaluation of these initiatives with systematic, cross-

national empirical research into comparable programs, their content, outcomes, and wider implications. Work must be intensified in designing cross-national indicators to serve as dependent variables, giving special attention to measures of political knowledge.

In completing my book on civic literacy (Milner 2002a) almost a decade ago, I pondered the long-term implications of its analysis. The final paragraph is as fitting an ending for this book as for that one. Rereading those words almost a decade later, and focusing on young people, I find that they are still appropriate. It is true that more rapid advances in communications technology than I predicted are turning the digital divide referred to into one based more on skills than on access, but the implications are no less daunting.

Economic globalization and the danger of a widening digital divide add an element of urgency to the choice confronting democratic societies. All face the prospect of mirroring a globalized world economy with its minority of "winners," and majority of "losers"—losers not only as a result of economic deprivation, but, increasingly, as a result of their inability to take informed action to make their society better for themselves and others. Only high civic-literacy societies institutionally arranged so that a substantial majority of their citizens have meaningful maps to guide them through the complexity of decisions that their community will face in the coming years, will, potentially, be equipped to meet the challenge. Only those communities can hope to fairly distribute the costs of globalization and new information technology so as to draw optimal advantage from their benefits.

Appendix

Political Knowledge Questions
United States and Canada

- As far as you know, does the federal government spend more on Social Security [for Canada, "old age pensions"] or on foreign aid?
- Would you say that one of the [for Canada, add "major"] parties is more conservative ["more to the right"] than the other on the national level? [If yes: "Which party is more to the right?"]
- Which of the following best describes who is entitled to vote in federal elections?

  residents

  taxpayers

  legal residents

  citizens

  don't know

  refused to answer

- Please name two members of the president's [for Canada, "federal"] cabinet and identify the department they are in charge of.
- Five countries have permanent seats on the Security Council of the United Nations. Which of these countries can you name?

  Canada only

• What is the maximum number of years between Canadian elections?

    1 three years

    2 four years

    3 five years

    4 six years

    5 other number of years

• Can you tell me which party has the *second* largest number of seats in the House of Commons?

    1 the Conservatives

    2 the Liberals

    3 the Bloc Quebecois

    4 the NDP

• Obviously, a person on a low income will pay less total money in income tax than someone on a high income. But do you think that a person on a low income pays:

    1 a bigger *proportion* of their earnings in income tax than someone on a high income

    2 the same *proportion*

    3 or a smaller *proportion* of their earnings in income tax

United States only

• How much of a majority is required for the u.s. Senate and House to override a presidential veto?

Notes

1. Why Political Dropouts Matter

1 In its synthesis of a number of studies commissioned to investigate the phenomenon, the Canadian Policy Research Network concluded that "for many youth, the term 'politics' has become a synonym for self-serving, narrow, partisan politics and, as such, is of little interest to them" (MacKinnon, Pitre, and Watling 2007, 9).

2 A good example is provided by the Canadian election of October 2008, in which the opposition Liberals, supported by the Greens, presented a carbon tax as the cornerstone of their electoral program and went down to defeat. Despite pro-Green attitudes expressed by young citizens in public-opinion polls, and a slightly higher proportion of Green voters among the young, there was no sign that the youth vote had mobilized behind the program.

3 While the numbers are not entirely comparable, we can see an increase in this phenomenon from the previous decade. In 1999, a report from the International Institute for Democracy and Electoral Assistance (International IDEA) examining political participation among young people in fifteen Western European countries found that, while young people usually were less likely to vote than their elders, by the early 1990s, the turnout gap between citizens aged eighteen to twenty-nine and those over thirty had grown to 12 percent.

4 In the 2001 U.K. election, overall turnout sank to a postwar low of just 59 percent, with only 39 percent of young people casting a vote (Electoral Commission 2002). The turnout of young people declined again in 2005, to 37 percent ("Voter Turnout by Age," International IDEA, http://www.idea.int/vt/by_age.cfm; accessed 19 September 2009).

5 We find a very high correlation between the Gini coefficient of income equality and indicators of nonmaterial redistribution in OECD countries, such as reading comprehension levels at the lower levels of education (Milner 2002a, 14).

6 A subsequent paper (Grönlund and Milner 2006) used political knowledge questions asked in national election surveys to test this contention, finding that in the more economically unequal countries, relative levels of education had a greater impact on political knowledge (see chapter 6). See, for example, the world database of happiness (http://worlddatabaseofhappiness.eur.nl/hap_nat/findingreports/RankReport 2006-1d.htm; accessed 19 September 2009), which scores countries based on responses

228 // NOTES TO PAGES 8–14

to a question about satisfaction with life. Four of the top seven were Scandinavian welfare states (Denmark, Iceland, Finland, and Sweden).

7 A user-friendly site with excellent graphic representation of comparative data can be found at Gapminder.org. The reader could usefully benefit from seeking information of this kind by consulting this site.

8 An excellent discussion of these approaches is found in Lively (1975, 132–41).

9 Barber (1998) argues that it is civic competence that is the irreplaceable ingredient of strong democracies.

10 Galston (2001, 223). See also Delli Carpini and Keeter (1996) and Popkin and Dimock (1999).

11 When Putnam invokes civic education, his emphasis is on community participation rather than on political knowledge (2000, 405), and when he worries about the effects of television watching, he stresses that it takes time from voluntary activities rather than that it provides less knowledge than newspapers used to (Milner 2002a, 127–29).

12 In this book, we will use the term "political literacy" to refer to individuals, reserving the term "civic literacy" for aggregates.

13 An analysis of this debate in a Canadian context concludes: "People who are most in need of information short-cuts are often the least likely to be able to make use of them . . . Even the 'simplest shortcut of all' will be of little help to people who tune out of politics so completely that they do not know who the party leaders are" (Gidengil, Blais, Nevitte, and Nadeau 2004, 80.)

14 Sunstein (2007) argues that deliberation among like-minded persons in fact produces more extremism and less diversity. He describes a Colorado experiment in which researchers brought people from liberal Boulder together in small groups to talk about climate change, same-sex civil unions, and affirmative action, and brought other people from conservative Colorado Springs together in separate groups to discuss the same topics. The researchers recorded their subjects' views anonymously before and after the groups met. Both the liberals and the conservatives started out somewhat open-minded about these issues, but after discussion, diversity was squelched and extremism increased. A parallel finding emerges from Hungarian survey data: Tóka (2008) finds that communication with peers may lead not to broadening citizens' horizons but to locking them into the narrow perspective that dominates their particular social milieu, from which all or most of their discussion partners come; spreading biased information; and anchoring political choices in the expressive and the psychologically comforting, rather than in politically instrumental logic.

15 In the case of British Columbia, it took two referendums to defeat the proposal. In 2005, the vote in favor did not miss the required 60 percent by much; in 2009, however, it was only 39 percent.

16 The quotes come from the February 2007 update sent out by the National Coalition for Dialogue & Deliberation, at thataway.org.

17 Peter Berkowitz, quoted by Hindman 2009, 139.

18 The work of Fishkin and Luskin, who have conducted more than twenty deliberative polls—which poll participants before and after informing them on the relevant issues—shows that ordinary citizens have altered views after being informed. Since each such poll, which involves several hundred participants, requires special efforts that cost time and money, the process can reach only a small fraction of any sizable population. From a democratic standpoint, while informing ordinary citizens is necessary and useful, any method that is limited to small groups is inadequate. See Luskin, Fishkin, and Jowell (2002).

19 For example, to involve young people in the process of drawing up the draft treaty, a youth convention in July 2002 brought together 210 Europeans aged eighteen to twenty-five to discuss issues relating to the future of Europe. The group was organized along the same lines as the European Convention, and its results were presented to the convention on 13 July. In March 2003, 5,501 school leaders were assembled for discussions and meetings with EU political leaders and experts.

20 I find it extremely telling that the coalition of eighty European federalist groups which delivered a "warning to governments" on June 8, 1996, called itself the Forum Permanent de la Société Civile. The statement denounced governments that "keep putting forward the archaic conception of 'national interests'" (http://www.forum-civil-society.org/spip.php?rubrique27, accessed July 3, 1996).

21 In the Eurobarometer survey after the 1989 parliamentary election, only 16 percent of respondents credited the campaign with bringing out differences between the parties on European matters (http://ec.europa.eu/public_opinion/archives/eb/eb31/eb31_en.pdf, accessed October 6, 2009).

22 The authors used survey data from the Finnish study of the national parliamentary election held in March 2007. The survey consisted of two stages: face-to-face interviews, with a total of 1,422 respondents; and a questionnaire returned by mail, answered by 1,033 respondents.

23 European Social Survey data are available at http://ess.nsd.uib.no.

24 For example, despite their sympathy for unconventional forms of participating, Stolle and Cruz are unable to identify a significant group who have rejected traditional participation in favor of those unconventional forms, concluding from the ESS data that "there is a gap between those youth who are broadly engaged in a myriad of both new and traditional channels and those youth who are not engaged at all" (2005, 96–97).

25 This is confirmed by a 2006 study in which 2,000 people in the Montreal area aged nineteen to thirty-one were surveyed by telephone. Of those who reported having participated in a demonstration, 80 percent also reported having voted in the last election. The authors, after controlling for overreporting, conclude that rather than being mutually exclusive, one activity tends to go hand in hand with the other (Fournier, Blais, Gidengil, and Dostie-Goulet 2007).

26 A Canadian example of such a "making a virtue out of necessity" approach can be found in a study that suggested, among other things, that participation be widely defined to include media consumer choices such as casting votes on *Canadian Idol* (Barnard, Campbell, Smith, and Embuldeniya 2003).

27 Taking a subjective approach is justified by Haste and Hogan: "Political science or philosophy may find it feasible to identify distinct moral and political domains. However, from the standpoint of education we must start from where the citizen is, and it is manifestly obvious that lay people do not make such a clear distinction" (2006, 474).

28 Dalton tends to regard citizen duty as conformist and outdated, but van Deth, using data from the European Social Survey, shows that those who eschew traditional organized political participation in favor of individual activities have low levels of support for the norms of citizenship: "Their idea of 'responsibility taking' is evidently self-centred and based on clear support for the norm to form your own opinions and a reluctance to support solidarity and social engagement" (2009, 21).

29 In fact, even Dalton's figures do not bear out his claim that political skills are increasing and that, therefore, more varied and assertive means of political action are taking place. His figure 3.1 shows that when you combine citizen duty and engaged citizens, the total is much lower for generation Y then for the earlier generations, while his figures 4.3 and 4.4 show that low percentages actually take any action except voting.

30 This helps explain why twice as many of the 57 percent of high-school seniors who reported doing volunteer work, compared to the 43 percent who did not report doing so, scored satisfactory or better (34 percent versus 16 percent) in the National Assessment of Educational Progress test of proficiency in civics from the National Center for Education Statistics (1999).

31 Dalton bases his analysis on data from the Citizenship, Involvement, Democracy (CID) survey conducted by the Center for Democracy and Civil Society at Georgetown University. The survey included several political knowledge questions (see chapter 5). Hence, Dalton could have incorporated the political knowledge dimension in his analysis.

32 In the last round of elections for the European Parliament, in June 2009, 57 percent of eligible voters stayed home.

2. Political Socialization, Social Class, and Technological Transformation

1 MacKinnon, Pitre, and Watling (2007) sum up how the literature describes the context in which the Internet generation came of age in the 1990s. Apart from the pervasive influences of changing information and communication technologies, the main developments were: the devaluation of politics; the rejection of hierarchical forms of political participation; the trumpeting of greater individual choice as a social good;

and the emergence of private-sector "client" orientations in government's relations with the public.

2 In Canada, for example, between 1981 and 2001, the proportion of adult children aged twenty-five to twenty-nine still living at home doubled, from 12 to 24 percent, and the 2006 Canadian census found that 43.5 percent (up from 41.1 percent in 2001) of those aged twenty to twenty-nine have either remained at home with their families or moved back in (MacKinnon, Pitre, and Watling 2007).

3 According to Conover and Searing: "While most students identify themselves as citizens, their grasp of what it means to act as citizens is rudimentary and dominated by a focus on rights, thus creating a privately oriented, passive understanding" (2000, 108).

4 In the late 1960s, more than 80 percent of college freshmen endorsed "the importance of developing a meaningful philosophy of life" as their top value. "The importance of being very well off financially" then ranked fifth or sixth. Soule notes: "These two values have switched places: the top value is now being very well-off financially (71%). Developing a meaningful philosophy of life now occupies sixth place (41%) . . . This is a generation that values self-fulfillment (75%) above patriotism (55%), religion (53%) or money (48%), but appears prepared to work hard (87%) to achieve financial success" (2001, 15).

5 The new generation is nearly one-third less trusting than their parents: 64 percent of young people agree that "government is run by a few big interests looking out for themselves, not for the benefit of all," and 57 percent think "you can't trust politicians because most are dishonest" (Astin, Parrot, Korn, and Sax 1997).

6 The phenomenon of male dropouts has come to be reflected in the education system itself. Kyle Smith writes: "In her book, *The Trouble with Boys*, journalist Peg Tyre investigates an education system in which women principals oversee women teachers who treat girl behavior as standard . . . normal male behavior . . . is redefined as antisocial, threatening, or (most sinister of all) indicative of 'special needs' . . . (Boys are diagnosed with attention disorders at four times the rate of girls)" ("Outlawing Boyhood," *New York Post*, 13 December, 2008).

7 A comparable European trend can be found in Finland. As reported by Tuomo Martikainen ("Young Helsinki Residents Turn Backs on Electoral Process," *Helsingin Sanomat*, international edition, 1 June 2001), in the Finnish national parliamentary election of 1999, the participation gap between Finns with and without a postsecondary education in those aged twenty-five to twenty-nine was an enormous 52 percentage points (83 percent compared to 31 percent).

8 Levinson 2007, 6. See also Fridkin, Kenney, and Crittenden (2006) and Sherrod (2003).

9 A detailed study by Strate, Parrish, Elder, and Ford (1989, 456) concludes that life experiences which enhance the level of political participation have their most profound effects on those who are otherwise least advantaged.

10 For example, Nguyen and Garand (2008), using aggregate data for the American states from 1960 to 2004, show that income inequality depresses voter turnout in the states.

11 When it comes to turnout, it should be noted that compulsory voting significantly reduces this class bias.

12 The 1999 International IDEA study of youth voter participation, based on figures from the mid-1990s, identifies the same patterns.

13 A later study (Grönlund and Milner 2006) found differences in the dispersion of political knowledge by levels of educational attainment, which confirmed the predicted relationship between civic literacy and policies aimed at the redistribution of resources (see chapter 5).

14 The 2004 data are from the International Social Survey Program. These data are updated by data from the European Social Survey and the World Values Survey.

15 An explanation may be found in a recent comparative analysis of texts used in civic education, which concluded that the older ones conveyed "a sense of the importance of citizenship . . . describing how citizens can get involved and affect politics. The newer texts are less empowering" (Macedo et al. 2005, 33).

16 Foreword, *Engaging Young People in Civic Life*, edited by James Youniss and Peter Levine (Nashville, Tenn.: Vanderbilt University Press, 2009), x.

17 The authors interviewed 476 students between fifteen and eighteen years old, from fifty-five representative schools.

18 This is one effect of election simulations. See part 3.

19 This is an important consideration, since "divorce is two and a half times as common as marriage by a resident parent and more than three times as likely as the death of a parent during the period of adolescence" (Sandell and Plutzer 2005, 134).

20 Of the 6,894 respondents whose parents were married in 1988, 458 reported at least one divorce between 1988 and 1992. The effect of divorce was found to be comparable to the net impact of parental education for white youth.

21 A recent study (Wernli 2007) found this to be the case as well in contemporary Switzerland, when it comes to transmission of political orientations.

22 The only recent study I have come across that concretely makes the link between peer groups and political activity is that of Kuhn (2004), who found that German adolescents' support for radical right-wing parties and the use of political violence was strongly predicted by the behavior of their best friends and peer group. Moreover, the relationship was strongest in cases where the adolescents frequently communicated with their peers about political issues.

23 Cited in "Nearer to Overcoming," *The Economist*, 10 May 2008, p. 34.

24 Controlling for size, economic development, and many other factors, residents of more diverse American communities display lower confidence in local government

and news media. They have less confidence in their own influence and are less likely to register to vote and work on a community project. Nevertheless, they also display more interest in and knowledge about politics. In a comparative study based on the IEA data for fourteen- and fifteen-year-olds combining school demographics and intention to vote, Wilkenfeld (2008) finds racially diverse neighborhoods had a significantly depressing effect on intention to vote—but, interestingly, only on girls.

25 A recent study suggests that it may no longer be the case in Canada that racial and ethnic diversity have negative effects on social capital. Harell and Stolle (2008) find that the existing negative relationship among adults does not seem to apply to younger Canadians, for whom more racial and ethnic diversity in their social networks corresponds to higher levels of generalized trust.

26 Widestrom argues that the notion that low-income citizens do not vote because of their individual economic status misses the fact that the disincentives from voting due to their own economic status are enhanced by social interactions in the context of an impoverished neighborhood.

27 Lay's study used data from students at twenty-nine representative public high schools (grades nine to twelve) in Maryland and Virginia, with the communities broken down by population density as more rural or more urban. The dependent variable was political knowledge, based on an index of the number of correct answers out of the seven knowledge-related questions.

28 Rothstein and Stolle (2003) suggest that institutions may in fact matter more than associations for generating social capital.

3. The Revolution in Information Technology

1 Roper Center of the University of Connecticut, *Public Attitudes toward Television and other Media in a time of Change* (New York: Television Information Office, 1985) and *America's Watching: Public Attitudes toward Television* (New York: Television Information Office, 1987).

2 Even among the university educated, television had a lead of 10 percentage points. This is compared to the early 1960s, when newspapers were still 5 percentage points ahead of television.

3 A 2006 Pew study on news consumption ("Online Papers Modestly Boost Newspaper Readership," http://people-press.org/report/282/online-papers-modestly-boost-newspaper-readership, accessed 5 October 2009), for example, found that young people are far less likely to read newspapers, with 24 percent of participants aged eighteen to twenty-nine reporting that they had read a paper the previous day, compared to 58 percent of those aged sixty-five or older. In the United Kingdom, there has been a 25 percent drop among youth who report watching television news (Schifferes and Lusoli 2007). The 2003 General Social Survey showed that only half of Canadians in their twenties follow the news daily, compared to 89 percent of seniors (Milan

2005). In addition, in 2000 not only did just 16 percent of those born after 1970 report newspapers were their primary source of election information, but the proportion was not much greater for those born earlier (26 percent) or for college graduates (32 percent) (Gidengil, Blais, Nevitte, and Nadeau 2004, 29). The current state of affairs in Canada is well captured in the conclusion of an investigation that found that "ICTs both reflect and reinforce the existing inequalities. The digital divide—whether conceived narrowly in terms of connectivity, or more broadly in terms of the ability and capacity to use ICTs in ways that enhance the autonomy of disadvantaged citizens—is an enduring reality in Canada's corner of cyber-space" (Barney 2005, 176–77).

4 A useful insight into the different effects on informed political participation by the media is provided by an Australian study (Edwards, Saha, and Print 2005). When asked, "Where do you get your information about voting in elections?" the student respondents placed television ahead of newspapers; but when the authors looked at the correlation between the amount of information from each source and student's intention to vote when eighteen, "even if voting were not compulsory," newspaper readership pulled well ahead of television.

5 For instance, Boiney notes: "We can retrieve meaning from televised communication [but] ... there's a trap ... [since we] assume that pieces of information communicated ... at the same time or in the same space, are consistent with one another ... When an ad fails to refer explicitly to some piece of information upon which an invited inference turns ... [viewers] without that information ... fill in the 'blank' with the interpretation that best fits with the scenario the ad has created, via mood-inducing music, attractive visuals, word choice, editing" (1993, 6–11).

6 For example, a European study revealed that "in most countries, higher levels of knowledge are positively and significantly correlated with preferences for public broadcasting, and in particular with preference for public TV combined with regular exposure to news" (Holtz-Bacha and Norris, 2001, 136). See also Aarts and Semetko (2003).

7 In an effort to measure this, I developed an indicator composed equally of average weekly television watching by country, and national per capita spending on television advertising. In the English-speaking and Southern European countries, typically four or five people read each copy of a daily newspaper that was sold, with commercial television watching widespread and frequent; in Northern Europe, two or three people read each newspaper, and commercial television was less popular.

8 Wattenberg adds that cable news networks, with combined ratings equal to 10 percent of those of the commercial networks (ABC, CBS, and NBC), could not be picking up the slack. One contemporary American phenomenon bears mentioning here: the political comedy shows, in particular Jon Stewart's *The Daily Show*—which, despite being on a cable channel with a relatively small audience, is watched regularly by millions of mainly young people. A study by Cao (2005) found young Americans especially likely to report in surveys that they learned about campaigns from political comedy shows.

9 At the end of the 1980s, there were on average thirty-eight fewer minutes of foreign news on combined weekly U.S. network news programs than at the beginning of the decade ("Harper's Index," *Harper's*, July 1993).

10 One comparison of responses to a survey question about the frequency of TV news watching in 1970 and 2000 in five European countries found an apparent increase in the overall percentage answering "every day" (Wattenberg 2007, 54).

11 One revealing study (Morris and Forgette 2004) used the Pew Research Center's 2004 Biennial Media Consumption Survey to identify "newsgrazers," respondents who agreed that, "I find that I often watch the news with my remote control in hand, flipping to other channels when I'm not interested in the topic." Newsgrazers were significantly less likely to follow news about people and events in national politics, international affairs, and local government, though not in sports, entertainment, culture and the arts, and the weather. Newsgrazers avoid news stories that present differing points of view, as well as those that feature in-depth interviews with political leaders and policymakers. Newsgrazing is "negatively associated with the ability to correctly identify the majority party in the US House of Representatives as well as the name of the terrorist organization responsible for the September 11 attacks . . . but not with knowledge of whether Martha Stewart was found guilty in federal court" (Morris and Forgette 2004, 101). It is also, once demographic factors are controlled for, negatively associated with voting, especially among those aged eighteen to twenty-four.

12 Lee Rainie and Janna Anderson, "The Future of the Internet III," http://www.pew internet.org/Reports/2008/The-Future-of-the-Internet-III.aspx (accessed 22 September 2009).

13 James V. Delong reports that in 2005 U.S. newspaper advertising reached its peak: "Papers collected $44.7 billion for print advertising . . . Online ads produced $2 billion, and $11 billion came from 54 million daily readers . . . Since then, it has been downhill . . . Ad revenues declined to $45.4 billion in 2007, followed by quarter-by-quarter falls of 12 percent to 20 percent during the catastrophes of 2008 . . . The most immediate threat from the Internet is classified ads . . . vulnerable to complete cannibalization by the Internet . . . Losing up to 30 percent of the revenues in a leveraged model is not good, but the real fear is that the rest of the advertisers will also leave" ("Preparing the Obituary," *The American*, March 3, 2009, http://american.com/archive/2009/february-2009/preparing-the-obituary/?searchterm=Preparing%20the%20Obituary (accessed 22 September 2009).

14 See John Nichols and Robert W. McChesney, "The Death and Life of Great American Newspapers," *The Nation*, 6 April 2009.

15 Eduardo Porter, "What Newspapers Do, Have Done and Will Do," *The New York Times*, February 13, 2009. Porter rejects the idea that the Internet and cable TV will fill the gap: "Cash-strapped TV stations depend on newspapers for much of their local news coverage. Cable news is increasingly commentary. And rather than a citizen reporter, the Internet has given us the citizen pundit, who comments on newspaper articles. Reporting the news in far-flung countries, spending weeks on investigations

of uncertain payoff, fighting for freedom of information in court—is expensive. Virtually the only entities still doing it on the necessary scale are newspapers. Letting them go on the expectation that the Internet will enable a better-informed citizenry seems like a risky bet."

16 In a study of 2,032 representative eight- to eighteen-year-olds, the Kaiser Family Foundation found that nearly half used the Internet on a typical day in 2004, up from just under a quarter in 1999. The average time that these children spent online on a typical day rose to one hour and forty-one minutes in 2004, from forty-six minutes in 1999. See Motoko Rich, "Literacy Debate: Online, R U Really Reading?" *The New York Times*, 27 July 2008.

17 A study of 210 college students by Aryn Karpinshki found Facebook users (see the discussion below) to have grades 10 percentage points lower than nonusers, and to study less than half as many hours each week (http://researchnews.osu.edu/archive/facebookusers.htm, accessed 5 October 2009).

18 Motoko Rich, "Literacy Debate: Online, R U Really Reading?" *The New York Times*, 27 July 2008. The site is http://zapatopi.net/treeoctopus.

19 In the United States, "more than 75 billion text messages are sent a month, and the most avid texters are 13 to 17, say researchers. Teens with cellphones average 2,272 text messages a month, compared with 203 calls, according to the Nielsen Co." (Donna St. George, "6,473 Texts a Month, But at What Cost?" *The Washington Post*, 22 February 2009).

20 The article concludes: "A decade ago, a zealot seeking to prove some absurd proposition—such as the denial of the Nazi Holocaust, or the Ukrainian famine—might spend days of research in the library looking for obscure works of propaganda. Today, digital versions of these books, even those out of press for decades, are accessible in dedicated online libraries" ("The Brave New World of E-hatred: Social Networks and Video-sharing Sites Don't Always Bring People Closer Together," *The Economist*, 24 July 2008).

21 Eli Saslow, "In Flag City USA, False Obama Rumors Are Flying" *The Washington Post*, 30 June 2008. And Nicholas D. Kristof reports: "A Pew Research Center survey released a few days ago found that only half of Americans correctly know that Mr. Obama is a Christian. Meanwhile, 13 percent of registered voters say that he is a Muslim, compared with 12 percent in June and 10 percent in March. More ominously, a rising share—now 16 percent—say they aren't sure about his religion because they've heard 'different things' about it" ("The Push to 'Otherize' Obama," *New York Times*, 20 September 2008).

22 An example of the potential benefits of this technology is the case of John Philip Neufeld, a twenty-one-year-old music student at Concordia University in Montreal, who sometimes acts as moderator on a website where people can upload computer-generated animation. When surfing the Web just before dawn on 17 March 2009, "he stumbled on a fresh posting that made him nervous. 'It said: "Today at 11:30, I am going to blow up my school. Those bastards are going to pay," [along with] a photo-

graph of himself holding a gasoline canister . . . Having spotted a link on the posting to a news site in England's Norfolk region, Mr. Neufeld tracked down the phone number for police in the area . . . Mr. Neufeld said police, who had received another warning from a British web surfer, took the tip seriously . . . Police were waiting at Attleborough High School when a 16-year-old boy arrived around 11:30 a.m. armed with a knife, matches and a canister of what appeared to be flammable liquid" (Peggy Curran, "Montreal Student Helps Avert British School Attack," *Canwest News Service*, 20 March 2009).

23 See Louise Story, "To Aim Ads, Web Is Keeping Closer Eye on You," *The New York Times*, 10 March 2008. Another disturbing element emerges from a Canadian survey of 308 Facebook users, which found the more time they spent on the site, the more suspicious they became of their partners: "The researchers argue that the social-networking site provides a vast catalogue of potentially painful artifacts . . . the site gives people unprecedented access to the 'off hours' of their significant others . . . 'You get a news feed telling you who posted on your partner's wall, who said what, what friends have been added.' . . . even those who refrain from spying on their partners are not immune . . . 'Friends end up providing you with information that 10, 15 years ago you would never have found out about . . . And suddenly you're exposed to every-body else's misattribution of what's going on in the pictures and comments'" (Zosia Bielski, "Facebook Is . . . Breeding Spying, Jealous Lovers," *The Globe and Mail*, 9 April 2009).

24 In an interview with Salon.com, Sunstein expresses the fear that "when it comes to the Internet, we demand the right to reinforce our own beliefs without embracing the responsibility to challenge them." He finds a danger to democratic discourse in "all the excitement about personalization and customization, hearing people saying 'this is unbelievably great that we can just include what we like and exclude what we dislike,' when his research into jury behavior was "finding that like-minded jurors, when they talk to one another, tend to get more extreme" (http://www.salon.com/news/feature/2007/11/07/sunstein, accessed 22 September 2009). Hindman (2009, 66) cites a study showing that only 2.6 percent of the traffic of the top fifty American political websites crosses ideological lines, a situation well captured by Manjoo (2008), who describes Americans as organizing themselves into "echo chambers." The earliest thinker along these lines was Nicholas Negroponte, the founder of MIT's Media Lab, who coined the term "the Daily Me" to describe a virtual daily newspaper customized for an individual's tastes.

25 This is not necessarily a universal phenomenon, however. A study of Finland, a society with very high Internet usage and high civic literacy, found a somewhat different situation: while highly motivated Finns do make use of the Internet to obtain political information, the overall relationship between such use and level of political knowledge is still quite weak (Grönlund 2007).

26 We need to be somewhat skeptical of the finding that reading Internet news is the most strongly correlated with high levels of interest and knowledge, since some deliberate intent and effort is often needed in order to access political news online. But it is

also true that commonly used portals like Yahoo and MSN place news headlines on their home pages, while Google, like others, offers an immediate link to its news pages.

27 Sherr suggests that the latter had greater credibility, which is a significant factor in determining the degree to which subjects retain the information provided. Another experiment showed that providing young people with a CD containing useful political information gave them a meaningful opportunity to engage in the world of politics (Iyengar and Jackman 2004).

28 The term "netizen" was coined in 1992 by the computer specialist Michael Hauben, to refer to an Internet user with a sense of civic responsibility to the online community corresponding to a citizen's duty to his country.

29 Iyengar and Jackman note: "In the words of a 17 year-old respondent in a recent Pew Internet and American Life survey, 'I multi-task every single second I am online. At this very moment I am watching TV, checking my email every two minutes, reading a newsgroup about who shot JFK, burning some music to a CD, and writing this message'" (2004, 3).

30 "Starting in July, telecommunication companies in the northern European nation will be required to provide all 5.2 million citizens with Internet connection that runs at speeds of at least 1 megabit per second" (Saeed Ahmed, "Finland Declares High-Speed Internet Access a Legal Right," CNN Wire, http://cnnwire.blogs.cnn.com/2009/10/15/finland-declares-high-speed-internet-access-a-legal-right, accessed 15 October 2009).

31 Cited by Hindman (2009, 69).

32 Jenkins describes these skills as follows: "Play—the capacity to experiment with one's surroundings as a form of problem-solving; Performance—the ability to adopt alternative identities for the purpose of improvisation and discovery; Simulation—the ability to interpret and construct dynamic models of real-world processes; Appropriation—the ability to meaningfully sample and remix media content; Multitasking—the ability to scan one's environment and shift focus as needed to salient details; Distributed Cognition—the ability to interact meaningfully with tools that expand mental capacities; Collective Intelligence—the ability to pool knowledge and compare notes with others toward a common goal; Judgment—the ability to evaluate the reliability and credibility of different digital information media; Transmedia Navigation—the ability to follow the flow of stories and information across multiple modalities; Networking—the ability to search for, synthesize, and disseminate information; Negotiation—the ability to travel across diverse communities, discerning and respecting multiple perspectives" (2006, 4).

33 These forms, as identified by Jenkins (2006, 3), include digital sampling, skinning and modding, fan videomaking, fan fiction writing, zines and mashups—and I admit to having no idea what most of them mean.

34 When Canadians were asked (in the 2000 Canadian Election Study) if they ever used the Internet to inform themselves about politics, by far the most important dis-

criminating factor was education, with income second (Gidengil, Blais, Nevitte, and Nadeau 2004, 33).

35 Using the international student-level PISA (Programme for International Student Assessment) database, Fuchs and Woessmann (2004) show that the positive correlation between student achievement and the availability of computers both at home and at school becomes negative for home computers, and insignificant for school computers, once they control for family background and school characteristics.

36 Indymedia, for example, had its origins in 1999 in the lead up to the protests against the World Trade Organization meetings in Seattle. It grew into a global network of over 135 news websites, where volunteer contributors post news with local, regional, and international content (Chadwick 2006). An example of a more nonpartisan site is "TakingITGlobal" (see Raynes-Goldie and Walker 2007), oriented to enhancing youth participation.

37 According to *Advertising Age*, 90 percent of Canadian undergraduate students report using Facebook daily (Zosia Bielski, "Facebook Is . . . Breeding Spying, Jealous Lovers," *The Globe and Mail*, 9 April 2009).

38 Here is a story that suggests that people put very little weight on their online commitments: "One day this past summer, I logged on to Facebook and realized that I was very close to having 700 online 'friends' . . . So I decided to have a Facebook party. I used Facebook to create an 'event' and invite my digital chums . . . Facebook gives people the option of RSVP'ing in three categories—'attending,' 'maybe attending' and 'not attending' . . . Fifteen people said they were attending, and 60 said maybe . . . one person showed up. I would learn, when I asked some people who didn't show up the next day, that 'definitely attending' on Facebook means 'maybe' and 'maybe attending' means 'likely not'" (Hal Niedzviecki, "Facebook in a Crowd," *The New York Times*, 26 October 2008).

39 Hindman (2009), tracking nearly three million websites, finds that the Internet in fact empowers a small set of mainly familiar elites, and that online organizing is dominated by a few powerful interest groups. He concludes that the Internet has neither diminished the audience share of corporate media, nor given greater voice to ordinary citizens.

40 Virginia Heffernan, "The Medium: Clicking and Choosing," *The New York Times Magazine*, 16 November 2008.

41 Danielle Allen, "Citizenship 2.0," *The Washington Post*, 25 November 2008.

42 At the end of February 2008, when his campaign really took off, Obama had 300,000 friends on Facebook (Hillary Clinton had 85,000). On both MySpace and YouTube, there were almost three times as many sites for Obama as for Clinton. Among the YouTube election-related clips, the five most popular Clinton ones were seen by an average of 383,000 viewers, compared to 847,000 viewers on average for Obama's top five clips. And Obama's campaign raised many millions of dollars in small donations via these sites (Karine Prémont, "L'Internet favorise Obama," *La Presse*, 22 February 2008).

43 Baumgartner and Morris (2008). Similarly, Cantioch and San Martin (2008) find that in Spain, exposure to political content on the Internet does not affect voter turn-out, which was not the case with traditional media.

44 Danielle Allen, "Citizenship 2.0," *The Washington Post*, 25 November 2008.

45 The first major test of the network took place in March 2009, when it sent people door to door to sell Obama's budget. A similar initiative took place over health care later in the spring.

46 Such an assessment needs to take into consideration the fact that social network-ing sites have also ushered in new forms of mischief. In response to a Canadian survey, 21 percent of high-school students in the Toronto area stated that they had been bul-lied, 35 percent admitted having bullied, 11 percent said that they had been threatened, and 18 percent said that someone had posed as them (Tim Johnson, "The Wild Web," *University Affairs*, November 2008, 10–11).

47 "Internet Overtakes Newspapers as News Outlet," *News Interest Index*, 23 Decem-ber 2008, http://people-press.org/report/479/internet-overtakes-newspapers-as-news-source (accessed 23 September 2009). The Obama effect seems to have sped this pro-cess along; no similar development was perceived in Canada, where "even among the 18–29 and 30–39 demographic age groups, who do use the Internet more than news-papers as a news source . . . TV's share is dominant" (Nik Nanos, "TV Is Still Top and Most Trusted News Source; Newspapers Second, and Internet Last,"*Policy Options*, June 2009, p. 1).

4. Political Participation: Do Young People Still Vote?

1 For example, McCann (2008) finds that American voters are significantly more so-cially and politically engaged than nonvoters, even when we control for age, education, etc.

2 The exception is U.S. party membership, but this high number is in fact more a re-flection of the percentage registered to vote, since Americans register as Democrats, Republicans, or independents.

3 See, for example, Milner (2002a) for comparative analysis based on average turnout in municipal elections. It proved very difficult to get good comparable data, especially for federal countries like the United States and Canada. It would be almost impossible at this point to obtain age-based, comparative turnout data.

4 Part, but not all, of the decline is attributable to the inclusion of eastern European countries, starting in the 1990s.

5 The shrinking of party memberships is very much a generational phenomenon (Goerres 2008; Sloam 2007; Electoral Commission 2002; Cross and Young 2004; O'Neill 2001).

6 Table 4.1 uses data mainly from the minority of democratic countries that make available recorded data about which individuals actually voted, which allows for link-

ing voting with certain attributes specified on the voters' list: e.g., gender and, usually, age.

7 For example, in the Canadian Election Study of 2000, 83 percent of respondents reported having voted, while the official turnout was under 61 percent (Rubenson et al. 2004, 408).

8 Pammett and LeDuc developed and applied a weighting factor to maintain the number of respondents who reported not voting, but discounted (i.e., negatively weighed) the scores of those who reported having voted, to force the data as a whole to reflect the aggregate turnout percentage (61.3 percent).

9 An illustration of this phenomenon emerges from the work of two French political scientists who made a sustained effort to track down political abstainers in La Cité de Cosmonautes, a working-class district in Saint-Denis, north of Paris. It became clear that those residents who could be reached and were willing to fill out a questionnaire, and to do so honestly, were not at all representative of the overall population. The authors conclude: "In trying to understand . . . the electoral demobilization that especially affects popular districts, the traditional sociological methods that are used seem manifestly inadequate. Due to their being unavailable or refusing to respond or concealing . . . [such behaviors as] failing to register or vote . . . [the underclass] is invariably poorly represented in surveys" (Braconnier and Dormagen 2007, 12–13, my translation).

10 It is prohibited by law in the United States and elsewhere to make cellphone numbers available for unsolicited calls, including surveys; yet even if such surveys were permitted, response rates would surely be low.

11 Potential participants who are not already on the Internet are sent an Internet appliance and receive an Internet service connection provided by Knowledge Networks. People who already have computers and Internet service can participate using their own equipment. Panelists receive unique log-in information for accessing surveys online (see http://www.knowledgenetworks.com/ganp/index.html).

12 "Youth Voter DNA Report," 2006, http://www.d-code.com/pdfs/YouthVoterDNA .pdf (accessed 23 September 2009).

13 The findings from this study are consistent with those of other such analyses. In a study combining longitudinal and cross-sectional analyses using Eurobarometer data, Wattenberg (2007, 124) shows that age-based variations were minimal in Germany, Italy, Denmark, the Netherlands, and Ireland, and moderate in France and the United Kingdom in 1979; they remained minimal in Italy and Denmark, and moderate in France, in 1999. There was a change from minimal to moderate in Germany and the Netherlands, while Ireland and the United Kingdom bounded to high levels of age-based inequality in 1997. Another study using Eurobarometer data adds Greece and Spain to the countries where youth turnout was significantly lower than other age categories (Anduiza Perea 1995).

14 For Sweden, the cutoff age was thirty.

15 In Finland, for reasons explained elsewhere in this book, social class plays an especially important role in fueling the decline. As noted in chapter 2, in the Finnish national parliamentary election of 1999, only 31 percent of those aged twenty-five to twenty-nine who had no postsecondary education voted, compared to 83 percent who had.

16 Data provided by Professor Bernt Aardal, at the Institutt for Samfunnsforskning (ISF; the Institute for Social Research), Oslo, 16 September 2009. In 1999, only 31 percent of those born after 1975 voted in local elections (Bjorklund 2000, 19).

17 For example, Anduiza Perea (2002, 9) sums up the situation in Spain: "non voters . . . are younger than voters. They have paid less attention to the campaign and they have talked little about politics during the campaign."

18 Using data from International IDEA (2004, 131) to convert the official 2004 Canadian rate of 60.9 percent of registered voters into potential voters to make it comparable to U.S. data, we arrive at a figure of approximately 53 percent.

19 John B. Anderson and Ray Martinez II, "Voters Ed" (*The New York Times*, 6 April 2006.)

20 It was in 1972 that eighteen-year-olds first became eligible to vote in the United States, and this change is in part responsible for the drop. But there is more to it: a wider generational phenomenon is at work (see Blais, Gidengil, Nevitte, and Nadeau 2004; Franklin, Lyons, and Marsh 2004).

21 Doug Hess, "Analysis of the 2008 Current Population Survey (CPS) Voter and Registration Supplement," http://www.projectvote.org/images/publications/Reports%20on%20the%20Electorate/Analysis%20of%20the%202008%20CPS%20Voting%20Supplement.pdf (accessed 5 October 2009).

22 This turnout rate was calculated for states that had both Republican and Democratic exit polls in 2000 and 2008—except for Rhode Island, where there was only a Democratic exit poll (Scott Keeter, "Young Voters in the 2008 Presidential Primaries," Pew Research Center for the People and the Press, 11 February 2008; http://pewresearch.org/pubs/730/young-voters (accessed 5 October 2009); see also Kirby, Marcelo, Gillerman, and Linkins, 2008).

23 Karlo Barrios Marcelo and Emily Hoban Kirby, "The Youth Vote in the 2008 Super Tuesday States," http://www.civicyouth.org/PopUps/FactSheets/FS08_supertuesday_exitpolls.pdf (accessed 5 October 2009). See also Lopez, Kirby, and Sagoff (2005).

24 Reported voter turnout numbers in Canadian federal elections since 1968 suggest that an individual's propensity to vote typically increases by about 15 percentage points between ages twenty and fifty (Gidengil, Blais, Nevitte, and Nadeau 2004).

25 Elections Canada used actual electoral data to create a sample made up of all electors who voted at an advance poll, by special ballot, or at a polling station on Election Day, combined with a sample drawn from actual recorded votes in fifty constituencies.

26 The 2004 general election was held in late June, when college students were at
home; the 2006 general election, however, took place on 23 January, at the start of the
semester. Because students could choose whether to vote at their campus or family
home, Elections Canada chose to take this geographic concentration into account.
Consequently, electoral districts with at least one large campus were included in the
sample (all the provinces except Ontario and Quebec had only one district in the
sample). Elections Canada used a weighting procedure to correct for the deliberate
sampling of districts with colleges, but it is not clear to me that it eliminated all overrepresentation of students within the age cohort. If it was able to do so, the fact that
the sampling in the 2004 study paid no attention to whether the districts chosen contained campuses, it is possible that since there were thus too few districts with universities in 2004 could explain the apparent jump in turnout in 2006 among the older
young voters.

27 Switzerland is another country with traditionally low turnout that has seen some
improvement in recent years. According to International IDEA, it gradually rose from
a low of 42.2 percent in 1995 to 48.3 percent in 2007 (http://www.idea.int/vt/country
_view.cfm?CountryCode=CH, accessed 24 September 2009).

28 This effect could prove to be short-lived. Consider the turnout for the second-
round senatorial election in Georgia, which, had their candidate won, could have given
the Democrats the magic filibuster-breaking number of 60 members in the Senate.
However, Robbie Brown and Carl Hulse reported: "Many of the Democrats who
turned out last month in enthusiastic support of Barack Obama apparently did not
show up at the polls on Tuesday. 'For a lot of African-American voters, the real election was last month,' said Merle Black, an expert in Southern politics at Emory University ... A little more than two million people voted in the runoff, compared with 3.7
million on Nov. 4"("Republican Wins Runoff for Senator in Georgia," *The New York
Times*, 2 December 2008).

29 The Swedish National Board for Youth Affairs, "Young People with Attitude,"
http://www.ungdomsstyrelsen.se/ad2/user_documents/Youngpeoplewithattitude.pdf
(accessed 5 October 2009).

30 This is not all that unusual. In Canada, with its high age gap in turnout, levels of
cynicism are actually slightly higher among those over thirty than those aged eighteen
to twenty-five (Rubenson et al. 2004, 418–19).

5. The Political Knowledge of Emerging Generations

1 Luskin concludes from the results of more than twenty deliberative polls (see chapter 1) that better informed publics have markedly different preferences for policies and
election outcomes due to substantial information gains and frequent and substantial
changes of attitude (2002). Tóka (2002) shows that across twenty-odd Czech, Hungarian, Polish, and Slovak surveys, the association between party preference, on the one
hand, and economic evaluations and left-right self-placement, on the other hand, is

almost always stronger at higher levels of information about the party composition of the national government.

2 The unpublished study, titled "Some Findings from an Analysis of the Roper Social Capital Benchmarck 2000 Survey," was conducted on my behalf in August 2002 by Richard E. DeLeon of San Francisco State University.

3 The overall finding is based on responses to a telephone survey in 2000 of a U.S. sample of almost 30,000 respondents from thirty-nine communities, with independent samples ranging from 388 to 1,505 respondents using logistic regression modeling. The finding holds up after statistically controlling for the effects of the other predictors. Separate logistic regression on each of the thirty-nine community samples found that statistically controlling for the effects of all other predictors in the model, the political knowledge predictor was statistically significant in twenty-seven of the thirty-nine communities.

4 Similarly, a study of 1,500 respondents in late 1995 found that "those in the highest third of the survey in terms of political knowledge were twice as likely to have voted in the 1994 presidential election as those in the lowest third" (Morin 1996, 7). The difference is even larger in off-year legislative elections (Popkin and Dimock 1999, 137). An interesting confirmation is provided by an experiment concerning a Copenhagen referendum on decentralization. Residents in four of fifteen districts received additional information about the effects of decentralization, resulting in "a sizeable and statistically significant causal effect of being informed on the propensity to vote" (Lassen 2005, 103).

5 The European Social Survey came close to including six such questions in its second round, but they were dropped at the last minute for lack of space.

6 Norris (2000) looked at answers to several such political knowledge questions and found, for example, that two-thirds of respondents knew that most EU institutions were in Brussels or Luxembourg, and half knewthat the European flag had a blue background and yellow/gold stars, but less than a fifth were able to name Jacques Santer as president of the EU Commission.

7 The International Adult Literacy Survey tested the comprehension of a large sample of the population aged sixteen and over in twenty-two industrial democracies, using three types of written materials: narrative prose; documents, such as train schedules and medication instructions; and problems requiring the application of basic arithmetic skills (Organisation for Economic Co-operation and Development 1997, 2000).

8 I use this score rather than average IALS score because civic literacy is a measure of the proportion of citizens with the minimal knowledge and skills to participate effectively. The functionally illiterate are effectively excluded: they are, with few exceptions, condemned to be political dropouts.

9 Respondents were asked to identify the U.N. Secretary General from a list of five names, and to name a U.N. agency (Millard 1993).

10 For example, a recent study (Aalberg and Strabac 2008) used response data from the last European Social Survey and the similar U.S. Citizenship, Involvement, Dem-

ocracy (CID) Survey from 2005 to a question that asked respondents to estimate the proportion of immigrants in their country's population. The U.S. respondents proved to be further from the actual number in their average estimates than those from every European country surveyed except France.

11 I have not included the scores on the question about the length of the election cycle, given the fixed election date in Finland, but had I done so, the difference in correct scores on that question between Finland (91 percent) and Canada (23 percent) would have significantly increased the overall difference.

12 These data were given me by Kimmo Grönlund of the Abo Academy, in Finland, 9 June 2002.

13 A similar phenomenon has been taking place in Sweden. According to Sören Holmberg, the director of the Swedish Election Study, the age difference in political knowledge increased even more in the latest survey, taken during the 2006 election (personal communication, March 2007).

14 "Public Knowledge of Current Affairs Little Changed by News and Information Revolutions: What Americans Know: 1989–2007," http://people-press.org/report/319/public-knowledge-of-current-affairs-little-changed-by-news-and-information-revolutions (accessed 5 October 2009). The low levels of U.S. political knowledge were revealed in earlier national surveys. Using the results of another Pew survey, Parker and Deane (1997) found that, on average, 36 percent of the respondents under thirty answered the information questions correctly, compared to 45 percent of those over thirty. Only 26 percent of young people answered campaign-related questions correctly, compared to 38 percent of those aged thirty to forty-nine, and 42 percent of those aged fifty or older.

15 The latter showed respondents a list of ten prominent political figures, of which two were Canadian, and asked them to identify the country and position of each, and a list of Canada's ten provincial premiers and asked them to identify each premier's province. The 2000 CES included questions asking the names of party leaders, the finance minister, and the premier of the province.

16 We know from an analysis of the 1997 Canadian Election Study data that the more politically knowledgeable were 9 percent more likely to have voted, a percentage higher than for all the other nineteen tested variables—including level of education and political interest—except age (Coulson 1999).

17 In a 1990 survey, 5 percent of Canadians could not name the prime minister; in a survey in March 2000, 11 percent could not do so. In 2000, when asked to identify the prime minister, finance minister, and official opposition party, 67 percent of those aged eighteen to twenty-nine answered only one of the three correctly, compared to 46 percent for the sample as a whole (Howe 2001).

18 A modicum of similarity emerges due to their content being chosen in such a way that the three questions are expected to be answered correctly by, respectively, roughly one-third, one-half, and two-thirds of the respondents.

19 I exclude the results of the Civic Education Study (discussed in chapter 9), which tested nearly 90,000 fourteen-year-old students in twenty-eight countries and 50,000 students aged seventeen to nineteen in sixteen countries on political knowledge, skills, and attitudes (Torney-Purta, Lehmann, Oswald, and Schulz 2001). The questions in that study exclude facts and thus do not permit a clear, comparative assessment of political knowledge. Instead, they test understanding of the logic of democracy and the functions of institutions in a democracy.

20 For example: "The Taliban and al Qaeda movements were both based in which country?" "Which two countries have had a longstanding conflict over the region of Kashmir?"

21 Although only young people were included in the survey, we can compare rankings for earlier generations by going back to the once-well-known study conducted for *National Geographic* (Gilbert M. Grosvenor, December 1989, 816–18), which asked a sample of the population in many of the same ten countries to locate sixteen places on a map of the world. Sweden came in first, with 11.6 average right answers; Germany, Japan, France, and Canada followed with, 11.2, 9.6, 9.3, and 9.2, respectively; and then came the United States and the United Kingdom, with 8.6 and 8.5. The only major change was the significant improvement of Italy, from eighth to third place.

22 The number surveyed was actually higher, but I do not include the data from the survey of oversamples of African Americans, Latinos, and Asian Americans aged fifteen to twenty-five conducted online. No such effort was undertaken in Canada, both because there is no comparable population, and also because there is reason to suspect that Internet survey respondents behave differently from respondents contacted in other ways. As noted in chapter 4, for online surveys, respondents are drawn from a list of people who have expressed initial interest in participating in surveys, and the methodology used to create Internet samples in Canada is more problematic than that used by Knowledge Networks, which carried out the U.S. Internet survey.

23 The sample was drawn using standard list-assisted, random digit dialing (RDD) methodology. The telephone interviewing oversampled those aged fifteen to twenty-five by setting a quota for respondents aged twenty-six and older. After that quota was filled, all remaining interviews were conducted with respondents aged fifteen to twenty-five. Interviews were conducted with fifteen-year-olds only after getting their parents' consent.

24 The U.S. survey, which drew on greater financial resources, made a greater effort to track down difficult–to-reach potential respondents. In the end, the response rate for those aged fifteen to twenty-five in the U.S. survey was 24.7 percent, while in the Canadian survey it was only 9.7 percent. It is clearly becoming extremely difficult to conduct telephone surveys, especially of young people. For Canada especially, that is clearly shown by the fact that reported voting was much higher than that found by Elections Canada—another reason I give little weight to reported voting. In many instances, low response rates make conclusions dubious, since those not responding are likely to differ from those responding on the attitudes being surveyed. (A glaring

example is a survey headlined in Montreal's *La Presse* on 4 July 2007, stating that 86 percent of young Quebeckers were happy.) As far as political knowledge is concerned, if the low response rate skewed the outcome, it most likely did so in the direction of higher levels of political knowledge. Hence there is no reason to believe that it affected the basic findings, except that the differential in response rate could account in part for the lower level of knowledge of the Americans.

25 Thomas and Young (2006) show a clear gender gap in political knowledge in Canada. College-educated women are roughly as knowledgeable about conventional politics as are men without a college education, which translates into a persistent gender gap among young people who have gone to college.

26 This was corroborated in a survey conducted by the Pew Research Center for the People & the Press, which found that among young adults, "just a quarter could identify Condoleezza Rice as the current secretary of state, compared with 46% of older Americans" ("How Young People View Their Lives, Futures and Politics: A Portrait of "Generation Next," http://people-press.org/reports/pdf/300.pdf, accessed 5 October 2009).

27 Canadian numbers are similarly low on such questions, but circumstances made them harder to answer: the Canadian government had been in power only eight months when the survey was conducted. Hence there were no equivalents of Donald Rumsfeld and Condoleezza Rice in public prominence. Moreover, since the name of the governing party is the Conservative Party, the formulation that had to be used was more difficult for Canadians: "which party is more to the right?"

28 To place this number in comparative perspective, Swedish political scientists describe as an indicator of the low political knowledge of Swedes the fact that "only" 48 percent were able to state the number of parties in the governing coalition in an open-ended question, and that by far the most common wrong answer was seven—i.e., the respondents mistook presence in Parliament for membership in the government (Oscarsson 2007).

29 All Quebec students who wish to continue their education after the final year of high school must first attend junior college.

30 The survey was described as being about "youth attitudes," and participants were told they would receive $25.

31 This expectation has sometimes led to a reluctance to include political knowledge questions in surveys, a reluctance that, at least as far as young people are concerned, is unjustified.

32 This is now a common practice among polling firms, as is the fact that all Quebec respondents were surveyed in French and all those in the rest of Canada were surveyed in English.

33 N = 289 for those aged fifteen to twenty-five, and 146 for those twenty-six and older.

34 Claes, Stolle, and Hooghe surveyed 3,334 sixteen- and seventeen-year-olds in eighty-one schools in Quebec and Ontario.

35 We should note here that the knowledge questions are oriented toward national— i.e., Canadian, rather than Quebec province—politics and institutions.

36 Another possible additional explanatory factor is the effect of politicization, given the polarization in Quebec during this period over the question of independence from Canada and the use of French and English in the province. Yet this does not easily fit the fact that Quebeckers over twenty-five are less politically knowledgeable than their English Canadian peers. Moreover, we do not see evidence of the significant attitudinal differences that one would expect from a more politicized population.

6. How Institutions Can Boost Informed Political Participation

1 This is borne out empirically in a recent study by Arnold (2007), who also finds that political knowledge is lower in countries with greater income equality.

2 The households are divided into deciles based on income, from the poorest 10 percent up to the richest 10 percent, and the Gini coefficient is based on the sum of the distances for each decile between the actual distribution and a theoretically equal one, in which each decile would receive the same total income.

3 If Belgium is excluded, the correlation rises to a high 0.68. The findings here correspond to the picture gained from the limited data available, which suggests that Belgium is lower in civic literacy than other Northern European countries (Milner 2002a, 60–61), yet its level of redistribution is similar to theirs. Explaining this anomaly constitutes an interesting question for future research.

4 A confirmation of this relationship is provided by Iversen (2008), who shows that, all else being equal, taking part in political discussion makes it significantly more likely that those with an economic predisposition to vote for a party of the Left—i.e., those who are lower in income and education—in fact do so. Interestingly, political discussion has very little effect on the choices of those whose income and education predisposes them to vote for parties of the Right.

5 Note that unitary systems can be highly decentralized. When it comes to the proportion of spending determined at the local level, the Scandinavian countries are more decentralized than many federal countries, including Australia (see Lijphart 1999).

6 Milner (2002a), chapters 7 and 8.

7 Levine (2007, 204) cites a 1998 National Election Study in which none of the 169 randomly selected young people in the sample reported making a contribution to a candidate or party (compared to 11 percent of respondents in their forties and fifties).

8 The United States does provide public money to candidates for president in the form of matching grants. Candidates become eligible for such funds by raising at least $5,000 in twenty different states from individuals contributing less than $250 each. Given the high costs of television campaigns, these funds do not, as we see below,

counter the dependency on privately raised money in American politics—especially unregulated "soft money." Note also that Obama, like George W. Bush, refused the matching grants and thus was not subject to these limits. Clearly, the late January 2010 Supreme Court ruling declaring restrictions on contributions by corporations and trade unions as unconstitutional can only exacerbate the influence of big money.

9 This editorial in *The New York Times* continues: "One of the main reasons voting is in such bad shape is that the states have far too much leeway in running elections, ranging from what ID they require to the number of polling places they open and the allocation of voting machines, which has a big impact on how long the lines are on Election Day. Registering to vote and casting ballots in federal elections are federal acts, which should be governed by uniform national standards" (18 March 2009).

10 Nonpartisan reform is blocked by the fact that it must take place at the state level, where it clearly has partisan consequences. For example, the Republicans would lose seats if reform came to Texas, while the Democrats would lose them if it took place in California. Were reform instituted nationally, the partisan advantages lost in one state would be balanced by the gains in the other.

11 Using Eurobarometer data, Anduiza Perea (1995, 24) shows that the "citizens with a high degree of identification are very likely to vote in every country independently of the country they live in," while for others voting is dependent on their circumstances.

12 Eurobarometer data assembled by Anduiza Perea (1995) shows that the stronger a person's party identification, the likelier the person is to vote, but the effects differs: it is strong in Portugal, France, and the Netherlands, and weak in Germany and the United Kingdom.

13 In 2000, only one in twenty Canadians between the ages of eighteen and thirty had ever belonged to a political party, compared with one-third of those over sixty (O'Neill 2001).

14 Young and Cross also surveyed young members of issue-oriented interest groups. Only 10 percent rated parties as an effective vehicle, compared to 30 percent for lawful demonstrations.

15 Thibault, Albertus, and Fortier (2007, 9) suggest that young people in Quebec are less likely to see voluntary associations as preferred substitutes for political parties, in part because volunteerism has been traditionally associated with the outmoded, church-linked elites of an earlier era.

16 See Birch (2009) for a fair and comprehensive book-length discussion of the subject.

17 Twenty countries use fines. The amounts vary by country, though most are nominal, and enforcement can be minimal or even nonexistent.

18 Some oppose compulsory voting on the basis of the supposed right to not vote. I am unconvinced by this argument, since one can always cast a blank ballot.

19 The survey was conducted at Vanier College, a Montreal English-language junior college, with over 5,000 students from a variety of socioeconomic groups and a wide

number of ethnicities, the majority of whom plan to continue their education after graduating. Less than a quarter of the students spoke French at home, and their political knowledge scores were notably higher than the rest of the respondents. This was to be expected from the fact that provincial elections are followed generally more closely by the Francophone majority. But it is also the case that the Francophones were not necessarily representative, being members of a self-selected minority that chose to attend junior college in their second language.

20 In Quebec, turnout is higher for provincial than for federal elections.

21 The requirement that all participants be entitled to be paid was a requirement of the Director General of Elections (DGE), so in a formal sense this was not a matter of paying people to vote. The office of the DGE is responsible for the administration of elections in the province, including the registration of voters and the administration of polling stations. Its cooperation made it possible to verify if the subjects voted.

22 Other questions were, for example, "Do you play sports on campus?" "Do you own a cellphone?" and "Do you plan to go on to university?"

23 Overall, 52 percent of subjects completed the first survey online, while the remainder filled out a paper copy.

24 In order to verify that they had voted, all subjects had to complete and sign a research consent form in person, giving the college permission to provide the DGE with their names and addresses.

25 We also excluded those whom the DGE could not find on a voters' list.

26 We measured political discussion using four questions: how often respondents follow what is occurring in "government and public affairs"; how closely they have followed the Quebec election; how often they discuss current events with friends; and how often they discuss them with family members. Each respondent was scored based on an average of the four. Media usage was similarly scored based on the subject's average response as to on how many days a week he or she reads a newspaper, watches the national news on television, listens to news on the radio, or reads news on the Internet. Our final variable measures the average number of days a week an individual consumes all of these media.

27 Nine repeated the previous questions verbatim, two repeated them in altered form, and nine new questions were added, almost all of which were closely linked to developments in the campaign.

28 Only one in twenty subjects said they had ever written to a newspaper or contacted a television or radio program regarding a political issue. Half of the subjects reported having signed a written or e-mail petition.

29 This question of whether the nonvoters' turning up to vote would have changed electoral outcomes has been tested in two recent studies: one of Sweden (Oscarsson 2007), and one of Canada (Blais, Gidengil, Fournier, and Nevitte 2009).

30 It is argued that refusing to participate can be a form of expression, that people need the power to withdraw legitimacy from their governments, and that refusal to

NOTES TO PAGES 132–136 // 251

vote is one of the most peaceful ways to do this. Moreover, compulsory voting does not address the underlying causes of low voter turnout, but masks them instead. If citizens are not voting, then it is incumbent on governments and political parties to address those causes.

31 Such assemblies have the merit of making some effort to be representative, which is often not the case with the various consultative councils discussed in chapter 1 that claim to speak for "the people." See Peters and Abud (2009) for a useful, if perhaps overly optimistic, portrayal of the potential of online forums drawing on four case studies, three from Canada and one from New Zealand.

32 It could be argued that the electoral formulas proposed by the assemblies were sub-optimal from the point of view of selling them to the public. Certainly that was the case in Ontario. The process requires (and makes it possible for) ordinary citizens to become quasi-experts on a complex subject, while still perceiving themselves to be ordinary citizens. Hence, unlike commission experts, assembly members tend to assume that a system meeting their own personal preferences does the same for ordinary citizens.

33 Agnes Vanya, "The Students' Assembly on Electoral Reform Draft Report," http://www.studentsassembly.ca/dwn/presentationreport.pdf (accessed 26 September 2009).

34 According to Althaus (2003), without incorporating the political knowledge dimension in attitudinal surveys on politically related issues, we are failing to take into account the quality of the opinions expressed, and thus failing to distinguish meaningful opinions held by respondents from artifacts of the interview process.

35 A good Canadian example of how this can be misleading is a poll conducted immediately upon Stéphane Dion's becoming leader of the Liberal Party, in which 60 percent of Quebeckers reacted positively. The poll prompted the distinguished columnist Geoffrey Simpson, among others, to conclude that Quebeckers were much more sympathetic to Dion's federalist views than Quebec's political elite was. In fact, only the political elite knew Dion's views on federalism. For most of those polled, Dion was someone with a French Canadian name who, as the question told them, had become Liberal leader.

36 A survey covering political issues in general, and energy policy in particular, had been sent to a random sample of 2,500 people in the Turku region. They were also invited to take part in the deliberative experiment; in the end, 135 took part. In the initial stages, the participants read balanced information on nuclear energy and heard proponents and opponents of nuclear power—an expert and a politician on each side—who made short presentations and answered questions from the participants. Three hours of deliberation, led by trained moderators, took place in twelve small groups, to which participants were randomly allocated. At the end of the process, the groups voted on to whether a sixth nuclear power plant should be built in Finland.

37 We do not know exactly how many users there were, since some used smartvote more than once.

38 See http://www.parteienkompass.ch and http://www.my-vote.ch (both accessed 26 September 2009).

39 See www.20min.ch (accessed 26 September 2009).

40 For a list of all media partners, see http://www.smartvote.ch/side_menu/partner/partners.php?who=v (accessed 26 September 2009).

7. The Electoral System

1 Lijphart originally conceived of federalism as an element of consensualism, a position different from that taken here, but later he distanced himself from that conceptualization.

2 In the spring of 2009, British Columbia rejected a semi-PR variant known as STV (single transferable vote), which used in Ireland and Malta.

3 Proportional representation was instituted in some local elections throughout the United States, including a number of city and school district elections in the twentieth century, though it was repealed due to various public fears, including worries that African Americans or Communists could take power.

4 There is some debate over whether STV qualifies as a PR system, and it will not be considered here.

5 A New Zealand royal commission proposed MMP, and the people ratified it in 1992 and 1993 referendums. After New Zealand, forms of MMP came to Britain, the new Scottish and Welsh assemblies, and the Greater London Council.

6 Germany avoids this by adding additional members in regions where there are not enough list seats to fully compensate the underrepresented parties.

7 There are two quota methods: Hare, which sets the quota at V (votes) divided by S (seats), and Droop (V divided by S+1). There are also two divisor methods: D'hondt (which successively divides the votes of each party by the series 1, 2 , 3 . . .) and Saint-Lague (which divides by the series 1, 3, 5 . . .).

8 While the Liberals averaged around 40 percent of the overall vote in the 1993, 1997, and 2000 federal elections, no other party could win nearly enough seats to form any kind of effective opposition or government in waiting.

9 In 1993, the voters repudiated the ruling Progressive Conservatives, but the electoral system decimated Canada's oldest party. Rather than the forty-six members of Parliament (MPs) that a PR system would have given them, they managed to elect only two.

10 In 1997, two-thirds of all the Liberal MPs were elected from Ontario, where the Liberals won only 48.5 percent of the vote but 101 of 103 seats. This left almost none for the Reform Party; yet Reform received many more votes in Ontario than it did in Alberta, where it won 92 percent of the seats with 55 percent of the votes.

11 Elections in New Brunswick, Prince Edward Island, and British Columbia ended up kicking the party in power not just out of the government, as the voters wanted, but also—effectively—out of the legislature.

12 In the Quebec election in 1998, with their support concentrated in non-Francophone constituencies, the Provincial Liberals garnered the most votes (43.6 percent to the Parti québécois' 42.9 percent) but elected only forty-eight members of the national assembly, compared to the Parti québécois' seventy-six.

13 In the 1998 Quebec election, no room was left for parties representing the middle group of Quebeckers, who prefer a compromise short of sovereignty and do not define themselves politically along the federalist-sovereignist fault line. The Action démocratique, which takes such a position, was effectively marginalized, averaging only two seats (out of 125) in the three previous elections, despite being supported by about one-sixth of Quebeckers. At the same time in Ontario, successive elections produced majority governments ideologically more extreme than the majority of Ontario voters—first, the New Democratic Party on the left, then the Harris Conservatives on the right—though neither won anywhere near 50 percent of the votes.

14 The exception is when residential patterns result in specific minorities' being concentrated into what SMP effectively turns into ghetto constituencies.

15 Estimates based on earlier data were higher: for Lijphart (1997a), it was about 9 percent, a difference similar to that found by International IDEA (1999), using voting age populations rather than registered voters.

16 See also Ladner and Milner (1999; 2006).

17 Gordon and Segura continue: "Lack of sophistication need not indicate an inherent weakness of mass publics; this shortcoming may, instead, be a product of the systems—and the individual choices structured by those systems—within which it emerges . . . Assessing capabilities by measuring performance, therefore, is problematic since the measure assumes the availability of accurate information and is driven both by genuine cognitive capacity as well as by the existence of variations in the value and accessibility of information. Capable people, in environments where information is available, may choose to be uninformed if that information is expensive and difficult to accumulate, or if the use of that information is of limited utility" (1997, 129).

18 Moreover, in comparing differences between average national turnout and average local turnout under SMP and PR, I found a significantly larger gap in the countries in which national parties play little or no role in local politics—such as the United States, Canada, and New Zealand—than in the European countries where they are very much involved (see Milner 2002a, chapter 5).

19 A New Zealand law allows local authorities to conduct elections under STV as well as SMP. For the 2004 municipal elections, only ten localities chose the former (see http://www.dia.govt.nz/diawebsite.nsf/wpg_URL/Resource-material-stv-Information-Index?OpenDocument#four, accessed 26 September 2009).

20 Using data from the Comparative Study of Electoral Systems, Karp and Banducci (1999) find that supporters of small parties are more likely to be dissatisfied with the political process, and that this dissatisfaction is likely to reduce the likelihood of their voting in plurality systems, but not in PR systems.

21 In a study for Elections Canada, Pammett and LeDuc (2003, 17) asked abstainers why they failed to vote in the 2000 election, and found respondents aged eighteen to twenty-four had the lowest tendency (27.3 percent versus 34.4 percent overall) to cite a failing in the political process as a reason.

22 From 2000 to 2004, turnout in the presidential elections rose in the twelve most competitive states by 9 percentage points, to 63 percent, while it barely moved in the twelve least competitive states, rising 2 percentage points to 53 percent. More than half of all presidential campaign advertisements shown during the peak campaign season were aired in just three states, and 99 percent of spending occurred in just sixteen states. Not a single ad was aired in twenty-three safe states (Hill and McKee 2005, 710).

23 This trend is likely to grow, since the number of battleground states decreased from twenty-two in 1992 to only thirteen in 2004. The number of completely uncompetitive states increased from five in 1992 to twenty in 2004 (see FairVote, "Presidential Elections Inequality: The Electoral College in the 21st Century," 18, http://www.fairvote .org/?page=1729, accessed 26 September 2009).

8. Who Should Vote, and When?

1 In a survey of 805 county party leaders, Shea (2009) found a significantly greater likelihood on the part of local parties to register and reach young citizens in competitive districts.

2 It was, for example, presented as a real possibility in the International IDEA (1999) report on youth political participation.

3 Most studies on lowering the voting age from twenty-one to eighteen find that this decrease in age resulted in decreased turnout. Blais and Dobrzynska (1998) found a 5 percent decrease in turnout as a result of the expansion of the electorate in the United States, and a 3 percent decrease in most other democracies that have lowered their voting age to eighteen, since those aged eighteen to twenty-one are less likely to vote, and individuals' voting patterns are established during the first few elections for which they are eligible.

4 A Statistics Canada study confirms this to be true of Canadians: "A strong sense of belonging to the community as a young adult resulted in higher odds of voting" (Milan 2005, 4).

5 In my comparative study of young Americans and Canadians (Milner 2007), discussed in chapter 5, I could find no independent effect of length of residence on political knowledge or reported voting.

6 There is a connection between the lowering of the voting age and the rapid aging of the population, of maintaining generational balance in a country where those aged sixty-five and older exceed the population aged fifteen and under.

7 See "Policy Briefing: Advance Voter Registration in Rhode Island," www.fairvote .org/ri/advance_registration_briefing.pdf (accessed 26 September 2009).

8 It might be argued, especially in light of the mobilizing action around the Obama campaign, that the system of primaries that allow popular participation in the nomination of candidates is another distinct American institution that facilitates youth participation. Clearly primaries provide an arena for active involvement unavailable elsewhere, but that involvement, however intense, is short-lived—tied to a particular candidate who seeks a particular office at a particular time. It is an open question if historically, compared to the less intense but more structured forms of participation in party activities in parliamentary systems with proportional elections, primaries foster greater levels of informed political participation.

9 This clause states: "Nothing in this section affects the powers of the Governor General, including the power to dissolve Parliament at the Governor General's discretion."

10 In choosing a date that optimizes reelection prospects, the leader needs to take into account the possibility of punishment for abusing this power. The degree of such subjective constraint will differ in different societies, even when the legal or regulatory environment is the same. Such subjective factors cannot be systematically incorporated into the kind of empirical comparative analysis undertaken here, but it is a dimension that should be kept in mind.

11 Norwegian law states that the Storting (the Norwegian parliament) may not be dissolved, and new elections may not be called, outside the regular general Election Day (on a Monday in September, every four years), forcing the parliamentarians to replace governments that resign prematurely from among themselves.

12 There are several ways for fixing the date of the regular election that will end the term of the prematurely elected legislature. The simplest and "most fixed" variant occurs in countries like Finland, where the exact date is unchangeable. In such instances, limits are also typically set on how late in the regular term premature elections can take place. The second variant is found in the Netherlands and Hungary, among other countries. Unlike Finns, who know that regular legislative elections will take place every four years in March no matter what, Hungarians know that the next general election will be held in April or May of the fourth year following the election of the previous parliament. A greater element of flexibility is added in a third variant, used for example in Belgium. Here, when the assembly is dissolved prematurely, the fixed term (of four years) begins when the new parliament is installed. Thus the date of the fixed election can shift from one time of year to another.

13 Two months seems to be the greatest period of flexibility employed in fixed term systems. Greater consistency is attained in cases where the actual months and weeks are specified, as in the Hungarian case. In contrast, German law states that the new election of the Bundestag shall be held on a Sunday or statutory public holiday at least forty-six months and at most forty-eight months after the beginning of the electoral period.

14 In borderline cases, where it is unclear how to classify a given country, I was guided by the consistency of actual election dates.

15 See Sawer and Kelly (2005) and Milner (2005a) for useful summaries of the main arguments, pro and con.

16 Other potential administrative advantages of fixed election dates take the form of better policy planning in the bureaucracy, in the use of more effective investigative commissions and the like, simply because officials will be able to better plan how to use limited resources, including available participants. Members of parliamentary committees are able to set out their agendas well in advance, which leads to more efficiency given the many calls on parliamentarians' time.

17 This could both save money and result in better planning, as was apparently the case in British Columbia. Jennifer Miller, an information officer at Elections B.C., is quoted as saying that the fixed election date "enabled us to plan and administer the election much better. Electoral district officers had the time to find facilities and train staff so that the election was very successful" (quoted in Gerry Bennett, "Fixed Election a Boon to Planning for Big Day," *Vancouver Sun*, 19 May 2005). In addition, setting dates for by-elections, especially through avoiding them late in the term, becomes simplified, and costs are reduced, when the date of the next general election is known.

18 Roughly 10 percent of Canadian students live in British Columbia.

19 A recent example of these recommendations was put forward by the Canadian province of New Brunswick's Commission on Legislative Democracy (http://www.gnb.ca/0100/FinalReport-e.pdf, accessed 27 September 2009; see chapter 5).

20 There has been some easing of the U.S. voting and registration process in recent years. The 1993 National Voter Registration Act, called the motor voter law, allows citizens to register by mail or at a variety of sites, such as state motor-vehicle offices. In addition, more than half the states now allow citizens to vote ahead of time, through absentee ballots or at advance polls, and seven states allow voters to register on Election Day. Still, universal registration, in which the government takes responsibility along with the citizen to ensure that all eligible voters are registered, seems a long way off.

21 Naureen S. Malik wrote: "The next generation of voters also gave Barack Obama a landslide victory. A mock election involving one million of America's youth—the vast majority of whom are too young to vote—went 60%–36% for Obama. It was also a record turnout for the online, K-12 student-only election hosted by the Youth Leadership Initiative of the University of Virginia's Center for Politics. The polls were open Oct. 20–30" ("Obama Wins Student Mock Election," *Wall Street Journal*, 5 November 2008).

22 "Still Broken," 17 March 2009.

23 A specific instance is found in measures enacted in a number of states to keep former felons from voting (given the overrepresentation of African Americans among them, former felons are very likely to vote for Democratic candidates, if they vote at all). This is an abusive measure, which can be interpreted in an abusive manner to block access to the ballot box even of those who are not former felons, as became clear

in the investigations into how Florida Republicans managed to declare George W. Bush the winner of that state in 2000. See the editorial "Felons and the Right to Vote" (*The New York Times*, 11 July 2004).

24 Of the 1,200 applications received, 142 grants were approved, the largest number going to municipalities, adult education associations, immigrant organizations, and disabled people's groups ("Democracy Policy," Swedish Ministry of Justice Fact Sheet, December 2004).

25 Immigrants who are not Swedish citizens can vote in municipal elections.

26 An evaluation in 2004 found that in the first eighteen months, 125 municipal councils took action in this area, while another 100 were considering the idea. A total of 981 citizens' proposals were received by the councils covered by the study. The proposals usually concerned social services, and were, as a rule, handled in the same way as ordinary motions, so they did not entail appreciably heavier workloads. Approximately 10 percent of the 296 proposals that came before the councils were approved.

27 The Chief Electoral Officer, Jean-Pierre Kingsley, put it this way: "We also developed a series of outreach initiatives for young people . . . [We appointed] community relations officers for youth identified neighborhoods with high concentrations of students . . . assisted in locating polls in places easily accessible to youth, and informed the community and youth leaders about registration and voting" ("Chief Electoral Officer's Message," *Electoral Insight*, July 2003, 1).

28 The four were the Canadian Federation of Students, the Fédération étudiante universitaire du Québec, the New Brunswick Student Alliance, and the Canadian Alliance of Student Associations. A total of 3,200 posters were sent to these associations for distribution to their 119 member associations.

29 Rush the Vote is an organization that aims to increase youth voter turnout and political awareness through edutainment. It is affiliated with the u.s. program Rock the Vote.

30 YouthLinks is a free, online education program that links students in Canada and abroad; it operates in some 400 high schools across Canada. "Voices," launched in late fall 2004, was designed to provide a practical teaching tool on elections and the democratic process.

9. Civic Education outside the Classroom

1 This is suggested by Conover and Searing (2000, 111–13), who note that the informal civic education that occurs in such non-civics courses as English literature may be more effective than civic education, as it is currently taught.

2 For the next round, in the field as this is being written, the civic knowledge instrument is expected to contain eighty questions, with nineteen actually testing the cognitive domain of knowing, and sixty-one testing analyzing and reasoning ("International Civic and Citizenship Education Study (iccs): Presentation to the iea General

Assembly," Berlin, 6–8 October 2008, www.iea.nl/uploads/media/ICCS_01.ppt, accessed 27 September 2009). However, among the countries that signed up, missing are the United States, Canada, the United Kingdom, France, Germany, Japan, and Australia (http://iccs.acer.edu.au/index.php?page=participating-countries, accessed 5 October 2009).

3 Part of the explanation may lie in the gradations allowed by the wording of possible answers. The first question is a simple yes or no, while the second goes from never (1) to often (4). This explanation is suggested by the small differences in the beta coefficients.

4 In addition, ironically—if not surprisingly, given what we have seen in part 1— Campbell (2006) finds that students who attend racially diverse schools are less likely to report open classrooms, suggesting that discussions of diverse or controversial opinions are more likely to be encouraged in racially homogeneous classrooms.

5 The sample is composed of all those who voted in 1,000 polling divisions (out of 58,017), fifty in each of twenty electoral districts.

6 The course is broken down into three units, respectively fifteen, twenty-five, and fifteen hours: "Democracy—Issues and Ideas," "The Canadian Context," and "Global Perspectives." The curriculum guidelines stress the historical and institutional approach, with emphasis on knowledge of government procedures, as well as teaching Canadian civic virtues—especially tolerance of diversity and commitment to the democratic process.

7 The confidence levels are based only on the sample of people previously registered who voted at the polls on Election Day, ignoring the additional almost three million people who registered at the polls and voted on Election Day, and those who voted at advance polls and by special ballot. It is not possible to calculate an exact figure by which bringing them into the analysis would reduce the confidence levels, since they must be treated as separate populations due to the fact that there will likely be a larger proportion of young voters among those registering on Election Day. But their inclusion certainly allows for a more solid estimate.

8 A u.s. study similarly found practically no positive effects on later voting from exposure to various forms of civics courses in high school (Lopez 2003).

9 I know of no quantitative studies of how these forty hours have actually been used, but anecdotal evidence suggests that most students follow the path of least resistance in meeting these requirements—hardly changing their behavior, but dressing it up in language that allowed them to claim they had met the requirements.

10 The students were also saddled with the additional difficulties entailed in adjusting to the shortening of the high-school curriculum by a year, in which the last year of high school included a double cohort—something experienced in no other province. Could this also have had a negative effect on turnout once they were eligible to vote?

11 In addition, in the schools where permission was granted, a certain self-selectivity of teachers with a particular interest in the subject was inevitable.

12 Westholm, Lindquist, and Niemi (1990) found that upper secondary students taking civics courses were 11 percent more likely to retain knowledge about international organizations, and 6 percent more likely to remember international events when retested two years later, than a comparable group of students who were in programs that did not require them to take the course.

13 See http://www.ecs.org/html/issue.asp?issueid=109 (accessed 5 October 2009).

14 See http://www.ecs.org/ecs/ecscat.nsf/WebTopicView?OpenView&count=-1& RestrictToCategory=Service+Learning/Community+Service (accessed 27 September 2009).

15 An example is the "Youth Voices" program described by Barbara Ferman ("Youth Civic Engagement in Practice," *The Good Society* 14 (3): 45–50). Examples of such projects in the United Kingdom can be found on the website of the British Youth Council (www.byc.org.uk; accessed 27 September 2009).

16 See, e.g., the Council of Europe's website on "Education for Democratic Citizenship and Human Rights" (http://www.coe.int/t/dg4/education/edc/default_en .asp, accessed 27 September 2009).

17 A variation of the study for U.S. readers was prepared for the Center for Information and Research on Civic Learning and Engagement (CIRCLE; see Milner, 2008, "The Informed Political Participation of Young Canadians and Americans," CIRCLE Working Paper 60, http://www.civicyouth.org/PopUps/WorkingPapers/WP60Milner.pdf, accessed 27 September 2009). Tossutti (2004) examines existing data and similarly concludes that there is little evidence that voluntarism leads to political engagement for young Canadians.

18 The idea that political involvement is distinct from, even inconsistent with, community service is a process termed "political evaporation," and Eliasoph (1998) portrays it as characteristic of many U.S. voluntary groups.

19 This was the conclusion of a weekend exchange, sponsored by the Johnson Foundation, among twenty representative Wisconsin college students and politicians.

20 Examples of Americorps projects in the state of Washington include: trail restoration, a fundraising bake sale for the humane society, campus beautification, mentoring younger students, presenting residents of a retirement home with a safety brochure and helping them create emergency packs, and removing and painting over graffiti on school grounds ("Roadmap to Civic Engagement: Executive Summary," http://encorps .nationalserviceresources.org/2006/10/roadmap_to_civic_engagement_ex.php, accessed 14 October 2009).

21 Quoted in Walker (2000, 647); see also Theiss-Morse and Hibbing (2005, 234). Walker relates her experiences with the National Education for Women leadership program of the Center for American Women and Politics: As one participant in the program put it: "Service was a friendly, morally pure alternative to the messy, dirty, compromise-filled world of politics."

22 The initiative is based at the Center for Politics of the University of Virginia (www
.youthleadership.net/index.jsp; accessed 27 September 2009).

23 I also found that a comparatively high proportion of those young Quebeckers who
see politics as a means for the less powerful to compete (rather than as a means for
the powerful to keep power for themselves) report that they always vote or intend to
vote.

24 If this is the case, it suggests that in the North American context, Quebec stands
out in a manner analogous to Denmark in Europe. According to Hahn (1998, 101–2),
Danish students live in a more political culture than students in England, Germany,
and the Netherlands.

25 A review of provincial civics documents suggests that Canada is indeed following
the United States along this path (see Llewellyn et al. 2007).

26 I have written elsewhere that Quebec, which in the late 1960s established junior
colleges along the lines of Scandinavian upper secondary institutions, should follow
their practices with regard to civic education (Milner 2002a, chapter 15).

10. The Challenge of Civic Education in the Internet Age

1 This is especially true for African American students (see Finkel and Ernst 2005; Lay
2006).

2 This was perhaps less true in the past. According to Jennings and Stoker (2001, 18),
there has been a generational shift in the United States: only 27 percent of those aged
eighteen to thirty at the time of the authors' research had run for elected office when
they were in school, compared to 50 percent for their parents' generation.

3 Kahne and Middaugh (2009, 33) cite a wide literature, on the basis of which they
include engaging in simulations as a "best practice" in civic education.

4 The Pace students drafted convention rules and procedures for committee chairs,
ran mock committee hearings for the chairs in the weeks leading up to the three-day
conventions, and generally prepared all the documentation and schedules for the conventions. On the first full day of each convention, the delegates divided into committees, and debated and drafted platforms on eight issues. Two high-school delegates
presented each plank to the entire relevant convention for discussion, amendments,
and a vote.

5 The program appears to enhance students' attentiveness to politics in the media and
home, and leads to higher turnout among parents as well as making them become better informed about politics through interaction with their children (Golston 1996).
Other research found that it sharpens students' critical thinking and narrows the gender and socioeconomic gap in civic education (McDevitt and Kiousis 2004).

6 See http://youthleadership.net/whysignup/mockelections.jsp;jsessionid=503B07D7
4D5F0FA2AF205A9B036158F2.N4 (accessed 28 September 2009).

7 The results were presented live, alongside the official adult vote, on CBC television. On the whole, the students took the exercise seriously, with civics or history classes often taking the lead in engaging and informing the student body during the campaign.

8 The relatively strong showing of the Greens and the social democratic New Democratic Party, and the relative weakness of the Conservatives, well reflected the leanings of the minority of young Ontarians who had an interest in partisan politics.

9 Quebec schools were especially underrepresented (Verboczy and Giguère 2004). Surveys were carried out by Student Vote 2004 to test the impact of the simulation. The presurvey, completed prior to participation in the program, had 14,344 responses, but only 2,841 responded to the postelection survey. (The falloff means that we cannot be sure how much weight to give to the improved intention-to-vote figures.) In the presurvey, 71 percent said they would vote if they had the opportunity. After participating in the simulation, 88 percent said they would do so (see http://www.student vote.ca/pages.php?pageid=3, accessed 5 October 2009).

10 See http://www.newswire.ca/en/releases/archive/April2009/29/c6624.html (accessed 5 October 2009).

11 See http://www.studentvote.ca/federal (accessed 5 October 2009).

12 See http://www.regeringen.se/sb/d/6148/a/55918 (accessed 28 September 2009).

13 The data allow for a longitudinal comparison of attitudes of subgroups in the group aged fifteen to nineteen and with the general population (see http://www.skolenettet .no/moduler/Module_FrontPage.aspx?id=39844&epslanguage=NO / (accessed 28 September 2009).

14 Starting with the 2009 election, the survey is conducted only online.

15 For the case of Norway, see http://www.tinget.no/no/Toppmeny/Minitinget/ (accessed 5 October 2009).

16 In Norway, students have looked at bills relating to whether students in upper secondary school should be paid wages, whether the government should establish ethnic zones in housing projects, whether domestic animals should be fenced in, and whether identity chips should be made compulsory.

17 A 2007 study, conducted by the independent firm RMC Research Corporation, found that Project Citizen students gained significantly more in their knowledge of public policy than comparison students. Project Citizen students also demonstrated superior writing ability in articulating, researching, and advocating policy solutions in essays addressing public policy problems (http://www.civiced.org/pdfs/PC/Project Citizen%20FullReport%202007.pdf, accessed 14 October 2009).

18 An example of the close link between school civics courses and the political process is found in the strategy adopted by the parliamentary commission mandated to take relevant EU issues to the Swedish population. The commission targeted study circles and other activities associated with adult education, but, most of all, the civics-related classes and activities of senior upper-secondary students. In advance of the

2003 referendum, for example, spokespersons on both sides were systematically invited to civic classes to present their cases for or against adopting the Euro.

19 For a discussion of the application of the German VAA, the Wahl-o-Mat, see Marschall and Schmidt (2008).

20 In fact, the number of countries is slightly lower, since separate data for four Canadian provinces are included.

21 The civics courses taken one hour weekly in seventh and eighth grades by almost all German students seem to have little effect (Händle, Detlef, and Luitgard 1999). In Australia, Hugh MacKay concludes, "typically, teenagers find little to interest or inspire them in the political process, and they often report that politics is the most boring subject discussed at home" (quoted in Civics Expert Group 1994,182). See also Dekker and Portengen (2000).

22 The Education Commission of the States compiles and makes available quantitative information comparing the states' efforts in:
- Citizenship education
- Civics or citizenship education standards
- High-school graduation requirements in civics or citizenship education
- Civics or citizenship education curriculum framework
- Civics, citizenship education, or social studies included in state assessments
- State assessments in civics, citizenship education, or social studies
- State laws that address civics, citizenship education, or social studies
- Recently enacted or pending civics, citizenship education, or social studies policies
- State education agency websites

23 Or, as Beem (2005, 7) puts it, they must develop opportunities to engage in political realities, including "partisanship."

24 The latter program is known as Congress in the Classrooms (see http://www.dirk sencenter.org/print_programs_CongressClassroom.htm, accessed 5 October 2009).

25 An early example of an effort in this direction was the "newspapers in the schools" program to introduce contemporary civics material into classrooms in Argentina, which, despite untrained teachers and limited class time, appears to have resulted in participating students' displaying greater political knowledge, more democratic values, and somewhat greater political interest. Because of the high dropout rate, the program was aimed at children in the sixth and seventh grades, reaching over 125,000 students (Morduchowic, Catterberg, Niemi, and Bell 1996).

26 Though directed at a group other than potential political dropouts, the experience of the Canadian Parliament to Campus program is valuable in this regard. It was launched in 2008 by the Canadian Association of Former Parliamentarians to provide free visits by former parliamentarians to campuses across Canada. In its first year, twenty-three such visits took place, giving students real insight into the realities of political life (see http://www.exparl.ca/home_e.asp, accessed 28 September 2009).

27 This information comes from a recent content analysis of the seven textbooks commonly used in civic education in Norway (Borhaug 2009).

28 The numbers come from a visual search through the printed questionnaires. Further interpretation awaits a statistical analysis of the data, to be undertaken by my colleagues.

29 The kind of partisanship based on different principles fostered in a PR environment, unlike the more inauthentic partisan conflicts built into the logic of majoritarian systems, can actually stimulate informed political participation. We know that parental partisanship remains a key factor in boosting the political participation of young people (Plutzer 2002), especially those still under their parents' roof.

30 One possible source is the Education for Democratic Citizenship and Human Rights project, which has developed "a set of practices and activities" related to human rights education, civic education, peace education and intercultural education "for equipping young people and adults to play an active part in democratic life and exercise their rights and responsibilities in society" (http://www.coe.int/t/dg4/education/edc/1_What_is_EDC_HRE/What_%20is_EDC_en.asp#TopOfPage, accessed 14 October 2009).

Conclusion

1 The figure of 80,000 is, no doubt, somewhat inflated, since at the time the current rules regarding accurate reporting of such numbers were not in place.

2 For the other Swedish parties, the participation of young people is more of a mixed bag. The smaller parties with more narrowly focused messages, like the Greens and the Christian Democrats, are holding their own, and the libertarian Pirate Party is reputed to have more young members than the Social Democrats.

3 Alongside the Green Party is the locally focused Stockholm Party and other local parties, environmentalist groups in the other parties, and an assortment of civil-society-based organizations.

4 The congestion fees had been brought in by the outgoing Social Democrat–led coalition as a pilot project. They were opposed by the main parties of the center right that are strong in the region surrounding Stockholm, who won in the 2006 national elections. Nevertheless, the fees were made permanent.

5 On the most recent Earth Hour (28 March 2009), 133 Swedish municipalities were estimated to have participated, out of 2.712 municipalities in eighty-three countries (see http://www.wwf.se/v/klimat/earth-hour/1196404-earth-hour-2009-startsida, accessed 28 September 2009), and the decrease in Swedish power consumption is projected to be equivalent to approximately half a million out of 4.5 million households.

6 As recounted earlier, Denmark has the highest levels of noncompulsory turnout. But it has been less successful than Sweden in integrating immigrants into its society, a dimension of civic engagement that needs to be explored as well.

7 Delli Carpini 2000, 343 (his emphasis and parentheses).

8 This is obvious, but it goes against the very grain of Canadian federalism. One part of the solution lies in asymmetric federalism, accepting the demands of moderate Quebec nationalists for greater institutional autonomy, especially and understandably in the areas of culture, education, and communications. Treating all provinces equally inhibits the remaining nine from closer coordination with federal policies in these areas.

Bibliography

Aalberg, Toril, and Zan Strabac. 2008. "Influence of TV-viewing on Knowledge about Immigration: An Analysis of Data from 18 Countries." Paper presented at the annual meeting of the American Political Science Association, Boston.

Aars, Jacob, and Kristin Strømsnes. 2007. "Contacting as a Channel of Political Involvement: Collectively Motivated, Individually Enacted." *West European Politics* 30 (1): 93–120.

Aarts, Kees, and Charlotte van Hees. 2003. "Lowering the Voting Age: European Debates and Experiences." *Electoral Insight* 5 (2): 42–46.

Aarts, Kees, and Holli A. Semetko. 2003. "The Divided Electorate: Media Use and Political Involvement." *Journal of Politics* 65 (3): 759–84.

Althaus, Scott L. 2003. *Collective Preferences in Democratic Politics: Opinion Surveys and the Will of the People.* Cambridge: Cambridge University Press.

——— and David Tewksbury. 2000. "Patterns of Internet and Traditional News Media Use in a Networked Community." *Political Communication* 17 (1): 21–45.

———. 2002. "Agenda Setting and the 'New' News: Patterns of Issue Importance among Readers of the Paper and Online Versions of the New York Times." *Communication Research* 29 (2): 180–207.

Amnå, Erik, Tiina Ekman, and Ellen Almgren. 2007. "The End of a Distinctive Model of Democracy? Country-diverse Orientations among Young Adult Scandinavians." *Scandinavian Political Studies* 30 (1): 61–86.

Amnå, Erik, Ingrid Munck, and Pär Zetterberg. 2004. "Meaningful Participation: Political Efficacy of Adolescents in 24 Countries." Paper presented at the European Consortium for Political Research (ECPR) Joint Sessions of Workshops, Uppsala University, Sweden.

Amy, Douglas J. 1989. *Real Choices/New Voices.* New York: Columbia University Press.

Andersson, Jan Otto. 2009. "Finland—Twelve Points!" *Inroads* 25: 118–35.

Andolina, Molly, Scott Keeter, Cliff Zukin, and Krista Jenkins. 2002. *The Civic and Political Health of the Nation: A Generational Portrait.* College Park, Md.: National Alliance for Civic Education.

Anduiza Perea, Eva. 1995. "Looking for the Impact of Institutions on the Individual Determinants of Electoral Participation." Paper presented at the European Consortium of Political Research (ECPR) Joint Sessions of Workshops, Bordeaux University, France.

———. 2002. "Campaign and Participation in the Spanish Election of 2000." Paper presented at the European Consortium of Political Research (ECPR) Joint Sessions of Workshops, University of Turin, Italy.

————, Aina Gallego Dobón, Marta Cantijoch, and Josep San Martin. 2008. "Online Resources, Political Participation and Equalities." Paper presented at the annual meeting of the American Political Science Association, Boston.

Anduiza Perea, Eva, Aina Gallego Dobón, and Laia Jorba. 2009. "New Media Exposure, Knowledge and Issue Polarization." Paper presented at the European Consortium for Political Research (ECPR) Joint Sessions of Workshops, University of Lisbon.

Archer, Keith, and Jared Wesley. 2006. "And I Don't Do Dishes Either: Disengagement from Civic and Personal Duty." Paper presented at the annual meeting of the Canadian Political Science Association, York University, Toronto.

Arnold, Jason Ross. 2007. "Contextualizing Political Knowledge: A Cross-National, Multi-level Approach." Paper presented at the annual meeting of the Midwest Political Science Association, Chicago.

Astin, Alexander W., Sarah A. Parrot, William S. Korn, and Linda J. Sax. 1997. *The American Freshman: Thirty Year Trends, 1966–1996*. Los Angeles: Higher Education Research Institute.

Ballinger, Chris. 2007. "Compulsory Voting: Palliative Care for Democracy in the UK." Paper presented at the European Consortium of Political Research (ECPR) Joint Sessions of Workshops, Helsinki University, Finland.

Barber, Benjamin. 1998. *A Passion for Democracy*. Princeton, N.J.: Princeton University Press.

Barker, Paul. 1994. "Voting for Trouble." In *Crosscurrents: Contemporary Political Issues*, 2nd ed., edited by Mark Charlton and Paul Barker. Scarborough, Ontario: Nelson Canada.

Barnard, Robert, Denise Andrea Campbell, Shelley Smith, and Don Embuldeniya. (2003). "Citizen Re:Generation: Understanding Active Citizen Engagement among Canada's Information Age Generations." Toronto: D-Code. http://www.d-code.com/pdfs/CitizenReGen 2003.pdf (accessed 15 October 2009).

Barney, Derek. 2005. *Communication Technology*. Vancouver: University of British Columbia Press.

Barnhurst, K. G. 1998. "Politics in the Fine Meshes: Young Citizens, Power and Media." *Media, Culture & Society* 20:201–18.

Bauerlein, Mark. 2008. *The Dumbest Generation: How the Digital Age Stupefies Young Americans and Jeopardizes Our Future*. New York: Jeremy P. Tarcher/Penguin.

Baumgartner, Jody C., and Jonathan S. Morris. 2008. "MyFaceTube Politics: Assessing the Impact of Social Networking Websites on the Political Attitudes and Knowledge of Young Adults during the Early 2008 Presidential Primary Season." Paper presented at the annual meeting of the American Political Science Association, Boston.

Beem, Christopher. 2005. "From the Horse's Mouth: A Dialogue between Politicians and College Students." Center for Information and Research on Civic Learning and Engagement (CIRCLE) Working Paper 27, http://www.civicyouth.org/PopUps/WorkingPapers/WP 27Beem.pdf (accessed 5 October 2009).

Bellamy, Robert V., and James R. Walker. 1996. *Television and the Remote Control: Grazing on a Vast Wasteland*. New York: Guilford.

Bengtsson, Asa, and Mikko Mattila. 2008. "Direct Democracy and Its Critics." Unpublished manuscript.

Bennett, Earl, and Linda L. M. Bennett. 2001. "What Political Scientists Should Know about the Survey of First-year Students in 2000." *PS: Political Science and Politics* 34 (2): 295–99.

Benz, Jennifer, Pamela Johnston Conover, and Donald Searing. 2008. "Placing Political Socialization in Context: The Role of Communities in Molding Citizens." Paper presented at the annual meeting of the American Political Science Association, Boston.

Bernèche, Francine, and Bertrand Perron. 2005. "La littératie au Québec: Faits saillants— Enquête internationale sur l'alphabétisation et les compétences des adultes 2003." Quebec: Institut de la statistique du Québec.

Bilodeau, Antoine, and André Blais. 2005. "Le vote obligatoire a-t-il un effet de socialisation politique?" Paper presented at the International Colloquium on Compulsory Voting at the Innstitute of Political Studies, Lille, France, October.

Birch, Sarah. 2009. *Full Participation: A Comparative Study of Compulsory Voting.* New York: United Nations University Press.

Bjorklund, Tor. 2000. "The Steadily Declining Voter Turnout: Norwegian Local Elections 1963–1999." Paper presented at a conference arranged by Della Societa Italiana di Studi Elettorali, Naples.

Blais, André. 2000. *To Vote or Not to Vote: The Merits and Limits of Rational Choice Theory.* Pittsburgh, Pa.: University of Pittsburgh Press.

——— and Agnieszka Dobrzynska. 1998. "Turnout in Electoral Democracies." *European Journal of Political Research* 33 (2): 239–62.

Blais, André, Elisabeth Gidengil, Patrick Fournier, and Neil Nevitte. 2009. "Information, Visibility and Elections: Why Electoral Outcomes Differ When Voters Are Better Informed." *European Journal of Political Research* 48 (2): 256–80.

Blais, André, Elisabeth Gidengil, Neil Nevitte, and Richard Nadeau. 2002. *Anatomy of a Liberal Victory: Making Sense of the Vote in the 2000 Canadian Election.* Peterborough, Ontario: Broadview.

———. 2004. "Where Does Turnout Decline Come From?" *European Journal of Political Research* 43:221–36.

Blais, André, and Peter John Loewen. 2009. *Youth Electoral Engagement in Canada.* Ottawa: Elections Canada.

Boiney, John. 1993. "You Can Fool All of the People . . . Evidence on the Capacity of Political Advertising to Mislead." Paper presented at the annual meeting of the American Political Science Association, Washington.

Borhaug, Kjetil. 2008. "Educating Voters: Political Education in Norwegian Upper Secondary Schools." *Journal of Curriculum Studies* 40 (5): 579–600.

———. 2009. "Outdated Political Education? A Critical Examination of Norwegian Social Studies Textbooks." Paper presented at the World Congress of Political Science, Santiago, Chile.

Bowler, Shaun, Elisabeth Carter, and David M. Farrell. 2000. "Studying Electoral Institutions and Their Consequences: Electoral Systems and Electoral Laws." Paper presented at the World Congress of Political Science, Quebec.

Boyte, H. C., and N. N. Kari. 1996. *Building America: The Democratic Promise of Public Work.* Philadelphia: Temple University Press.

Braconnier, Céline, and Jean-Yves Dormagen. 2007. *La démocratie de l'abstention.* Paris: Gallimard.

Brayboy, Bryan, Angelina Castagno, and Emma Maughan. 2007. "Equality and Justice for All? Examining Race in Education Scholarship." *Review of Research in Education* 31: 159–94.

Brooks, Neil, and Thaddeus Hwong. 2006. *The Social Benefits and Economic Costs of Taxation: A Comparison of High- and Low-Tax Countries*. Ottawa: Canadian Centre for Policy Alternatives.

Calenda, Daviede, and Lorenzo Mosca. 2007. "Logged On and Engaged? The Experience of Italian Young People." In *Young Citizens in the Digital Age: Political Engagement, Young People, and New Media*, edited by Brian D. Loader. New York: Routledge.

Campbell, David. 2006. *Why We Vote: How Schools and Communities Shape Our Civic Life*. Princeton, N.J.: Princeton University Press.

———. 2007. "Sticking Together: Classroom Diversity and Civic Education." *American Politics Research* 35 (1): 57–78.

Cantijoch, Marta, and Josep San Martin. 2008. "Exposure to Political Information in New and Old Media: Which Impact on Political Participation?" Paper presented at the annual meeting of the American Political Science Association, Boston.

Cao, Xiaoxia. 2005. "Political Comedy Shows and Knowledge about Primary Campaigns among Young Americans." Paper presented at the annual meeting of the American Political Science Association, Washington.

Carlson, T. 2008. "Riding the Web 2.0 Wave: Candidates on YouTube in the Finnish 2007 Election." Unpublished paper.

Chadwick, A. 2006. *Internet Politics: States, Citizens and New Communication Technologies*. Oxford: Oxford University Press.

Chareka, Ottilia, and Alan Sears. 2006. "Civic Duty: Young People's Conceptions of Voting as a Means of Political Participation." *Canadian Journal of Education* 29 (2): 521–40.

Civics Expert Group. 1994. *Whereas the People: Civics and Citizenship Education*. Canberra: Australian Government Publishing Service.

Claes, Ellen, Dietlind Stolle, and Marc Hooghe. 2007. "How Citizenship Education and Students' Political Resources Influence the Socialisation of New Citizens in Canada." Paper presented at the European Consortium of Political Research (ECPR) biennial conference, University of Pisa, Italy.

Claes, Ellen, and Marc Hooghe. 2008. "Citizenship Education and Political Interest: Political Interest as an Intermediary Variable in Explaining the Effects of Citizenship Education." Paper presented at the Civic Education and Political Participation Workshop, University of Montreal, 17–19 June.

Clark, W. 2007. "Delayed Transitions of Young Adults." *Canadian Social Trends*, September, 13–21.

Colville, Robert. 2008. *Politics, Policy and the Internet*. London: Centre for Policy Studies.

Comber, Melissa K. 2006. "Equalizing Political Participation Abilities: Civic Education and Cognitive Civic Skills." Paper presented at the International Civic Education Conference, Orlando, Fla., 17–19 January.

Conover, P. J., and D. D. Searing. 2000. "A Political Socialization Perspective." In *Rediscovering the Democratic Purposes of Education*, edited by L. M. McDonnell, P. M. Timpane, and R. Benjamin. Lawrence: University Press of Kansas.

Côté, J., and J. M. Bynner. 2008. "Changes in the Transition to Adulthood in the UK and Canada: The Role of Structure and Agency in Emerging Adulthood." *Journal of Youth Studies* 11 (3): 251–68.

Coulson, Tony. 1999. "Voter Turnout in Canada: Findings from the 1997 Canadian Election Study." *Electoral Insight* 1 (2): 18–22.

Council of Baltic Sea States. 2006. *Study on Citizens' Participation in the Baltic Sea Region.* Stockholm: Council of Baltic Sea States Secretariat.

Cross, W., and L. Young. 2004. "The Contours of Political Party Membership in Canada." *Party Politics* 10 (4): 427–44.

Czesnik, Mikolaj. 2007. "Is Compulsory Voting a Remedy? Evidence from the 2001 Polish Parliamentary Elections." Paper presented at the European Consortium of Political Research (ECPR) Joint Sessions of Workshops, University of Helsinki, Finland.

Dalton, Russell. 2006. *The Good Citizen: How a Younger Generation Is Reshaping American Politics.* Washington: Congressional Quarterly Press.

Dee, Thomas S. 2004. "Are There Civic Returns to Education?" *Journal of Public Economics* 88 (9–10): 1697–1720.

Dekker, Henk. 2007. "Political Cynicism, Its Origins and Its Effects on Political Cohesion." Paper presented at the International Political Science Association RC 21-29 Conference, Antwerp, Belgium, September.

———— and R. Portengen. 2000. "Political Knowledge: Theories and Empirical Research." In *Democracies in Transition: Political Culture and Socialization Transformed in West and East,* edited by Russell F. Farnen, Henk Dekker, Dan B. German, and Rudiger Meyenberg. Oldenburg, Germany: BIS Verlag.

Dekker, Paul, and Andres van de Broeck. 1998. "Civil Society in Comparative Perspective: Involvement in Voluntary Associations in North America and Western Europe." *Voluntas* 9 (1): 11–38.

Delli Carpini, Michael X. 1999. "In Search of the Informed Voter." Paper presented at The Transformation of Civic Life Conference, Middle Tennessee State University, Nashville, 12–13 November.

————. 2000. "Gen.com: Youth, Civic Engagement, and the New Information Environment." *Political Communication* 17:341–49.

———— and Scott Keeter. 1996. *What Americans Know about Politics and Why It Matters.* New Haven, Conn.: Yale University Press.

Dennis, Jack, ed. 1973. *Socialization to Politics: A Reader.* New York: Wiley.

Di Gennaro, Corinna, and William Dutton. 2006. "The Internet and the Public: Online and Offline Political Participation in the United Kingdom." *Parliamentary Affairs* 59 (2): 299–313.

Donovan, Todd, and Caroline Tolbert. 2007. "State Electoral Context and Voter Participation: Who Is Mobilized by What?" Paper presented at the annual meeting of the American Political Science Association, Chicago.

————. 2008. "Effects of State-level and US House District Electoral Competition on Interest and Participation." Paper presented at the annual meeting of the American Political Science Association, Boston.

Drotner, Kirsten. 2007. "Leisure Is Hard Work: Digital Practices and Future Competencies." In *Youth, Identity, and Digital Media,* edited by D. Buckingham. Cambridge, Mass.: MIT Press.

Dudley, Robert L., and Alan R. Gitelson. 2002. "Political Literacy, Civic Education, and Civic Engagement: A Return to Political Socialization?" *Applied Developmental Science* 6 (4): 175–82.

Eagles, Monroe, and Russell Davidson. 2001. "Civic Education, Political Socialization, and Political Mobilization." *Journal of Geography* 100:233–42.

Earl, Jennifer, and Alan Schussman. 2008. "Contesting Cultural Control: Youth Culture and Online Petitioning." In *Civic Life Online: Learning How Digital Media Can Engage Youth*, edited by W. Lance Bennett. Cambridge, Mass.: MIT Press.

Easton, David, and Jack Dennis. 1969. *Children in the Political System: Origins of Political Legitimacy*. New York: McGraw-Hill.

Easton, David, and Robert D. Hess. 1962. "The Child's Political World." *Midwest Journal of Political Science* 6 (3): 229–46.

Edwards, Kathy, Lawrence J. Saha, and Murray Print. 2005. *Youth Electoral Study (YES). Report 3: Youth, the Family, and Learning about Politics and Voting.* http://www.youth .infoxchange.net.au/news/items/2006/10/107886-upload-00001.pdf (accessed 15 October 2009).

Ehman, Lee H. 1980. "The American School in the Political Socialization Process." *Review of Educational Research* 50 (1): 99–119.

Electoral Commission. 2002. *Voter Engagement and Young People*. London: Electoral Commission.

Electoral Commission. 2004. *The Age of Electoral Majority: Report and Recommendations*. London: Electoral Commission.

Eliasoph, N. 1998. *Avoiding Politics: How Americans Produce Apathy in Everyday Life*. Cambridge: Cambridge University Press.

Elklit, Jørgen, Palle Svensson, and Lise Togeby. 2005. "Why Is Voter Turnout Not Declining in Denmark?" Paper presented at the annual meeting of the American Political Science Association, Washington.

Ellis, Andrew, John H. Pammett, Maria Gratschew, and Erin Thiessen. 2007. *Engaging the Electorate: Initiatives to Promote Voter Turnout from around the World, Including Voter Turnout Data from National Elections Worldwide 1945–2006*. Stockholm: International Institute for Democracy and Electoral Assistance (International IDEA).

Engelen, Bart, and Marc Hooghe. 2007. "Compulsory Voting and Its Effects on Political Participation, Interest and Efficacy." Paper presented at the European Consortium of Political Research (ECPR) Joint Sessions of Workshops, University of Helsinki, Finland.

European Parliaments Research Initiative (EPRI). 2006. "Connecting Parliaments and Citizens." EPRI Workshop, 24 April, Austrian Parliament, Vienna. http://www.epri.org/ epriknowledge/contents/Material_2nd_EPRI_workshop/WorkshopReading.pdf (accessed 27 September 2009).

Farrell, David M. 2001. "The United Kingdom Comes of Age: The British Electoral Reform 'Revolution' of the 1990s." In *Mixed-Member Electoral Systems: The Best of Both Worlds?* edited by Matthew Shugart and Martin Wattenberg. Oxford: Oxford University Press.

Ferguson, Ross. 2007. "P2P Politics: Young People and Policy Deliberation Online." In *Young Citizens in the Digital Age: Political Engagement, Young People, and New Media*, edited by Brian D. Loader. New York: Routledge

Fieldhouse, Edward, Mark Tranmer, and Andrew Russell. 2007. "Something about Young People or Something about Elections? Electoral Participation of Young People in Europe: Evidence from a Multilevel Analysis of the European Social Survey." *European Journal of Political Research* 46 (6): 797–822.

Finkel, Steven E., and Howard R. Ernst. 2005. "Civic Education in Post-apartheid South Africa: Alternative Paths to the Development of Political Knowledge and Democratic Values." *Political Psychology* 26 (3): 333–36.

Fishkin, James, Shanto Iyengar, and Robert Luskin. 2004. "Virtual Democratic Possibilities: Creating and Sustaining Informed Opinion through Online and Face-to-Face Deliberative Polling." Paper presented at the annual meeting of the International Communication Association, New Orleans.

Fitzgerald, Mary. 2003. "Easier Voting Methods Boost Youth Turnout." Center for Information and Research on Civic Learning and Engagement (CIRCLE) Working Paper 1, http://www.civicyouth.org/PopUps/WorkingPapers/WP01Fitzgerald.pdf (accessed 24 September 2009.

Flanagan, C. A. 2003. "Developmental Roots of Political Engagement." *PS: Political Science and Politics* 36 (2): 257–61.

Fournier, Patrick, André Blais, Elisabeth Gidengil, and Eugénie Dostie-Goulet. 2007. "The Determinants of Youth Political Participation: Conventional Versus Non-conventional." Paper presented at the European Consortium of Political Research (ECPR) biennial conference, University of Pisa, Italy.

Franklin, Mark. 1999. "Electoral Engineering and Cross-National Turnout Differences: What Role for Compulsory Voting?" *British Journal of Political Science* 29:205–24.

———. 2004. *Voter Turnout and the Dynamics of Electoral Competition in Established Democracies since 1945.* Cambridge: Cambridge University Press.

———. 2005. "You Want to Vote Where Everybody Knows Your Name: Anonymity, Expressive Engagement, and Turnout among Young Adults." Paper presented at the annual meeting of the American Political Science Association, Washington.

Franklin, Mark, Patrick Lyons, and Michael Marsh. 2004. "The Generational Basis of Turnout Decline in Established Democracies." *Acta Politica* 39:115–51.

Fridkin, Kim, Patrick J. Kenney, and Jack Crittenden. 2006. "On the Margins of Democratic Life: The Impact of Race and Ethnicity on the Political Engagement of Young People." *American Politics Research* 34 (5): 605–26.

Friedland, Lewis A., and Shauna Morimoto. 2006. "The Lifeworlds of Young People and Civic Engagement." In "Youth Civic Engagement: An Institutional Turn," edited by Peter Levine and James Youniss. Center for Information and Research on Civic Learning and Engagement (CIRCLE) Working Paper 45, http://www.eric.ed.gov/ERICDocs/data/eric docs2sql/content_storage_01/0000019b/80/29/dd/8a.pdf (accessed 24 September 2009).

Fuchs, Thomas, and Ludger Woessmann. 2004. "Computers and Student Learning: Bivariate and Multivariate Evidence on the Availability and Use of Computers at Home and at School." CESifo Working Paper Series 1321.

Gallego Dobón, Aina. 2007. "Changing Repertoires of Political Action: Which Impact on Equality in Participation?" Paper presented at the European Consortium of Political Research (ECPR) biennial conference, University of Pisa, Italy.

———. 2009. "Where Else Does Turnout Decline Come From? Education, Age, Generation and Period Effects in Three European Countries." *Scandinavian Political Studies* 32 (1): 23–44.

——— and Laia Jorba. 2008. "Does New Media Use Lead to a Widening Knowledge Gap and Declining Participation?" Paper presented at the Youth and Politics: Strange Bedfellows? Comparative Perspectives on Political Socialization Conference, Bruges, Belgium, 3–4 July, organized by the Comparative Youth Survey Project, Catholic University of Leuven.

Galston, William. 2001. "Political Knowledge, Political Engagement, and Civic Education." *Annual Review of Political Science* 4:217–34.

Geissel, Brigitte. 2008. "Reflections and Findings on the Critical Citizen: Civic Education—What For?" *European Journal of Political Research* 47 (1): 34–63.

Gibson, Rachel, Wainer Lusoli, and Stephen Ward. 2005. "Online Participation in the UK: Testing a 'Contextualised' Model of Internet Effects." *British Journal of Politics and International Relations* 7:561–83.

Gibson, Rachel, and Stephen Ward. 2008. "E-Politics: The Australian Experience." *Australian Journal of Political Science* 43 (1): 111–31.

Gidengil, Elisabeth, André Blais, Neil Nevitte, and Richard Nadeau. 2004. *Citizens.* Vancouver: University of British Columbia Press.

Gidengil, Elisabeth, Brenda O'Neill, and Lisa Young. 2008. "Her Mother's Daughter? The Influence of Childhood Socialization on Women's Political Engagement." Paper presented at the annual meeting of the American Political Science Association, Boston.

Gimpel, James G., and J. Celeste Lay. 2006. "Youth At-Risk for Non-Participation." In "Youth Civic Engagement: An Institutional Turn," edited by Peter Levine and James Youniss, Center for Information and Research on Civic Learning and Engagement (CIRCLE) Working Paper 45, http://www.eric.ed.gov/ERICDocs/data/ericdocs2sql/content_storage_01/0000019b/80/29/dd/8a.pdf (accessed 24 September 2009).

——— and Jason E. Schuknecht. 2003. *Cultivating Democracy.* Washington: Brookings Institution Press.

Goerres, Achim. 2008. "Are Parties 'Old School'? An Analysis of Age Group Differences in Party Membership across Europe." Paper presented at the annual Elections, Public Opinion and Parties (EPOP) Conference, University of Manchester.

Golston, Syd. 1996. "Never Too Young: Kids Voting USA." *Social Education*, October, 344–48.Goodyear-Grant, Elisabeth, and Cameron Anderson. 2008. "Adolescents' Attitudes toward Political Participation: Assessing Recent Evidence from Ontario." Paper presented at the Civic Education and Political Participation Workshop, University of Montreal, 17–19 June.

Goot, Murray. 2008. "Is the News on the Internet Different? Leaders, Frontbenchers and Other Candidates in the 2007 Australian Election." *Australian Journal of Political Science* 43 (1): 99–110.

Gordon, Stacy B., and Gary M. Segura. 1997. "Cross-national Variation in the Political Sophistication of Individuals: Capability or Choice?" Journal of Politics 59:126–47.

Greenstein, Fred I. 1960. "The Benevolent Leader: Children's Images of Political Authority." *American Political Science Review* 54 (4): 934–43.

———. 1965. *Children and Politics.* New Haven, Conn.: Yale University Press.

Grönlund, Kimmo. 2007. "Knowing and Not Knowing: The Internet and Political Information." *Scandinavian Political Studies* 30 (3): 397–418.

———, and Henry Milner. 2006. "The Determinants of Political Knowledge in Comparative Perspective." *Scandinavian Political Studies* 29 (4): 386–406.

Grönlund, Kimmo, and M. Setälä. 2004. "Low Electoral Turnout: An Indication of a Legitimacy Deficit?" Paper presented at the European Consortium of Political Research (ECPR) Joint Sessions of Workshops, Uppsala University, Sweden.

Hahn, Carole L., ed. 1998. *Becoming Political: Comparative Perspectives on Citizenship Education.* Albany: State University of New York Press.

Händle, Christa, Oesterreich Detlef, and Trommer Luitgard. 1999. "Concepts of Civic Education in Germany Based on a Survey of Expert Opinion." In *Civic Education across*

Countries, edited by Judith Torney-Purta, John Schwille, and Jo-Ann Amadeo. Amsterdam: International Association for the Evaluation of Educational Achievement.

Harell, Allison, and Dietlind Stolle. 2008. "Ethnic Ties in Multinational States: Ethnic Diversity and the Development of Generalized Trust." Paper presented at the annual meeting of the American Political Science Association, Boston.

Hargittai, Eszter, and Gina Walejko. 2008. "The Participation Divide: Content Creation and Sharing in the Digital Age." *Information, Communication & Society* 11 (2): 239–56.

Haste, Helen, and Amy Hogan. 2006. "Beyond Conventional Civic Participation, beyond the Moral-political Divide: Young People and Contemporary Debates about Citizenship." *Journal of Moral Education* 35 (4): 473–93.

Hébert, Yvonne. 2008. "Youth's Understandings of Civic and Political Issues: First and Second Generation and Youth of Non-immigrant Origins." Paper presented at the Civic Education and Political Participation Workshop, University of Montreal, 17–19 June.

Henderson, Ailsa, Steven D. Brown, Mark Pancer, and Kimberly Ellis-Hale. 2007. "Mandated Community Service in High School and Subsequent Civic Engagement: The Case of the 'Double Cohort' in Ontario, Canada." *Journal of Youth and Adolescence* 36 (7): 849–60.

Henn, Matt, and Mark Weinstein. 2003. *First-Time Voters' Attitudes towards Party Politics in Britain*. Swindon, U.K.: Economic and Social Research Council.

Henzey, Debra. 2003. "North Carolina Civic Index: A Benchmark Study Impacts State-level Policy." *National Civic Review* 92 (1): 27–36.

Hepburn, Mary A. 1990. "Educating for Democracy: The Years Following World War II." *Social Studies* 81 (4): 153–60.

Hess, Robert D., and Judith Torney. 1967. *The Development of Political Attitudes in Children*. Chicago: Aldine.

Hibbing, John R., and Elizabeth Theiss-Morse. 2002. *Stealth Democracy: Americans' Beliefs about How Government Should Work*. Cambridge: Cambridge University Press.

Hill, David, and Seth McKee. 2005. "Mobilization and Turnout in the 2000 Presidential Election." *American Politics Research* 33:710–25.

Hillygus, D. Sunshine. 2005. "The Missing Link: Exploring the Relationship between Higher Education and Political Engagement." *Political Behavior* 27 (1): 25–47.

Hindman, Matthew. 2009. *The Myth of Digital Democracy*. Princeton, N.J.: Princeton University Press.

Holtz-Bacha, Christina, and Pippa Norris. 2001. "To Entertain, Inform, and Educate: Still the Role of Public Television." *Political Communication* 18 (2): 123–40.

Hooghe, Marc, and Yves Dejaeghere. 2007. "Does the 'Monitorial Citizen' Exist? An Empirical Investigation into the Occurrence of Postmodern Forms of Citizenship in the Nordic Countries." *Scandinavian Political Studies* 30 (2): 249–71.

Hooghe, Marc, and Dimokritos Kavadias. 2005. "Determinants of Future Willingness to Vote: A Comparative Analysis of 14 Year Olds in 28 Countries." Paper presented at the European Consortium of Political Research (ECPR) biennial conference, University of Budapest.

Howe, Paul. 2001. "The Sources of Campaign Intemperance." *Policy Options*, January–February, 21–24.

———. 2003. "Where Have All the Voters Gone?" *Inroads* 12:74–83.

———. 2006. "Political Knowledge and Electoral Participation in the Netherlands: Comparisons with the Canadian Case." *International Political Science Review* 27:137–66.

————. 2008. "Political Culture in the Age of Adolescence." Paper presented at the annual meeting of the Canadian Political Science Association, Vancouver.

Huckfeldt, Robert, and John Sprague. 1991. "Discussant Effects on Vote Choice: Intimacy, Structure, and Interdependence." *Journal of Politics* 53:122–58.

Hultén, Olof. 2003. "Value for Money: Auditing Public Broadcasting Performance in Sweden." *The Public* 10 (3): 97–108.

Hunter, Susan, and R. A. Brisbin, Jr. 2000. "The Impact of Service Learning on Democratic and Civic Values." *PS: Political Science and Politics* 33 (3): 623–26.

Hyman, H. 1959. *Political Socialization.* Glencoe, Ill.: Free Press.

Inglehart, Ronald. 1997. *Modernization and Postmodernization: Cultural, Economic and Political Change in 43 Societies.* Princeton, N.J.: Princeton University Press.

———— and Gabriela Catterberg. 2002. "Trends in Political Action: The Developmental Trend and the Post-Honeymoon Decline." *International Journal of Comparative Sociology* 43 (3–5): 300–316.

International IDEA. 1999. *Youth Voter Participation: Involving Today's Young in Tomorrow's Democracy.* Stockholm: International Institute for Democracy and Electoral Assistance (International IDEA).

————. 2004. "Part III. The International IDEA Database: Voter Turnout from 1945 to 2003; Parliamentary Elections." In *Voter Turnout in Western Europe since 1945,* edited by Rafael López Pintor and Maria Gratschew. Stockholm: International Institute for Democracy and Electoral Assistance (International IDEA).

Iversen, Torben. 2008. "A Water Cooler Theory of Political Knowledge." Paper presented at the annual meeting of the American Political Science Association, Boston.

Iyengar, Shanto, and Simon Jackman. 2004. "Technology and Politics: Incentives for Youth Participation." Center for Information and Research on Civic Learning and Engagement (CIRCLE) Working Paper 24, http://www.civicyouth.org/PopUps/WorkingPapers/WP24 Iyengar.pdf (accessed 25 September 2009).

Jackson, L. A., A. von Eye, F. A. Biocca, G. Barbatsis, Y. Zhao, and H. E. Fitzgerald. 2006. "Does Home Internet Use Influence the Academic Performance of Low-income Children?" *Developmental Psychology* 24:413–37.

Jacobs, Lawrence, et al. 2004. "American Democracy in an Age of Rising Inequality." *Perspectives on Politics* 2 (4): 651–66.

Jacoby, Susan. 2008. *The Age of American Unreason.* New York: Pantheon.

Jaros, Dean. 1973. *Socialization to Politics.* New York: Praeger.

Jenkins, Henry. 2006. "Confronting the Challenges of Participatory Culture: Media Education for the 21st Century." Occasional Paper. Chicago: MacArthur Foundation.

Jennings, M. Kent, and Richard G. Niemi. 1974. *The Political Character of Adolescence.* Princeton, N.J.: Princeton University Press.

Jennings, M. Kent, and Laura Stoker. 2001. "Generations and Civic Engagement: A Longitudinal Multiple-Generation Analysis." Paper presented at the annual meeting of the American Political Science Association, San Francisco.

————. 2002. "Generational Change, Life Cycle Processes, and Social Capital." Paper presented at the Citizenship on Trial: Interdisciplinary Perspectives on the Political Socialization of Adolescents Conference, McGill University, Montreal, 20–22 June.

Junn, Jane. 1995. "Participation in Liberal Democracy: What Citizens Learn from Political Activity." Paper presented at the annual meeting of the American Political Science Association, New York.

Kahne, Joseph, and Ellen Middaugh. 2009. "The Civic Opportunity Gap in High School." In *Engaging Young People in Civic Life*, edited by James Youniss and Peter Levine. Nashville, Tenn.: Vanderbilt University Press.

Kandel, D. B. 1985. "On Processes of Peer Influences in Adolescent Drug Use: A Developmental Perspective." *Advances in Alcohol and Substance Abuse* 4:139–63.

Karp, Jeffrey A., and Susan A. Banducci. 1998. "The Impact of Proportional Representation on Turnout: Evidence from New Zealand." Paper presented at the annual meeting of the Australasian Political Science Association, Christchurch, New Zealand.

———. 1999. "Electoral Rules and Voter Participation: A Cross-national Analysis of Individual-level Behavior." Paper presented at the annual meeting of the American Political Science Association, Atlanta, Ga.

Kautto, Mikko, Johan Fritzell, Bjorn Hvinden, Jon Kvist, and Hannu Uusitalo. 2001. *Nordic Welfare States in the European Context.* London: Routledge.

Kavanaugh, Andrea, B. Joon Kim, Manuel A. Prez-Quiones, Joseph Schmitz, and Philip Isenhour. 2008. "Net Gains in Political Participation: Secondary Effects of Internet on community." *Information, Communication & Society* 11 (7): 933–63. http://www.informaworld.com/smpp/content~db=all~content=a904084056 (accessed 5 October 2009).

Keen, Andrew. 2007. *The Cult of the Amateur.* New York: Random House.

Keeter, Scott, Cliff Zukin, Molly Andolina, and Krista Jenkins. 2002. "The Civic and Political Health of the Nation: A Generational Portrait." Center for Information and Research on Civic Learning and Engagement (CIRCLE), http://www.eric.ed.gov/ERICDocs/data/ericdocs2sql/content_storage_01/0000019b/80/36/2c/9f.pdf (accessed 24 September 2009).

Kerr, David, Joana Lopes, Julie Nelson, Kerensa White, Elizabeth Cleaver, and Tom Benton. 2007. "Vision versus Pragmatism: Citizenship in the Secondary School Curriculum in England." Nottingham, U.K.: National Foundation for Educational Research.

Kidd, Quentin, and Erin Phillips. 2007. "Does the Internet Matter? Examining the Effects of the Internet on Young Adults' Political Participation." Paper presented at the annual meeting of the American Political Science Association, Chicago.

Kirby, Emily Hoban, Karlo Barrios Marcelo, Joshua Gillerman, and Samantha Linkins. 2008. "The Youth Vote in the 2008 Primaries and Caucuses." Center for Information and Research on Civic Learning and Engagement (CIRCLE) Fact Sheet. http://www.civicyouth.org/PopUps/FactSheets/FS_08_primary_summary.pdf (accessed 15 October 2009).

Kirlin, Mary. 2007. "A Developmental Framework of Civic Skill Acquisition: A Cross Disciplinary Approach to Advancing Our Understanding of Civic Education for Engagement." Paper presented at the annual meeting of the American Political Science Association, Chicago.

Krueger, Brian S. 2002. "Assessing the Potential of Internet Political Participation in the United States: A Resource Approach." *American Politics Research* 30 (5): 476–98.

Kuhn, H. P. 2004. "Adolescent Voting for Right-wing Extremist Parties and Readiness to Use Violence in Political Action: Parent and Peer Contexts." *Journal of Adolescence* 27: 561–81.

Laakso, M., and R. Taagepera. 1979. "'Effective' Number of Parties: A Measure with Application to West Europe." *Comparative Political Studies* 12:3–27.

Lacy, D., and B. C. Burden. 2000. "The Vote-stealing and Turnout Effects of Third-party Candidates in U.S. Presidential Elections, 1968–1996." American Political Science Association Working Paper.

Ladner, Andreas, and Henry Milner. 1999. "Do Voters Turn Out More under Proportional than Majoritarian Systems? The Evidence from Swiss Communal Elections." *Electoral Studies* 2:235–50.

———. 2006. "Can PR Voting Serve as a Shelter against Declining Turnout? Evidence from Swiss Municipal Elections." *International Political Science Review* 27 (1): 29–45.

Ladner, Andreas, Giorgio Nadig, and Jan Fivaz. 2009. "Voting Assistance Applications as Tools to Increase Political Participation and Improve Civic Education." In *Civic Education and Youth Political Participation*, edited by Murray Print and Henry Milner. Rotterdam: Sense.

Langton, Kenneth, and M. Kent Jennings. 1968. "Political Socialization and the High School Civics Curriculum." *American Political Science Review* 62:862–67.

Lassen, David D. 2005. "The Effect of Information on Voter Turnout: Evidence from a Natural Experiment." Economic Policy Research Unit Working Paper Series 04-03. Department of Economics, University of Copenhagen.

Lauf, Edmund. 2001. "The Vanishing Young Reader: Sociodemographic Determinants of Newspaper Use as a Source of Political Information in Europe, 1980–98." *European Journal of Communication* 16 (2): 233–43.

Lay, J. Celeste. 2006. "Learning about Politics in Low-income Communities: Poverty and Political Knowledge." *American Politics Research* 34 (3): 319–40.

Levine, Peter. 2007. *The Future of Democracy: Developing the Next Generation of American Citizens.* Lebanon, N.H.: University Press of New England.

Levinson, Meira. 2007. "The Civic Achievement Gap." Center for Information and Research on Civic Learning and Engagement (CIRCLE) Working Paper 51, http://www.civicyouth.org/PopUps/WorkingPapers/WP51Levinson.pdf (accessed 24 September 2009).

Lewis, J. P. 2009. "Is Civic Education the Answer? The Futile Search for Policy Solutions to Youth Political Apathy." In *Civic Education and Youth Political Participation*, edited by Murray Print and Henry Milner. Rotterdam: Sense.

Lijphart, Arend. 1984. *Democracies: Patterns of Majoritarian and Consensus Government in Twenty-One Countries.* New Haven, Conn.: Yale University Press.

———. 1997a. "Dimensions of Democracy." *European Journal of Political Research* 31: 195–203.

———. 1997b. "Unequal Participation: Democracy's Unresolved Dilemma." *American Political Science Review* 91 (1): 1–14.

———. 1999. *Patterns of Democracy: Government Forms and Performance in Thirty-six Countries.* New Haven, Conn.: Yale University Press.

Listhaug, Ola, and Lars Grønflaten. 2007. "Civic Decline? Trends in Political Involvement and Participation in Norway, 1965–2001." *Scandinavian Political Studies* 30 (2): 272–99.

Lively, Jack. 1975. *Democracy.* Oxford: Blackwell.

Livingstone, S., and P. Dahlgren. 2007. "Interactivity and Participation on the Internet: Young People's Response to the Civic Sphere." In *Young Citizens and New Media*, edited by S. Livingstone and P. Dahlgren. London: Routledge.

Llewellyn, Kristina R., Sharon Cook, Joel Westheimer, Luz Alison Molina Girón, and Karen Suurtaam. 2007. "The State and Potential of Civic Learning in Canada: Charting the Course for Youth Civic and Political Participation." Ottawa: Canadian Policy Research Networks.

Lopez, Mark Hugo. 2003. "Civic and Social Studies Course Taking and Civic Engagement." Paper presented at the International Conference on Civic Education Research, New Orleans, November.

——— and Emily Hoban Kirby. 2007. "U.S. Civics Instruction: Content and Teaching Strategies." Center for Information and Research on Civic Learning and Engagement (CIRCLE) Fact Sheet, http://www.civicyouth.org/PopUps/FactSheets/FS07_Civics_Classes.pdf (accessed 24 September 2009).

——— and Jared Sagoff. 2005. "The Youth Vote 2004." Center for Information and Research on Civic Learning and Engagement (CIRCLE) Fact Sheet, http://www.civicyouth.org/PopUps/FactSheets/FS_Youth_Voting_72-04.pdf (accessed 24 September 2009).

Lopez, Mark Hugo, Peter Levine, Deborah Both, Abby Kiesa, Emily Kirby, and Karlo Marcelo. 2006. "The 2006 Civic and Political Health of the Nation: A Detailed Look at How Youth Participate in Politics and Communities." Center for Information and Research on Civic Learning and Engagement (CIRCLE). http://www.civicyouth.org/PopUps/2006_CPHS_Report_update.pdf (accessed 5 October 2009).

Lukensmeyer, Carolyn J., and Lars Hasselblad Torres. 2006. *Deliberation: A Manager's Guide to Public Engagement.* Washington: IBM Center for the Business of Government.

Lupia, Arthur. 1994. "Shortcuts Versus Encyclopedias: Information and Voting Behavior in California Insurance Reform Elections." *American Political Science Review* 88 (1): 63–76.

Luskin, Robert C. 2002. "From Denial to Extenuation (and Finally Beyond): Political Sophistication and Citizen Performance." In *Thinking about Political Psychology*, edited by James H. Kuklinski. New York: Cambridge University Press.

———, James Fishkin, and Roger Jowell. 2002. "Considered Opinions: Deliberative Polling in Britain." *British Journal of Political Science* 32:455–87.

Macedo, Stephen, et al. 2005. *Democracy at Risk: How Political Choices Undermine Citizen Participation and What We Can Do about It.* Washington: Brookings Institution Press.

MacKinnon, Mary Pat, Sonia Pitre, and Judy Watling. 2007. "Lost in Translation: (Mis) Understanding Youth Engagement." Synthesis Report. Ottawa: Canadian Policy Research Networks.

Mahler, Vincent, and Sarah Skowronski. 2008. "Inequality, Redistribution and Electoral Turnout: A Cross-national Analysis of the Developed Countries." Paper presented at the annual meeting of the American Political Science Association, Boston.

Mair, P., and Ivan Biezan. 2001. "Party Membership in Twenty European Democracies, 1980–2000." *Party Politics* 7 (1): 5–21.

Malone, Christopher, and Julian Gregory. 2005. "Democratic Action Research (DARE) and Large Scale Simulations: Teaching Political Literacy and Civic Engagement at Pace University's Presidential Convention." *PS: Political Science and Politics* 38 (4): 771–76.

Manjoo, Farhad. 2008. *True Enough: Learning to Live in a Post-fact Society.* Hoboken, N.J.: Wiley.

Marschall, Stefan, and Christian K. Schmidt. 2008. "Preaching to the Converted or Making a Difference? Mobilizing Effects of an Internet Application at the German General Election 2005." In *Non-party Actors in Electoral Politics*, edited by David M. Farrell and Rüdiger Schmitt-Beck. Baden-Baden, Germany: Nomos.

Martikainen, Tuomo. 2000. "Disengagement from Politics: Part 1—Electoral Participation." Paper presented at the Democracy in Scotland and Scandinavia: Towards Spectator Democracy Workshop, Oslo, 28–29 October.

Mayer, Nonna. 2002. "La consistance des opinions." In *La Démocratie à l'épreuve*, edited by Gerard Grunberg, Nonna Mayer, and Paul Sniderman. Paris: Presses de Sciences Po.

McCann, James A. 2008. "Electoral Participation and Local Community Activism: Spillover Effects, 1992–1996." Paper presented at the annual meeting of the American Political Science Association, Boston.

McDevitt, Michael, and Steven Chaffee. 2000. "Closing Gaps in Political Communication and Knowledge: Effects of a School Intervention." *Communication Research* 27:259–92.

———. 2002. "From Top-Down to Trickle-Up Influence: Revisiting Assumptions about the Family in Political Socialization." *Political Communication* 19 (3): 281–301.

McDevitt, Michael, and Spiro Kiousis. 2004. "Education for Deliberative Democracy: The Long-term Influence of Kids Voting USA." Center for Information and Research on Civic Learning and Engagement (CIRCLE) Working Paper 22, http://www.civicyouth.org/PopUps/WorkingPapers/WP22McDevitt.pdf (accessed 14 October 2009).

Meirick, Patrick C., and Daniel B. Wackman. 2004. "Kids Voting and Political Knowledge: Narrowing Gaps, Informing Votes." *Social Science Quarterly* 85 (5): 1161–77.

Merelman, R. M. 1980. "Democratic Politics and the Culture of American Education." *American Political Science Review* 74: 319–32.

Micheletti, Michelle, Andreas Føllesdal, and Dietlind Stolle, eds. 2004. *Politics, Products, and Markets: Exploring Political Consumerism Past and Present*. New Brunswick, N.J.: Transaction.

Milan, Anne. 2005. "Willing to Participate: Political Engagement of Young Adults." *Canadian Social Trends*, Winter, no. 79.

Millard, William J. 1993. "International Public Opinion of the United Nations." *International Journal of Public Opinion* 5:92–99.

Milligan, Kevin, Enrico Moretti, and Philip Oreopoulos. 2003. "Does Education Improve Citizenship? Evidence from the U.S. and the U.K." National Bureau of Economic Research Working Paper 9584.

Milner, Henry. 2002a. *Civic Literacy: How Informed Citizens Make Democracy Work*. Hanover, N.H.: University Press of New England.

———. 2002b. "Civic Literacy in the Global Civil Society: Excluding the Majority from Democratic Participation." In *Global Civil Society and Its Limits*, edited by Sandra Halperin and Gordon Laxer. New York: Palgrave Macmillan.

———. 2005a. *Do We Need to Fix Our System of Unfixed Election Dates?* Montreal: Institute for Research in Public Policy.

———. 2005b. "Electoral Reform and Deliberative Democracy in British Columbia." National Civic Review 94 (1): 3–8.

———. 2007. Political Knowledge and Political Participation among Young Canadians and Americans. Montreal: Institute for Research in Public Policy.

———. 2009a. "Political Institutions, Political Knowledge and the Turnout of Young Citizens: A Nordic Comparison." Paper presented at the annual meeting of the American Political Science Association, Toronto.

———. 2009b. "Youth Electoral Participation in Canada and Scandinavia." In *Engaging Young People in Civic Life*, edited by James Youniss and Peter Levine. Nashville, Tenn.: Vanderbilt University Press.

Milner, Henry, Peter Loewen, and Bruce Hicks. 2007. *The Paradox of Compulsory Voting: Participation Does Not Equal Political Knowledge?* Montreal: Institute for Research in Public Policy.

Milner, Henry, Chi Nguyen, and Frances Boylston. 2008. "Variations in Civic Education: The IDEA Civic Education Database." Paper presented at the Citizenship on Trial: Interdisciplinary Perspectives on the Political Socialization of Adolescents Conference, McGill University, Montreal, June.

Morduchowicz, Roxana, Edgardo Catterberg, Richard G. Niemi, and Frank Bell. 1996. "Teaching Political Information and Democratic Values in a New Democracy." *Comparative Politics* 28 (4): 465–76.

Morin, Richard. 1996. "Turned Off: Millions of Americans Know Little about how Their Government Works." *Washington Post National Weekly Edition*, 5–11 February.

Morris, Jonathan S., and Richard Forgette. 2004. "News Grazers, Television News, Political Knowledge, and Engagement." *Press/Politics* 12 (1): 91–107.

Mossberger, Karen, Caroline J. Tolbert, and Ramona S. McNeal. 2008. *Digital Citizenship: The Internet, Society, and Participation.* Cambridge, Mass.: MIT Press.

Mutz, Diana C. 2006. *Hearing the Other Side: Deliberative Versus Participatory Democracy.* New York: Cambridge University Press.

Nguyen, Kim, and James Garand. 2008. "Income Inequality and Voter Turnout in the American States: 1960–2004." Paper presented at the annual meeting of the American Political Science Association, Boston.

Nie, Norman H., and D. Sunshine Hillygus. 2001. "Education and Democratic Citizenship: Explorations into the Effects of What Happens in Pursuit of the Baccalaureate." In *Education and Civil Society*, edited by Diane Ravitch and Joseph Viteritti. New Haven, Conn.: Yale University Press.

Nie, Norman H., Jane Junn, and Kenneth Stehlik-Barry. 1996. *Education and Democratic Citizenship in America.* Chicago: University of Chicago Press.

Niemi, Richard G. 2008. "Where Can and Should College Students Vote?" Paper presented at the Civic Education and Political Participation Workshop, University of Montreal, 17–19 June.

——— and Mary A. Hepburn. 1995. "The Rebirth of Political Socialization." *Perspectives on Political Science* 24 (1): 7–16.

Niemi, Richard G., and Jane Junn. 1998. *Civic Education: What Makes Students Learn.* New Haven, Conn.: Yale University Press.

Niemi, Richard G., and Nancy S. Niemi. 2005. "The Content and Focus of High School Civics Teaching." Paper presented at the European Consortium of Political Research (ECPR) biennial conference, University of Budapest.

Norris, Pippa. 2000. *A Virtuous Circle? Political Communications in Post-Industrial Democracies.* Cambridge: Cambridge University Press.

———. 2002. *Democratic Phoenix: Reinventing Political Activism.* Cambridge: Cambridge University Press.

———. 2003. "Young People and Political Activism: From the Politics of Loyalties to the Politics of Choice?" Paper presented at "Young People and Democratic Institutions: From

Disillusionment to Participation," a Council of Europe symposium, Strasbourg, France, 27–28 November.

Nurmi, Jonna. 2007. "Political Knowledge of Finnish 15 Year-Old Students." Paper presented at the European Consortium of Political Research (ECPR) biennial conference, University of Pisa, Italy.

O'Neill, Brenda. 2001. *Generational Patterns in the Political Opinions and Behaviour of Canadians: Separating the Wheat from the Chaff.* Montreal: Institute for Research in Public Policy.

––––––. 2009. "Democracy, Models of Citizenship and Civic Education." In *Civic Education and Youth Political Participation*, edited by Murray Print and Henry Milner. Rotterdam: Sense.

Organisation for Economic Co-operation and Development. 1997. *Literacy Skills for the Knowledge Society: Further Results from the International Adult Literacy Survey.* Paris: Organisation for Economic Co-operation and Development.

––––––. 2000. *Literacy in the Information Age: Final Report of the International Adult Literacy Survey.* Paris: Organisation for Economic Co-operation and Development.

Oscarsson, Henrik. 2007. "A Matter of Fact? Knowledge Effects on the Vote in Swedish General Elections, 1985–2002." *Scandinavian Political Studies* 30:301–22.

O'Toole, Therese, David Marsh, and Su Jones. 2003. "Political Literacy Cuts Both Ways: The Politics of Non-participation among Young People." *Political Quarterly* 74 (3): 349–60.

Owen, Diana. 2004. "Citizenship Identity and Civic Education in the United States." Paper presented at the Comparing International Approaches to Educating New Citizens Conference, San Diego, 26 September–1 October.

Paakkunainen, K. 2000. "Citizens' Identity and Disintegrating Nationalities in the Rhetoric of Youth Living by the Baltic Sea." Paper presented at the World Congress of Political Science, Quebec.

Pacheco, Julianna S. 2008. "Political Socialization in Context: The Effect of Political Competition on Youth Voter Turnout." *Political Behavior* 30 (4): 415–36.

–––––– and Eric Plutzer. 2007. "Stay in School, Don't Become a Parent: Teen Life Transitions and Cumulative Disadvantages for Voter Turnout." *American Politics Research* 35:32–56.

Pammett, Jon, and Larry Leduc. 2003. *Explaining the Turnout Decline in Canadian Federal Elections: A New Survey of Non-voters.* Ottawa: Elections Canada.

Parker, Kimberly, and Claudia Deane. 1997. "Ten Years of the Pew News Interest Index." Paper presented at the annual meeting of the American Association for Public Opinion Research, Norfolk, Va.

Patterson, Thomas. 2000. *Doing Well and Doing Good.* Cambridge, Mass.: Joan Shorenstein Center on the Press, Politics and Public Policy, Harvard University.

Persson, Mikael, and Henrik Oscarsson. 2008. "The Effects of an Egalitarian Educational Reform on Democratic Citizenship." Paper presented at the Youth and Politics: Strange Bedfellows? Comparative Perspectives on Political Socialization Conference, Bruges, Belgium, 3–4 July, organized by the Comparative Youth Survey Project, Catholic University of Leuven.

Peters, Joseph, and Manon Abud. 2009. *E-Consultation: Enabling Democracy between Elections.* Montreal: Institute for Research in Public Policy.

Phelps, Edward. 2005. "Young Voters at the 2005 British General Election." *Political Quarterly* 76 (4): 482–87.

Phillips, John Anthony. 2004. "The Relationship between Secondary Education and Civic Development: Results from Two Field Experiments with Inner City Minorities." Center for Information and Research on Civic Learning and Engagement (CIRCLE) Working Paper 14, http://www.civicyouth.org/PopUps/WorkingPapers/WP14Phillips.pdf (accessed 24 September 2009).

Phillips, Susan. 2006. "The Intersection of Governance and Citizenship in Canada: Not Quite the Third Way." Policy Matters 7 (4).

Plutzer, Eric. 2002. "Becoming a Habitual Voter: Interia, Resources, and Growth in Young Adulthood." American Political Science Review 96:41–56.

Popkin, Samuel, and Michael Dimock. 1999. "Political Knowledge and Citizen Competence." In Citizen Competence and Democratic Institutions, edited by Stephen L. Elkin and Karol Edward Soltan. University Park: Pennsylvania State University Press.

Postman, Neil. 1986. Amusing Ourselves to Death: Public Discourse in the Age of Show Business. New York: Penguin.

Prior, Markus. 2007. Post-broadcast Democracy: How Media Choice Increases Inequality in Political Involvement and Polarizes Elections. New York: Cambridge University Press.

Putnam, Robert D. 1993. Making Democracy Work: Civic Traditions in Modern Italy. Princeton, N.J.: Princeton University Press.

———. 2000. Bowling Alone: The Collapse and Revival of American Community. New York: Simon and Schuster.

———. 2007. "E Pluribus Unum: Diversity and Community in the Twenty-first Century." Scandinavian Political Studies 30 (2): 137–74.

Raynes-Goldie, Kate, and Luke Walker. 2007. "Taking IT Global: Online Community to Create Real World Change; A Case Study." In Civic Engagement, edited by L. Bennett. Cambridge, Mass.: MIT Press.

Reeher, Grant. 2006. "Log On, Tune Off? The Complex Relationship between Internet Use and Political Activism." Http://www.personaldemocracy.com (accessed 5 October 2009).

Robinson, Michael J. 1974. "The Impact of the Televised Watergate Hearings." Journal of Communication 24 (2): 17–30.

Rose, Lawrence. 2002. "Local Political Participation in Denmark and Norway: Does Information Make a Difference?" Paper presented at the European Consortium of Political Research (ECPR) Joint Sessions of Workshops, University of Turin, Italy.

Rosenstone, Steven J., and John Mark Hansen. 1993. Mobilization, Participation, and Democracy in America. New York: Macmillan.

Rothstein, Bo, and Dietlind Stolle. 2003. "Introduction: Social Capital in Scandinavia." Scandinavian Political Studies 26 (1): 1–26.

Rubenson, Daniel, André Blais, Patrick Fournier, Elisabeth Gidengil, and Neil Nevitte. 2004. "Accounting for the Age Gap in Turnout." Acta Politica 39 (4): 407–21.

Ruusuvirta, Outi, and Martin Rosema. 2009. "Do Online Selectors Influence the Direction and Quality of the Vote?" Paper presented at the European Consortium of Political Research (ECPR) biennial conference, University of Potsdam, Germany.

Saha, Lawrence J., Murray Print, and Kathy Edwards. 2005. Youth Electoral Study (YES). Report 2: Youth, Political Engagement and Voting. http://www.aec.gov.au/pdf/publications/youth_study_2/youth_electoral_study_02.pdf (accessed 20 September 2009).

Sandell, Julianna, and Eric Plutzer. 2005. "Families, Divorce and Voter Turnout in the US." Political Behavior 27:133–62.

Sanders, Lynn M. 1997. "Against Deliberation." *Political Theory* 25 (23): 347–76.

Sawer, Marian, and Norm Kelly. 2005. "Parliamentary Terms." Democratic Audit of Australia (February). http://democratic.audit.anu.edu.au/papers/20050702_sawer_kelly_parl_terms.pdf (accessed 15 October 2009).

Schaffner, Brian, and Matthew Streb. 2000. "Voters without Cheat Sheets: The Education Bias of the Non-partisan Ballot." Paper presented at the annual meeting of the American Political Science Association, Washington.

Scheufele, D. A., and M. C. Nisbet. 2002. "Being a Citizen On-line: New Opportunities and Dead Ends." *Harvard International Journal of Press/Politics* 7 (3): 53–73.

Schifferes, Ward, and Wainer Lusoli. 2007. "What's The Story . . . ? Online News Consumption in the 2005 UK Election." Unpublished manuscript.

Schudson, Michael. 1998. *The Good Citizen: A History of American Civic Life.* New York: Free Press.

Schwarz, Norbert, and Howard Schumer. 1997. "Political Knowledge, Attribution, and Inferred Interest in Politics: The Operation of Buffer Items." *International Journal of Public Opinion* 9:191–95.

Sears, D. O. 1990. "Whither Political Socialization Research? The Question of Persistence." In *Political Socialization, Citizenship Education, and Democracy*, edited by Ort Ichilov. New York: Teachers College Press.

Shea, Daniel M. 2009. "Local Political Parties and Young Voters: Context, Resources, and Policy Innovation." In *Engaging Young People in Civic Life*, edited by James Youniss and Peter Levine. Nashville, Tenn.: Vanderbilt University Press.

Sherr, Susan. 2005. "News for a New Generation: Can It Be Fun and Functional?" Center for Information and Research on Civic Learning and Engagement (CIRCLE) Working Paper 29, http://www.civicyouth.org/PopUps/WorkingPapers/WP29Sherr.pdf (accessed 24 September 2009).

Sherrod, Lonnie R. 2003. "Promoting the Development of Citizenship in Diverse Youth." *PS: Political Science and Politics* 36:287–92.

Siaroff, Alan. 2007. "An Empirical Overview of Voter Turnout and Political Party Membership in European Countries, the European Union, and Canada." Paper presented at the Citizen Participation in the EU and Canada: Challenges and Change Conference, Carleton University, Ottawa, 24–25 May.

Simon, James, and Bruce D. Merrill. 1998. "Political Socialization in the Classroom Revisited: The Kids Voting Program." *Social Science Journal* 35:29–42.

Sloam, James. 2007. "Rebooting Democracy: Youth Participation in Politics in the UK." *Parliamentary Affairs* 60 (4): 548–67.

Smets, Kaat. Forthcoming. "A Widening Generational Divide? Assessing the Age Gap in Voter Turnout between Younger and Older Voters." Ph.D. diss., European University Institute, Florence.

Soule, Suzanne. 2001. "Will They Engage? Political Knowledge, Participation and Attitudes of Generations X and Y." Paper prepared for the German and American Conference, "Active Participation or a Retreat to Privacy." http://www.civiced.org/papers/research_engage.pdf (accessed 15 October 2009).

Stolle, Dietlind, and Cesi Cruz. 2005. "Youth Civic Engagement in Canada: Implications for Public Policy." Social Capital in Action: Thematic Policy Studies. Ottawa: Privy Council, Policy Research Initiative.

Stolle, Dietlind, and Marc Hooghe. 2004. "Emerging Repertoires of Political Action? A Review of the Debate on Participation Trends in Western Societies." Paper presented at the European Consortium of Political Research (ECPR) Joint Sessions of Workshops, Uppsala University, Sweden.

Strate, John M., Charles J. Parrish, Charles D. Elder, and Coit Ford III. 1989. "Life Span Civic Development and Voting Participation." *American Political Science Review* 83:443–64.

Stroupe, Kenneth S., Jr., and Larry J. Sabato. 2004. "Politics: The Missing Link of Responsible Civic Education." Center for Information and Research on Civic Learning and Engagement (CIRCLE) Working Paper 18, http://www.civicyouth.org/PopUps/WorkingPapers/WP18Stroupe.pdf (accessed 24 September 2009).

Sunstein, Cass R. 2007. *Republic.com 2.0.* Princeton, N.J.: Princeton University Press.

Syvertsen, Amy K., Constance A. Flanagan, and Michael D. Stout. 2007. "Best Practices in Civic Education: Changes in Students' Civic Outcomes." Center for Information and Research on Civic Learning and Engagement (CIRCLE) Working Paper 57, http://www.civicyouth.org/index.php?s=stout (accessed 24 September 2009).

Tapscott, Don. 2008. *Grown Up Digital: How the Net Generation Is Changing Your World.* Dubuque, Iowa: McGraw-Hill Professional.

Teorell, J., M. Torcal, and J. R. Montero. 2007. "Political Participation: Mapping the Terrain." In *Citizenship and Involvement in European Democracies*, edited by J. W. van Deth, J. R. Montero, and A. Westholm. Milton Park, U.K.: Routledge.

Theiss-Morse, Elizabeth, and John R. Hibbing. 2001. "Citizenship and Civic Engagement." In *Social Capital and Participation in Everyday Life*, edited by E. M. Uslaner and P. Dekker. London: Routledge.

———. 2005. "Citizenship and Civic Engagement." *Annual Review of Political Science* 8: 227–49.

Thibault, André, Patrice Albertus, and Julie Fortier. 2007. *Rendre compte et soutenir l'action bénévole des jeunes.* Ottawa: Canadian Policy Research Networks.

Thomas, Melanee, and Lisa Young. 2006. "More Subject than Citizen: Age, Gender and Political Disengagement in Canada." Paper presented at the annual meeting of the Canadian Political Science Association, York University, Toronto.

Tóka, Gábor. 2002. "Issue Voting and Party Systems in Central and Eastern Europe." In *Citizens and Democracy in East and West: Studies in Political Culture and the Political Process*, edited by Dieter Fuchs, Edeltraud Roller, and Bernhard Wessels. Opladen, Germany: Westdeutscher.

———. 2008. "The Impact of Everyday Political Talk on Involvement, Knowledge and Informed Voting." Paper presented at the annual Elections, Public Opinion and Parties (EPOP) Conference, University of Manchester.

Torney-Purta, Judith. 2000. "Comparative Perspectives on Political Socialization and Civic Education." *Comparative Education Review* 44 (1): 88–95.

——— and Carolyn Henry Barber. 2004. *Strengths and Weaknesses in U.S. Students' Civic Knowledge and Skills: Analysis from the IEA Civic Education Study.* Center for Information and Research on Civic Learning and Engagement (CIRCLE) Fact Sheet, http://www.civicyouth.org/PopUps/FactSheets/FS_CivicKnowledge.pdf (accessed 24 September 2009).

Torney-Purta, Judith, Rainer Lehmann, Hans Oswald, and Wolfram Schulz. 2001. *Citizenship and Education in Twenty-Eight Countries: Civic Knowledge at Age Fourteen.* Amsterdam: Eburon-International Association for the Evaluation of Educational Achievement.

Torney-Purta, Judith, J. Schwille, and J. Amadeo. 1999. *Civic Education across Countries: Twenty-Four National Case Studies from the IEA Civic Education Project.* Amsterdam: International Association for the Evaluation of Educational Achievement.

Tossutti, Livianna. 2004. "Youth Voluntarism and Political Engagement in Canada." Paper presented at the annual meeting of the Canadian Political Science Association, Winnipeg.

Trippi, J. 2004. *The Revolution Will Not Be Televised: Democracy, the Internet, and the Overthrow of Everything.* New York: Regan.

Twenge, Jean. 2006. *Generation Me.* New York: Free Press.

van der Eijk, Cees, Mark Franklin, and Michael Marsh. 1996. "What Voters Teach Us about Europe-wide Elections: What Europe-wide Elections Teach Us about Voters." *Electoral Studies* 15 (2): 149–66.

Van Der Meer, T. W. G., and E. J. Van Ingen. 2009. "Schools of Democracy? Disentangling the Relationship between Civic Participation and Political Action in 17 European Countries." *European Journal of Political Research* 48 (2): 281–308.

van Deth, Jan. 2009. "New Modes of Participation and Norms of Citizenship." Paper presented at the European Consortium for Political Research (ECPR) Joint Sessions of Workshops, University of Lisbon.

Verba, Sidney, and Norman H. Nie. 1972. *Participation in America.* Chicago: University of Chicago Press.

Verba, Sidney, Kay Lehman Schlozman, and Nancy Burns. 2005. "Family Ties: Understanding the Intergenerational Transmission of Political Participation." In *The Social Logic of Politics,* edited by A. S. Zuckerman. Philadelphia: Temple University Press.

Verboczy, Akos, and Christian Giguère. 2004. "Électeurs en Herbe: Building Citizenship Step by Step; A Quebec Approach to Civic Education." *Inroads* 16:84–89.

Vowles, Jack, and Dan Stevens. 2008. "Turnout, Competitiveness, Age, and Generations in British Elections, 1964–2005." Paper presented at the annual meeting of the American Political Science Association, Boston.

Vromen, Ariadne. 2008. "Building Virtual Spaces: Young People, Participation and the Internet." *Australian Journal of Political Science* 43 (1): 79–97.

Wagner, Markus, and Outi Ruusuvirta. 2009. "Faulty Recommendations? Party Positions in Online Voting Advice Applications." Paper presented at the annual meeting of the American Political Science Association, Toronto.

Walker, Tobi. 2000. "The Service/Politics Split: Rethinking Service to Teach Political Engagement." *PS: Political Science and Politics* 33 (3): 647–49.

Walling, Donovan R. 2007. "The Return of Civic Education." *Phi Delta Kappan,* December, 285–89.

Warren, Marc E. 2008. "Governance-driven Democratization." Center for Democratic Network Governance, Roskilde University, Denmark, Working Paper 2008: 3. http://www.ruc.dk/upload/application/pdf/f51d6748/Working Paper 2008_3 Marc Warren_Governance Driven Democratization.pdf (accessed 20 September 2009).

Wattenberg, Martin. 2003. "Electoral Turnout: The New Generation Gap." *Journal of Elections, Public Opinion and Parties* 13 (1): 159–73.

———. 2007. *Is Voting for Young People?* New York: Longman.

———. 2008. *Where Have All the Voters Gone?* Cambridge, Mass.: Harvard University Press.

Wernli, Boris. 2007. "La transmission intergénérationnelle de l'orientation idéologique en Suisse dans les familles à plusieurs generations." *Swiss Political Science Review* 13 (2): 237–59.

Westheimer, Joel. 2006. "No Child Left Thinking: Democracy at Risk in American Schools." *Democratic Dialogue* No. 17: Ottawa: University of Ottawa.

——— and Joseph Kahne. 2004. "What Kind of Citizen? The Politics of Educating for Democracy." *American Educational Research Journal* 41 (2): 237–69.

Westholm, Anders. 1999. "The Perceptual Pathway: Tracing the Mechanisms of Political Value Transfer across Generations." *Political Psychology* 20:525–51.

———, Arne Lindquist, and Richard G. Niemi. 1990. "Education and the Making of the Informed Citizen: Political Literacy and the Outside World." In *Political Socialization, Citizenship Education, and Democracy,* edited by Ort Ichilov. New York: Teachers' College Press.

Whiteley, Paul. 2008. "Can Voting Be Taught? Citizenship Education and the Electoral Participation of Students." Unpublished paper.

Widestrom, Amy. 2008. "Neglected Neighborhoods: Economic Inequality, Residential Segregation and Declining Voter Turnout among Low-income Citizens." Paper presented at the annual meeting of the American Political Science Association, Boston.

Wilhelm, A. 1999. "Virtual Sounding Boards: How Deliberative Is Online Political Discussion?" In *Digital Democracy: Discourse and Decision Making in the Information Age,* edited by Barry N. Hague and Brian D. Loader. London: Routledge.

Wilkenfeld, Britt. 2008. "Civic Contexts: How Schools and Neighborhoods Influence Youth Political Engagement." Paper presented at the Youth and Politics: Strange Bedfellows? Comparative Perspectives on Political Socialization Conference, Bruges, Belgium, 3–4 July, organized by the Comparative Youth Survey Project, Catholic University of Leuven.

Wisse, Eva. 2006. "Promoting Democracy: An International Exploration of Policy and Implementation Practice." http://www.scribd.com/doc/9136492/Promoting-Democracy-Policy-and-Practice (accessed 24 September 2009).

Wolfinger, Raymond E., and Steven J. Rosenstone. 1980. *Who Votes?* New Haven, Conn.: Yale University Press.

Xenos, M. A., and W. L. Bennett. 2007. "Young Voters and the Web of Politics: The Promise and Problems of Youth-oriented Political Content on the Web." In *Young Citizens in the Digital Age: Political Engagement, Young People, and New Media,* edited by Brian D. Loader. New York: Routledge.

Young, Lisa, and William Cross. 2007. *A Group Apart: Young Party Members in Canada.* Ottawa: Canadian Policy Research Networks.

Youniss, James, Susan Bales, Verona Christmas-Best, Marcelo Diversi, Milbrey McLaughlin, and Rainer Silbereisen. 2002. "Youth Civic Engagement in the Twenty-First Century." *Journal of Research on Adolescence* 12:121–48.

Youniss, James, and Peter Levine, eds. 2009. *Engaging Young People in Civic Life.* Nashville, Tenn.: Vanderbilt University Press.

Zeiser, Pamela. 2001. "Building Better Citizens: Increasing the Level of Civic Education among Teens in Jacksonville, Florida." *National Civic Review* 90 (3): 289–91.

Zukin, Cliff, and Robin Snyder. 1984. "Passive Learning: When the Media Environment Is the Message." *Public Opinion Quarterly* 48:629–38.

Index

IEA (International Association for the Evaluation of Educational Achievement), 20, 95, 177–79, 197
immigrants, 99, 129, 145, 170
inequality, 14, 40–41, 49, 68, 70, 97, 118, 119
Inglehart, Ronald 18, 19, 20, 35
Internet, 3, 4, 5, 18, 29, 34, 50, 51, 52, 53, 57–73, 75-76, 80, 82, 98, 108–10, 117, 123, 131, 135–36, 167, 180, 195–96, 202, 206, 211, 214, 221, 223
Iraq, 7, 37, 40, 91, 92, 220
Ireland, 41, 85, 154
Italy, 86, 104, 144
Iyengar, Shanto, 134

J
Jackson, L. A., 61
Jacobs, Lawrence, 118
Jacoby, Susan, 60
Japan, 89, 104, 144
Jaros, Dean, 44
Jenkins, Krista, 36, 67, 106, 181
Jennings, M. Kent, 40, 42–44, 47
Jones, Su, 21
Jorba, Laia, 66, 70
journalism, 29, 60, 114, 203, 214. *See also* press
Jowell, Roger, 134
Junn, Jane, 44, 99, 200, 207

K
Kahne, Joseph, 190
Kandel, D. B., 48
Karp, Jeffrey A., 152
Kautto, Mikko, 218
Kavadias, Dimokritos, 83
Kavanaugh, Andrea D., 70
Keen, Andrew, 60, 62
Keeter, Scott, 36, 99, 106, 181, 208
Kerr, David, 196, 209–10
Kidd, Quentin, 66
Kids Voting USA, 200
Kirby, Emily H., 208, 212
Kirlin, Mary, 211
Knowledge Networks, 81–82, 241n11, 246n22
Krueger, Brian J., 70

L
Lacy, D., 144
Ladner, Andreas, 64, 136, 137, 151
Langton, Kenneth, 40, 42, 43
Lauf, Edmund, 55

Lay, J. Celeste, 31, 39, 49
legislatures, 28, 96, 118, 121–24, 139–43, 148, 160, 163, 164–65, 203–4; bicameral, 121, 140, 152, 222; unicameral, 12--22, 139–40, 218
Lehmann, Rainer, 178
Leu, Donald J., 62
Levine, Peter, 75, 124, 169
Levinson, Meira, 39
Lewis, J. P., 186
libraries, 175, 218
Lijphart, Arend, 129, 140
Lindquist, Aren, 207
Listhaug, Ola, 17
literacy, 11–12, 16–17, 25–6, 37, 53–54, 67–68, 70, 75, 94, 100–104, 112, 117, 121, 144–45, 158, 175–77, 187, 218, 220, 222, 224. *See also* reading
Livingstone, S., 72
Loewen, Peter, 92, 109, 129, 130, 132
Lopez, Mark H., 189, 208, 212
Lower Saxony, 158–59
Lukensmeyer, Carolyn J., 13
Lupia, Arthur, 11
Luskin, Robert C., 134
Lusoli, Wainer, 70, 71
Lutz, Georg, 137

M
Macedo, Stephen, 10, 118
Mahler, Vincent, 118
Mair, Peter, 127
Malone, Christopher, 200
Marsh, David, 21
Marsh, Michael, 121
Martikainen, Tuomo, 96
Mattila, Mikko, 17
Maughan, Emma, 42
Mayer, Nonna, 50
McDevitt, Michael, 45, 195
McNeal, Ramona S., 65
Meirick, Patrick C., 200
Merelman, R. M., 43
Merriam, Charles, 32
Merrill, Bruce D., 200
Micheletti, Michele, 21
Milan, Anne, 182
Milligan, Kevin, 176
Milner, Henry, 8, 18, 54, 56, 65, 68, 79, 96, 100–101, 103, 109, 118–19, 123, 127, 129, 130, 132–33, 143, 148, 151, 171, 175, 179, 189, 207, 224, 253
Minitinget, 205, 261n15